The DARKNESS AMONG US

The DARKNESS AMONG US

A Look at the Sinister Growth of the Occult and How Dangerously Close It Is To You

William C. Viser

BROADMAN
& HOLMAN
PUBLISHERS

Nashville, Tennessee

4260-75
0-8054-6075-6

Dewey Decimal Classification: 133
Subject Heading: OCCULTISM
Library of Congress Card Catalog Number: 93-13997
Printed in the United States of America

Library of Congress Cataloging-in-Publication Data

Viser, William C., 1947–
    The darkness among us : a look at the sinister growth of the occult and how dangerously close it is to you / William C. Viser.
        p.   cm.
    Includes bibliographical references.
    ISBN 0-8054-6075-6
    1. Occultism—Controversial literature.   2. Satanism.   I. Title.
BF1042.V58   1994
261.5'1—dc20   93-13997

To my precious wife, Susan,
and
my beautiful children, Ryan and Lauren,
who have made my life so complete.

Contents

Preface . . . . *ix*
Acknowledgments. . . . . *xi*
1. What...the Devil Is Going On? *3*
2. The Tempter's Tunes *28*
3. Get the Picture? Lucifer's Lessons Through the Media *50*
4. Satan in Scripture *81*
5. Seances and Spirits: Spiritism Today *98*
6. On the Road to Endor: Witchcraft in the United States *117*
7. The Devil You Say? The Spread of Satanism Today *132*
8. The Prince of Power of the Air: Prophecy and Astrology *151*
9. Where on Earth Is the Prince of the World? *170*
10. What's Got into You? Demon Possession *188*
11. Turning the Darkness into Sunshine *203*
Appendix A: Organizations *213*
Appendix B: Suggested Reading *223*
Appendix C: Scripture Index *227*
Endnotes. *231*

Preface

Darkness. Evil waits for the cover of darkness to slip in among us and do its damage. In the darkness, we are weaker. We are not watchful. Danger surrounds us on all sides, yet we sleep. And the enemy uses this darkness to his advantage.

I have written *The Darkness Among Us* from the personal conviction that God's adversary and our enemy is hard at work among us. His influence is spreading throughout our land and the world today in ways which we, as Christians, are often unaware.

I began my study of the occult in 1973 writing a series of articles, and I lived for ten years in the heart of Macumba, a voodoo-influenced cult in Rio de Janeiro, Brazil. It was not, however, until I returned to the United States in late 1988 and began my teaching and counseling responsibilities that I realized just how dark it was becoming for Christians everywhere.

Writing this book has certainly made me more aware of how cunning and subtle and persuasive Satan can be. This has not been an easy book to write. There are a host of subjects I would rather write about in the dark hours between midnight and 5:00 A.M. than the occult! Nonetheless, it is my sincere hope and prayer that the pages ahead will be a blessing to you. They should (1) help you see that the growing darkness among us is evidence that our Lord's return is drawing ever closer, (2) educate you as to how Satan works to keep in darkness the hearts and minds of people from all walks of life and ages, (3) prepare you to help those who struggle desperately to be free from their bondage to the occult, (4) aid you in seeing the warning signs in your own community and your home, and (5) equip you to combat the dark influence of the occult.

At the beginning of chapter one, you will meet Lauren, a fictional sixteen-year-old honor roll student. As each chapter opens, we will continue Lauren's story of increasing attraction to and involvement in the occult. You will see how subtle and dangerous the forces of darkness can be.

I have tried to maintain a balanced, thoroughly scriptural understanding of a very difficult and complex subject. Careful documentation has been provided to substantiate what you are about to read.

I have also tried to address the emotional vulnerability of children, youth, and adults in order to demonstrate how this can leave an individual open to the lure of the occult.

Finally, let us remember the urgency that undergirds our work for the Savior. For as He Himself reminded us, "As long as it is day, we must do the work of him who sent me. Night is coming, when no one can work" (John 9:4).

Acknowledgments

It is with grateful appreciation that I acknowledge the following, without whose help and support this manuscript would never have taken on form and substance:

To my students at Ouachita Baptist University, who read my chapters, listened to my lectures, and entered into meaningful dialogue with me.

To the administration of Ouachita Baptist University, for their encouragement and support, as well as to my departmental colleagues and DeGray Baptist Church, where I serve as pastor.

To Wanda Stephens, M.D., and the staff at Living Hope Institute of Little Rock, Arkansas, and Chicago, Illinois, for their helpful comments and moral support.

To my typists, Crystal Graves, Faith Kennedy, Becky Boyett, and Caroline Curry, for their good work and positive criticism.

To Cheryl Smith, Perry Alexander, Darin Peterson, John H. Viser III, and countless students who assisted me in my research.

To Truman Smith, senior family consultant at the Foreign Mission Board, and his staff, Mrs. Jane Hilgenhold, who circulated and returned my surveys.

To my missionary colleagues, who always respond so faithfully to my cries for help in seeking their opinion and stories.

To the following publishers for permission to include material in my manuscript: American Portrait Films, *Hell's Bells*; Bethany House, *Why Knock Rock?* by Dan and Steve Peters and Cher Merrill; Crossway Books, *Demon Possession and the Christian* by C. Fred Dickason; HarperCollins, *Painted Black* by Carl Raschke; Moody Press, *What Demons Can Do to Saints* by Merrill F. Unger; Newmarket Press, *Bram Stoker's Dracula: The Film and the Legend*, edited by Diana Landzu; Pocket Books, a division of Simon and Schuster, Inc., *Across the Border* by Gary Provost; Scripture Press, *Biblical Demonology* by Merrill F. Unger; The Myterious Press, *Satan Wants You* by Arthur Lyons; The Home Mission Board of the Southern Baptist Convention, "The Occult" by Gary Leazer; Tyndale House, *Demons in the World Today* by Merrill F. Unger; WORD Incorporated, *Counseling and the Demonic* by Roger Buford and *Sacrifice* by Jim Kilroy and Bob Stewart; Zondervan Publishing House, *Dictionary of Cults, Sects, Religions, and the Occult* by George A. Mather and Larry A. Nichols.

Finally, to nameless numbers who love me and promised to pray for me as I dealt with a difficult subject. You have truly helped pull me through.

LAUREN

That there is a Devil is a thing doubted by none but such as are under the influences of the Devil. For any to deny the being of a Devil must be from an ignorance of profaneness worse than diabolical.
— COTTON MATHER: *A Discourse on the Wonders of the Invisible World*

Lauren is sixteen, a tenth grader, and an honor roll student. She is your average adolescent with long blond hair and blue eyes. She was always well-dressed and active in her school organizations, at least until recently. Lauren's parents are the average middle-class mom and dad. They have tried to give Lauren what she needs plus a little more, but it takes its toll on their finances as there are two others behind Lauren. Her parents both work, so Lauren is one of approximately sixteen million students who come home after school to an empty house.[1]

Lauren's parents do not screen what Lauren watches on television. Lately, Lauren has been watching more and more shows with occult themes. Even Lauren's younger brother and sister watch the same programs. Everyone in the family agrees that they are strangely fascinating.

Her parents recently found a book on witchcraft in Lauren's room, but Lauren just mumbled something about a friend loaning it to her. Her parents did not pursue it any further.

I

Her younger brother and sister told their parents that Lauren's cassette tapes had pictures of the devil, demons and scenes from graveyards and hell but they dismissed it as "typical teenage music."

Lauren's parents are out of touch with their daughter. They know very little about Lauren's world, her friends, or the boys she dates. They do not know that Lauren's weight loss and slightly disheveled appearance has anything to do with the heavy burden she has been carrying deep in her heart. They don't know that Lauren's grades have begun to slip ever so gradually. They have no idea that Lauren's boyfriend of five months had been pressuring her to go all the way with him sexually. Lauren doesn't want to lose him, but she doesn't want a sexual relationship either. What should she do?

Lauren's girlfriends have invited her to a slumber party. Lauren says she wishes she knew what her future would be like so she would know what to do now. The girls laugh and say that's easy. Haven't you ever heard of a Ouija™ board? Candles are lit, the lights are turned off, and Lauren takes another step into a frightening and deceitful world...

O N E

*And I do not want you to be participants
with demons.*
— 1 CORINTHIANS 10:20

What...the Devil Is Going On?

The word "occult" comes from the Latin word *occultus* meaning "to conceal."[1] The origin of the word is fitting, since those involved in the occult world do not want anyone to see what they are doing. The *World Book Encyclopedia* defines occultism as a wide range of beliefs and practices involving magic or forces outside the natural world. Occultism includes astrology, fortune-telling, magic, and spiritualism, which is the belief that spirits of the dead communicate with the living. People who believe in occultism consider it based on hidden knowledge that ordinary individuals do not have.[2]

DENIAL OF ITS EXISTENCE

Why do some individuals choose not to believe in the occult?

Occultism draws Lauren and countless people into its beliefs and practices, yet many others still deny its existence or its ability to destroy lives.

Over the years, I have spoken often on the subject of the occult and talked to many people. I have discovered what I will call the "too" perspective—too sophisticated, too spiritually blind, too incredible, too distasteful, too scared, too naive, too faddish, and too doubtful.

(1) Too sophisticated. Mention the devil and many will imagine a red-skinned half-man/half-goat with horns, a goatee, and a pitchfork in hand. Others will remember "Saturday Night Live" and the popular sketch "Church Chat" with the "Church Lady." Dana Carvey portrays a woman in the ministry who, more often than not, makes reference to the devil as "SATAN," screaming it out to the delight and laughter of the studio audience. For many the devil is but an invention, like the bogeyman, made up to scare impressionable boys and girls.

(2) Too spiritually blind. In churches throughout our land, you will seldom hear a message on hell or Satan. Worse, some in the ministry today do not believe in a literal devil or hell. Sadder still, some students enter the ministry having been taught in their undergraduate or graduate programs to question the very existence of the devil. Is it any wonder that the average person who sits in the pew has not theologically thought through what he or she believes?

I know of a pastor in an evangelical denomination who was interviewing a prospective summer youth minister by phone. The interview was very thorough and was proceeding fairly nicely, until the pastor happened to ask the young seminary student what he thought about the devil. The young man paused and replied that he wasn't sure if he believed in him or not. Then he said something about his professor explaining that there was no "literal hell." He did not get the job.

(3) Too incredible. How does one explain what many claim occurs in occultic meetings? Has Satan actually appeared? Can demons really be conjured up from hell? Is it possible to talk with the dead? Can someone really know what the future holds? Can an individual truly be cursed? On and on we could go, and we will look at these and many other related matters in the chapters ahead. I believe the bottom line may well be just how much power

does Satan have in the world today? Chapter 4 will examine this in more detail from a scriptural point of view.

(4) Too distasteful, painful, or ugly. To talk about occultic practices is not only to talk about strange beliefs and their roots in the ancient past; it is also to talk about extortion, murder, child abuse, drugs, and pornography and other deviant sexual activity. I have made every effort to be as tasteful as possible in the pages ahead, but even so you will no doubt find the evidence disturbing.

(5) Too scared. Reading and thinking about Satanists, witches, seances, demons, and such just plain scares some individuals. Never mind that it is happening in their city, town, or possibly community. They just want to ignore it in hopes that it will go away.

(6) Too naive. This perspective says, "I cannot believe people would actually do such things. I never would, my friends never would, and neither would anyone else."

(7) Too faddish. This perspective is wishful thinking. It assumes that interest in the occult may be popular today but will be gone tomorrow, like trends in fashions. As we look more closely at various aspects of the occult, we will see that its roots go far back in time and numbers today do not indicate a fad, but rather steady growth. Satan has not been on vacation nor is he planning one anytime soon. He isn't going anywhere—until he goes to the lake of fire that God has prepared for him (Matt. 25:41).

(8) Too doubtful. This perspective is very dangerous. This individual may say, "I am not going to believe anything that I cannot verify with my own observations."

What an East Texas forest ranger saw one night nearly cost him his life in a close encounter with the occult. He thought he saw a fire in an isolated, wooded area. The uniformed officer left his car and walked briskly toward the smoke, pushing tree limbs away from his face. Then he saw a most unusual sight. As he drew closer to the orange glow, he began to make out silhouettes of robed figures. Rather than confronting them singlehandedly, he quietly retreated but gave away his presence by the snapping of a twig underfoot. The chase was on, and the ranger ran for his life. Fortunately for him, he did escape.

Dr. Paul Carlin, an occult researcher, firmly believes that, had the ranger been apprehended, he would have been killed by the members of the occult group upon which he stumbled.[3]

A State of Confusion

Satan wants to keep us off balance as to his work in the world today and, unfortunately, he has done a good job of it! As we observe closely the world around us today, we cannot help but see the state of disorder which exists.

C. S. Lewis once observed, "There are two equal and opposite errors into which our race can fall about the devils. One is to disbelieve in their existence. The other is to believe, and feel an excessive and unhealthy interest in them. They themselves are equally pleased by both errors and hail a materialist or a medium with the same delight."[4] A closer examination of several events will help explain why there is disbelief on the one hand and excessive interest on the other.

Disbelief: The Skeptics' Choice

Mention the words witchcraft, Satanism, black magic, and other occultic terms and you will likely be greeted with raised eyebrows, laughter, disbelief, and extreme suspicion, or outright ignored! The sad truth is many do not take occultic activity seriously at all. They find the facts confusing, as seen in the following examples:

Worldwide Satanic Convention in Washington, D.C.? Consider the "Satanist Convention" planned for September through November of 1990 in Washington, D.C.[5] According to a Christian who claimed to be the former number-two leader in the Church of Satan, the meeting was to take place from September through November with members converging on the nation's capital from all over the United States and throughout the world. Strategies to destroy the Christian church were to be discussed and rituals were to be performed in support of these strategies. Even Satanic baptisms and weddings were to be celebrated.

Women's Aglow Fellowship sent out a prayer alert to all fifty states. The convention was used in a fund-raising letter by one evangelistic organization and was mentioned by Pat Robertson on a "700 Club" broadcast of October 31. Even *USA Today* reported the rumors and the Christian countermeasures.

Was it true? Was there to be a convention? How had this entire story started?

A Fairfax, Virginia, pastor who heard the story from the former Satanist and wanted the opinions of colleagues sent out letters outlining the new convert's claims to twenty pastors and Christian leaders in his area "inviting them to evaluate this man's information and message." Unfortunately, the letters were further distributed, spread like wildfire, and were preached as fact. Further investigation would eventually cast extreme doubts as to the authenticity of the "Satanist's" background.

Understandably, the pastor was disturbed about the way Christians had handled the story, remarking that "people reacted in two ways. They assumed what they heard was true and ran with it or they avoided the topic [of Satanism] altogether and denied its existence."

It sounds like what C. S. Lewis said forty-two years earlier, doesn't it?

Animal Mutilation: The Work of Satanists? A second example which cast doubt on occult activity took place in California. In the town of Tustin, officials from Orange County investigated a number of mutilated cats. The conclusion was that increased construction in the nearby foothills had driven coyotes down into the urban setting where they preyed upon household cats.

An article in *The Humanist* recounted the reaction gleefully:

> A tiny group saw the mutilation of the cats as evidence of ritual Satanic activity and refused to accept the initial conclusion of the animal control officers. The county was forced into an expensive, in-depth investigation expending hundreds of work hours and tens of thousands of taxpayers' dollars to make certain that no ritual Satanic cat mutilations were taking place. Ron Hudson, Chief of Field Services of Orange County Animal Control, had every mutilated cat submitted to a necropsy by a veterinarian. After examining over one hundred animals he announced that the evidence was consistent with the animal control investigators' initial conclusion—that coyotes were preying on the cats.

This was ignored by the local extremists who exploited the situation by bringing in one or two outside "experts," forming an organization, instituting citizen patrols, and offering a reward for information leading to the arrest of "Satanists" who were perpetrating this atrocity.[6]

The author then summed up the episode as follows:

Although Orange County Animal Control acted promptly and properly, the county taxpayers will have to foot the bill for the hundreds of additional work hours needed to address the rumor panic brought about by a handful of people who believed that Satanists were operating locally.[7]

Satan's Underground: Truth or Hoax? Confusion concerning occult activities is not limited to well-meaning Christian organizations, media, or industry. It can spill over into sources which are widely read for information, as our next account reveals.

A third example which has helped fuel the fires of disbelief occurred in 1988, when a book entitled *Satan's Underground* was released by Harvest House Publishers of Eugene, Oregon. Written by Laurel Rose Wilson under the pen name of Lauren Stratford, this book would eventually sell more than 130,000 copies before being withdrawn from circulation.

Stratford's book described a life filled with sexual abuse, pornography, prostitution, and eventually Satanism. Among her most shocking revelations was that she bore three children, two who were killed in "snuff" films (pornographic films in which the life of the victim is literally "snuffed out"), and a third, who was sacrificed in her presence during a Satanic ritual.[8]

The situations described by Stratford in the book were validated by Mike Warnke, author of *The Satan Seller*; Hal Lindsey, author of *The Late Great Planet Earth*; Kenneth Wooden, former producer for the ABC news program "20/20"; and Larry M. Jones, founder and director of the Cult Crime Impact Network, Inc. (CCIN) which publishes *File 18* directed toward law enforcement agencies and the clergy.

Anticult researchers Bob and Gretchen Passantino collaborated with the editor of the *Cornerstone*, a Chicago-based Christian magazine, to investigate Stratford's claims after noting a lack of specific names, dates, and places in the story.

In an article setting forth apparent contradictions in her account of her family and her involvement in Satanic rituals, the researchers stated:

> The information supplied from interviews with family members, a former pastor and close friends reveal a very different person depicted in *Satan's Underground.* Over the years Stratford told many different stories to many different people and at one point even faked blindness—all it seems with the motive of receiving attention and love.[9]

Public records were examined in an attempt to verify the authenticity of Stratford's story. Stratford herself was contacted on three different occasions and was asked for documentation of her story. She turned down these requests.

The writers concluded that they could find no evidence, for example, to corroborate Stratford's claim of three pregnancies. They also pointed to numerous contradictions involving people and dates, including the date of Stratford's father's death, a turning point in her life.[10]

We should make two points regarding this controversy.

First, the Passantinos do not believe the alleged fraud was committed for financial gain. Nor do they deny that ritual abuse takes place or that people may have been helped by Stratford's testimony. But because her story is not true, her qualifications as an expert and counselor are "nonexistent."

Second, Stratford's supporters, such as pediatrician Lyn Laboriel, have been critical of the Passantinos' methods and motives as well as their conclusions. It is their position that problems with memory gaps, sequence of events, and, indeed, storytelling are characteristic of victims of abuse. "If I did not see that kind of pattern, I would have a more difficult time believing the story is true," Laboriel said.[11]

In an interview on Detroit radio station WWCM conducted after the release of the *Cornerstone* article, Stratford admitted she had lied about incidents in her life and that she continues to reconstruct memories. But her confusion, she said, is typical of victims of abuse. "That does not discredit the book," she said.[12]

So what does one conclude? Do you fall into the error of concluding that all this points to individuals with an overactive imagination? Do you choose to disbelieve in the existence of devils? Before deciding, let's look at the second of Lewis' errors from which many become victims today.

Excessive Interest: The Other Side of the Coin

Interest in the devil and the occult has literally exploded into alarming proportions.

On October 25, 1988, television viewers tuned to the NBC program, "Devil Worship: Exposing Satan's Underground" were greeted by host Geraldo Rivera with this statement:

> Satanic cults! Every hour, every day, their ranks are growing. Estimates are there are over one million Satanists in this country. The majority of them are linked in a highly organized, very secret network. From small towns to large cities, they've attracted police and FBI attention to their satanic ritual child abuse, child pornography and grisly satanic murder. The odds are this is happening in your town.[13]

Many people must have tuned in to find out just what was happening in their town. So many, in fact, that audience ratings for the two-hour documentary went through the roof.[14]

Chicago police detective Robert Simandl thinks investigating satanic crime may be a growth industry. He calls it "the crime of the 90s," and has led more than two hundred seminars for law-enforcement professionals on recognizing earmarks of the occult in crimes ranging from church burglaries to child abuse. Each day he gets at least a dozen calls from colleagues around the country perplexed over headless hens, spray-painted pentagrams—and worse.[15]

The police are not the only ones to receive phone calls. Gary Leazer, formerly the assistant director (field staff) for the Southern Baptist Convention's Home Mission Board Interfaith Witness Department, said that the number of requests his department received for information about the occult in the last five years have mushroomed: "Before 1985, it was very seldom that we'd get more than one call per year on the occult. Now the occult and New Age Movement are the top two areas that we get requests about."[16]

Requests for information on the occult may not always be positive. Some request more information and become involved in the occult. A national hotel chain in Little Rock, Arkansas, was the scene of a two-day conference. Billed as a "Psychic Fair," it featured items for sale such as crystals, Indian talismans, "I Love My Psychic" bumper stickers, and other assorted items as well as card and palm readings for twenty dollars a session.

One customer told a local newspaper reporter that her psychic predicted that her house would be vandalized. About three months later, it was. The woman said that the psychic knew things about her personal problems that no one else knew.[17]

Not too many people knew of General Manuel Noriega's interest in the occult. When U.S. soldiers stormed one of his guest houses in Panama City, Panama, they narrowly missed capturing four Brazilian voodoo witches who performed rituals for his protection, according to an article by Stephen Komarow.

The so-called "witch house," a fortified structure specially built for Noriega, contained an estimated fifty pounds of cocaine, a bucket of blood, voodoo artifacts, and a brewery for making concoctions and potions.[18]

Interest in the occult has also moved into the classroom. Theological schools such as Southwestern Baptist Theological Seminary in Fort Worth, Texas, offer a course entitled "Christian Mysticism and the Occult," while Fuller's School of World Missions has five courses related to the subject.[19]

At Ouachita Baptist University my course entitled "Counseling and the Occult" has been offered every year for the past two years and never lacked for students.

The "School Intervention Report," a publication which focuses on what is happening in schools around the country, recently devoted an entire issue to the subject "Satanism and Schools."[20]

Unfortunately, it is not a problem limited to the United States. Herr Hans Schwier, education minister of Northrhine-Westphalia, issued an "urgent appeal" to teachers in West Germany's biggest federal state warning them against underestimating the dangers of "the new drug of occultism" among the young. In fact 85 percent of teachers completing a questionnaire had dealt with the subject of the occult in class, in most cases in response to pupils' questions. Most of the teachers felt they were not well enough informed to deal with the issue adequately.[21]

Herr Kare Hillermeir, Bavaria's social affairs minister, related that experimenting with cards and pendulums and contacting "spirits" through a moving glass or a tapping table were "a common enough phenomenon" among Bavarian children.[22]

In Brazil, Argentina, and other countries, the Cult of the Holy Daime is rapidly increasing in popularity among the people. Men, women, and children line up to drink the brew Indians use to induce visions, heal the sick, and communicate with spirits. Daime centers have sprung up in major cities and "the daimistas" have a powerful political lobby in Brazil. In 1991 they were granted $230,000 by the Brazilian government for a nutprocessing plant to be established and run by the cult. To these cultists, Daime is God, "your best counsel and your best friend."[23]

Cults such as the daimistas may seem to be far removed from the youth of your community, but make no mistake, cults are a problem, as the 1993 Branch Davidian tragedy in Waco, Texas proves.

Approximately 50 percent of the high school students surveyed in 1985 by Stanford University psychologists Philip Zimbardo and Cynthia Hartley reported that they had been approached by cult recruiters.[24] Some cults specifically target middle level and even elementary school children.

Even comic books are not immune to the occult. Gospel-pop singer Amy Grant sued Marvel Comics to stop the use of what she said was her likeness on a comic book that has occult subject matter. She said a photo from one of her album covers was copied for an issue of "Dr. Strange, Sorcerer Supreme."[25]

WHY SO MUCH INTEREST IN THE OCCULT?

The 1970s saw an intense interest in the occult with a proliferation of articles and books on the subject. The 1990s are seeing a tremendous upswing in occult interest by all ages. What causes individuals and even Christians of all ages to become interested in the occult? I believe there are six explanations.

(1) Its mysteriousness. The way it seems to defy explanation lures many people. As we saw in the example of Lauren, she was faced with pressures and questions for which she had no answer. She had no faith to fall back on nor did any of her friends, and her parents were out of touch with her concerns. Where was she to turn?

In El Paso, Texas, Christina Mireles was lured into a satanic cult when she was fourteen. She said, "It seemed like fun, like an adventure. It was mysterious."[26] But, like everyone else who enters an occult group, Christina could not see what lay ahead for her. The mystery turned to violence as she was savagely beaten for refusing to have sex with one of the members.

Another victim, Steven Lee, recalled his initiation into terror: "It was like a roller coaster. It started out slow and high—then it plunged straight down." When Lee finally wanted out of the cult, his fellow members, worried about exposure, placed a crown of thorns on his head and beat him until he could barely stagger out the door.[27]

Fortunately for Tony Drake, he was able to see where his involvement was leading him and was able to get out just in time. "I thought at first I could be a Satanist on just a philosophical level," he said. "But I could feel that Satan wanted me to go on to a bigger level—to sacrificing bigger animals, then maybe to humans, then even to my life." Realizing he had a serious problem, Drake finally committed himself to an alcohol/drug-abuse and cult-rehabilitation program.[28]

(2) The instability in today's world. As the financial situation worsens and crime rates continue to rise, some youth look for answers in places they would not normally go.

(3) Unusually intense pressures. Stresses such as the breakup of the family unit, ever-changing social customs, cries that the church is irrelevant, and the erosion of confidence in our political system all may contribute to the pressures of daily life. Many people break under the load.

The alarming conclusions of a recently released report astonished even the commission's members. Thirty-six members—including former Surgeon General C. Everett Koop, pollster George Gallop, Jr., former Education Commissioner Ernest Boyer, Illinois Governor James Thompson, California school chief Bill Honig, and other leaders in the medical and educational fields—reported that America is raising a generation of adolescents plagued by pregnancy, illegal drug use, suicide, and violence.

"We are absolutely convinced that if we don't take action immediately, we're going to find ourselves with a failing economy and social unrest," said Roseann Bentley of the National Association of State Boards of Education. The commission's report concluded that "young people are less healthy and less prepared to take their places in society than were their parents."[29]

Among the commission's findings were the following:

➤ One million teen-age girls—nearly one in ten—become pregnant each year.

➤ Thirty-nine percent of high school seniors reported they had gotten drunk within the previous two weeks.

➤ Alcohol-related accidents are the leading cause of death among teenagers.

➤ The suicide rate for teens has doubled since 1968, making it the second leading cause of death among adolescents. Ten percent of teenage boys and 18 percent of teenage girls have attempted suicide.

➤ Teen-age arrests are up thirty-fold since 1950.

➤ Homicide is the leading cause of death among fifteen- to nineteen-year-old minority youths.

Inattention to these problems has left thousands of young people doomed to failure, "which for many will be the precursor to an adult life of crime, unemployment or welfare dependency," the commission report concluded.[30]

(4) Extreme loneliness. The feeling that no one cares may lead people to become involved in the occult.

Few people probably understand just how lonely many feel today or how prevalent this feeling is among people of all ages from the young to the elderly. Loneliness has been called "the world's most common mental health problem,"[31] "one of the most universal sources of suffering,"[32] and an "almost permanent condition for millions" of people.[33]

Having worked with youth for over twenty years, I can readily understand their feelings that no one cares. As a counselor, I hear more and more angry young people who feel that their parents place unrealistic expectations upon them. Straight A's on their report card, excelling as athletes, making the cheer leading squad—the pressure never stops. For many, achieving these elusive goals is equated with love and acceptance from their parents. Even if they should reach these goals, the price they have to pay to get there and stay on top can cause deep feelings of resentment that make them feel used. It isn't difficult to see why they are angry.

One other aspect that I see in counseling is the common complaint that "no one knows how I feel." This may well be true, since many parents often forget what it was like to be young. They no longer remember the problems they faced as adolescents and so are not likely to empathize with their own son(s) and/or daughter(s).

The common response to many problems goes something like this, "Don't worry about it. It's no big deal," or "Too bad."

These answers, quick and easy as they may be, do little to soothe the pains that many young people experience and further reinforce their feelings of loneliness.

A common misconception is that young people in the church have no problems or fewer problems than their peers who are not involved in church. But, as one youth minister pointed out, "Youth who come to church have the same types of problems as those who don't attend church." The church will have to change this attitude if it is to meet the needs of its youth.[34]

(5) Mysticism. The influence of Eastern religions in America, continued emphasis on psychic phenomenon, and mind-expanding drugs have turned many toward a mystical approach to life.

U.S.A. Weekend reported that Transcendental Meditation (TM) has made a "major comeback." Everyone from movie director David Lynch to Elizabeth Taylor to real-life baby boomers are doing it to fight stress and burnout. Even prisons use TM to defuse tension among inmates, according to the article. Since the sixties, 1.5 million Americans have learned this form of meditation. What began as a student fad is now embraced by middle America.[35]

Time-Life Books understands the popularity of psychic phenomenon. Television commercials promote their series of hardcover books, *Mysteries of the Unknown*. To add a little incentive to purchase the series, they promise to send you a black velvet bag with smooth stones and crystals which possess supernatural powers. These "powers" will heal you, improve your memory, and give you mental clarity, joy, happiness, creativity, prosperity, efficiency, relief from stress, an improved love life, wisdom, protection, and much, much more. Sounds like a bargain, doesn't it?

Popular radio personality Paul Harvey reported that half of all prison inmates are doing time for drug-related crimes. Furthermore, he said, more young people die every one hundred hours in mostly drug-related gang wars in the United States than were killed in the forty-three-day Persian Gulf War.[36]

(6) Christianity's Impact. Evangelist Billy Graham stated, "Satanism is growing because belief in Jesus is growing. The Devil is also making his pitch."[37]

(7) Heavy metal music with occultic themes. Gladys Alarcon, a detective with the Hillsborough (Florida) County Sheriff's Department, said every teen she has interviewed in relation to an occult crime has listened to black metal music, which glorifies Satanism.[38]

(8) Fantasy role-playing games. The next time you are in a shopping mall you might stop in a toy store and browse through the fantasy role-playing games. The most popular of them all has to be "Dungeons and Dragons," also known as D & D. Dr. Gary North in his book, *Dare Call It Witchcraft*, calls "Dungeons and Dragons" the most effective, most magnificently packaged, most profitably marketed, most thoroughly researched introduction to the occult in history.[39]

The books in the series lead the player to assume the identity of a given character which could be a fighter, a thief, a cleric, an elf, a magician, a dwarf, or a "halfling," a mixture of human and subhuman. The dungeon master gives direction to the game by creating the dungeon map and coordinating the game. Themes such as witchcraft, demonology, murder, rape, desecration, cannibalism, prostitution, blasphemy, suicide, sexual perversion, sadism, divination, and others equally negative are taught to the players. The length of time an individual spends playing this game may be hours, days, or even years. Today D & D has its own magazine, annual convention, and world headquarters in Lake Geneva, Wisconsin. The game continues to sell extremely well, gaining new fans daily.

Gary Gygax, inventor of the game, admitted the game can take over someone's personality. "When you start playing out a fantasy, it can eat up time and capture you totally," he says. "At the same time," he continues, "most people can handle it, but there probably are exceptions. You can get very emotionally involved."[40]

These exceptions may well come to a tragic end, for themselves as well as for others. In 1985 the National Coalition on Television Violence (NCTV) reported that more than twenty-seven deaths were associated with the playing of the game. They listed the deaths in two categories as follows:

(1) Where D & D was the decisive factor. These are usually suicides where full information is available, often with detailed suicide notes, and (2) Where D & D was a major factor in the lives of the young men at the time of their violent acts. These are usually murders and fuller details are less available because of at least four on-going murder trials.[41]

For many the warning has come too late. Consider these three examples.

One teenage boy in Phoenix, Arizona, became so involved in the game that one of his fellow players declared him "possessed." A bright young man with an I.Q. of 122, his studies began to slide as well as other interests. He became consumed with buying items to be used for satanic rituals; purchasing books about metaphysics, magic, and the occult; sketching strange pictures in his school notebooks of daggers and heads of creatures; and listening to heavy metal music with occult themes. Church attendance and his enjoyment of activities were replaced by outright hostility to the church and to God. His diary, found too late, revealed just how far he had digressed:

> Upon reading these words, you will know that I am dead. I have now started the lonesome journey to the bowels of the earth. I travel that twisted road that winds its way down to the forsaken pit. It is time to meet my lofty maker! My destination will be the foot of the throne, where I will kneel and greet my father. Thus, ending my travel. Wearily I will scale the great monument and seat myself by the side of my lord, bowing my head in shame for I had not the courage to continue my earthly existence. Though I am a shameful sight, my father will spread his wings and welcome me to his and my real home.[42]

Knowing that his parents would not be home for at least two hours or more, he slid into the seat of his family car in a closed garage, started the engine, and slipped out into eternity.

In 1986 young Sean Sellers held a distinction that no other young man held—or would want to hold. At seventeen years of age, he was the youngest man on death row in the Oklahoma State Penitentiary. Sean had been convicted and sentenced for the murder of three people: a convenience store clerk, his stepfather, and his mother.

Sean's introduction into the occult followed the same gradual pattern that others have found. He was a bright student who loved to read; science fiction and tales of the supernatural soon became his preferences. When a babysitter checked out some books about Satanism and witchcraft for him, Sean found the attraction irresistible. At twelve years of age he discovered "Dungeons and Dragons." The rest was downhill.

In his own story, Sean says,

> Beneath the few books I carried home with my football equipment was a notebook filled with Dungeons and Dragons material. I had four primary interests: I played football, practiced Ninjutsu (Japanese assassin rites), collected comic books, and played D & D.
>
> I was a Dungeon Master and I played a character. We ran three different campaigns. I DMed [dungeon mastered or planned the

game map and directed the flow of the game] in two of them and played my neutral/chaotic fighter in the third. Nobody understood the game as well as I. I read, I studied the manuals. I created new and more intense Dungeon modules. All of my spare time in school was taken up in my study of D & D.[43]

From D & D Sellers progressed ever deeper into the occult world, studying demonology, conducting and participating in satanic rituals, compiling his grimoire (a manual for invoking demons and spirits of the dead), and taking drugs.

Pat Pulling, a thirty-eight-year-old Richmond, Virginia, mother, lost her sixteen-year-old son to suicide, which she blames on "Dungeons and Dragons." "The dungeon master," she explains, "had issued a death curse instructing the boy to kill other people. He felt he couldn't kill other people so he killed himself."[44]

To combat the occult influence among youth, Pulling founded a national non-profit organization, BADD (Bothered About Dungeons and Dragons and other Harmful Influences on Children). The group seeks to help parents and whole communities deal with Satanism among youth. Would these young men be where they are today had it not been for D & D? We will never know.

(9) It's the "in thing" to do. Pat Pulling, who has testified as an expert in three different occult-related murder trials, elaborates on this aspect as she says, "The kids think it's neat. It [Satanism] is a way to amass power. They experiment, and the next thing you know…they start to believe they have powers and magic abilities.

"I have had parents say," she further explains, "'My kid wouldn't do this because he is a Christian.' But if a child can believe in a God he cannot see…, why can't the public see that he can believe in the opposite kind of supernatural forces, especially when they relieve him of all restrictions?

"Satanists live by the motto, 'Do what thou wilt.' What 15-18-year-old wouldn't love to adopt that philosophy?"[45]

(10) The decline of the family. The traditional family of mom, dad, and a child or two is getting harder to find. Only 11 percent of all U.S. households fit this description. Furthermore, 14.6 percent of the adult population is divorced.[46] A noticeable decline in the divorce rate is not expected.[47]

The sheer cost of beginning a family is staggering. The U.S. government estimates that it will cost $120,150 to raise a child to age eighteen for a middle-income family making between $29,900 and $48,300![48] Small wonder that more mothers are entering or returning to work than ever before. Many have no other choice financially, and more and more children will come home from school to an empty house.

A husband's unrealistic expectations that the wife combine the traditional housewife/homemaker and career roles, financial worries, and physical exhaustion have combined to take a devastating toll on marriages.

Dean Register, in a keynote address entitled, "Caring for the Family of the 90s," added a further disturbing thought when he wrote that mobility and urbanization will also increase in the very near future. Hundreds of thousands of children may soon not know what a hometown is, and millions will live in skyscraper neighborhoods inhabited by strangers.[49]

With the family in trouble, the ground becomes very fertile for occultic influence. For example, Sean Sellers was subject to constant mobility, a broken home at age three, continually being farmed out to relatives, frequent separations from his mother, and frequent reminders at home that he was not good enough. He would later remark, "If I had had a close family relationship, I might not have gotten into Satanism. There was an absence, and Satan filled that."[50]

PERSONALITY TYPES

Even though stress and uncertainty can help explain why people are attracted to the occult, we also need to ask if certain personality types are more likely to become involved in occult activity.

As a university counselor, I am daily reminded of Psalm 139:14 in which the psalmist says, "I praise you because I am fearfully and wonderfully made." Every person I meet is uniquely individual. It would be nice if we could place everyone in neat and simple categories that we could understand and rely on, but God's creation is simply too complex for such simplifications. This fact must be clear before this discussion of personality types.

An ever-expanding base of data is emerging in an effort to understand the personality of those involved in the occult. Many issues affecting this study are shrouded in controversy, such as the effect of fantasy-role playing games, the influence of black and heavy metal music, etc. These and other issues will be considered in depth a little later in this book.

People who get involved in the occult can generally be divided into four categories: (1) the fringe or thrill seekers, (2) the dabblers, (3) the orthodox (those who have made serious commitments), and (4) the criminal (those who commit serious crimes such as child abuse, rape, murder, etc.).

We will examine the first two levels now and save the last two for our discussion in chapter 7.

The Fringe or Thrill Seekers

Critics like to point out that playing with a Ouija™ board, tarot cards, and "Dungeons and Dragons," or listening to "satanic music" does not make one a practicing occultist. While this may well be true, it could be equally argued that every day someone gets behind the wheel of his car intoxicated and arrives at his destination without a serious problem. Would anyone want to use this as an excuse for drinking and driving? Drinking and driving don't mix: Every day someone will be seriously injured, maimed for life, or die because of an intoxicated driver. It isn't worth the risk to the driver or the innocent on the streets. Neither is flirting with the occult.

At the beginning of the chapter, we met Lauren and witnessed her introduction into the occult world. Was Lauren a deeply disturbed individual? She certainly faced moral questions that bother many young people today. By consulting a Ouija™ board to find the answers to her problems, Lauren was setting a dangerous precedent. Some of the girls around the Ouija™ board were involved in Sunday morning Bible study and in the youth program of their church. Had anyone told them about the dangers of flirting with the occult? Probably not. They would see no reason to deter Lauren. Who among Lauren's friends would have the slightest idea where Lauren's step that night would lead her?

Indeed, if you could see the end result of yielding to Satan's temptation in your life, would you be tempted in the first place?

What is this group like? Those on the fringe have an interest in occult movies and/or television programs with occult themes. Extrasensory perception (ESP) and psychic phenomenon may also attract them. They may try to understand the future through astrology, tarot cards, and the Ouija™ board. They may read books with occult subjects (fiction and non-fiction) and/or listen to music with occult subject matter. Fringe seekers may even dress in bizarre manners (such as all black) and exhibit body tattoos which are occult symbols. Girls may paint their fingernails black.

It is important not to overreact. One man told me that he felt as if he and his family were "under siege" because two mischievous friends of his daughter had decorated his house with toilet paper and sprayed red paint on portions of his driveway. He was quite certain that one of the youths was involved in Satan worship and pointed to the red color of the paint as representing blood.

A personality profile of the fringe or thrill seeker category will, for the most part, reveal no particularly serious personality problems. This will not hold true for the second category.

Dabblers

Some individuals are not connected to orthodox occult groups and create their own religion, borrowing perhaps from *The Satanic Bible,* written by Anton LaVey, an occult-related movie, or some other occult object. These individuals are known as dabblers.

Noted authority Arthur Lyons believes these are socially alienated teenagers whose occult rituals revolve around wish fulfillment such as acquisition of money and sexual gratification, and may involve infatuation with the game "Dungeons and Dragons," heavy drug use, and devotion to heavy metal rock music.[51]

Perhaps the most significant word in understanding the depth of involvement in the dabbler category is the word "unusual." Upon close observation this level of involvement may not be that difficult to assess.

Individuals in this category will show an *unusual* amount of interest in watching occult-related movies or television material.

The same interest is also often evident in the individual's music preference.

When such unusual interest is accompanied by noticeable behavioral changes, there is a good possibility that this individual is in the dabbler category. At this point, we need to be alert for other indications of occult activity.

WARNING SIGNS OF ADOLESCENT OCCULTIC INVOLVEMENT

The following are some of the warning signs that someone may be interested or involved in the occult. Behavioral changes and the presence of certain occultic paraphernalia in his or her bedroom merit attention. One or more of these signs does not necessarily mean that adolescents have an interest or are involved in the occult. These signs should be taken into consideration with other factors such as gradual or abrupt behavioral changes and patterns. It is imperative that parents be involved with their teenagers and that communication lines always remain open.

➤ Abrupt emotional changes
➤ Animal masks
➤ Ashes, gongs, drums, and/or bells
➤ Bizarre haircuts, hair color
➤ Black dress, unusually long fingernails (sometimes painted black)
➤ Body paint, face paint
➤ Bull whip, cat-o'-nine-tails
➤ Changes in school habits
➤ Coffin
➤ Crystals in various shapes and sizes (balls, domes, etc.)
➤ Ferns, palms
➤ Flash powder, smoke bombs
➤ Goblet or chalice
➤ Graph paper for fantasy games, dice (maybe oddly shaped configurations with numbers on them)
➤ Heavy wooden staff, swords, and knives

➤ Human or animal bones (especially skull, long bones, finger bones), flesh
➤ Incense
➤ Large ruby or red stone ring worn on the first finger of the right hand
➤ Masks like Halloween (horror type) and costumes
➤ Medallions with satanic symbols or other occult jewelry
➤ Meditations, chanting, use of new vocabulary
➤ Metal crown with four candle holders
➤ Obsession with rock music using satanic symbols or references
➤ Occult drawings on notebooks, tattoos
➤ Paraphernalia in and related to clothing and/or weapons associated with martial arts (ninja costumes, etc.)
➤ Phallus
➤ Poems and prose with themes of blood, death, murder, Satan, evil, dying, and suicide
➤ Possession or use of games with occultic themes (Ouija™ board, tarot cards, fantasy role-playing games, I Ching, crystal ball, etc.)
➤ Posters of heavy metal/punk rock stars
➤ Posters of mythological beings, animals, half man/half beast
➤ Posters of nightmarish pictures
➤ Posters of sexual nature, particularly sado-masochistic
➤ Rejection of friends
➤ Rejection of parental values
➤ Right-hand black satin or velvet glove
➤ Ritual books, black books, diaries (such as the *Book of Shadows*, which might be handwritten)
➤ Small animals in cages or empty cages
➤ Small metal figures of a mythological nature
➤ Small scarlet velvet pillow
➤ Unusual interest in books of Satanism, black magic, witchcraft, or other occult subjects.

WHAT YOU CAN DO

If you know someone who may be demonstrating interest in or is already involved in the occult, you need to consider the following:

➤ Make your concern a matter of urgent prayer as you determine the steps you should take under the guidance of God's Holy Spirit.

➤ Seek out your pastor, minister of education, or youth minister and share your concern confidentially with them. They may be able to offer you sound spiritual advice in addition to praying with you about the matter.

➤ Call or write to one of the organizations listed in appendix A for further information.

➤ Above all, do not react hysterically. Be sure of your facts before you talk with an individual or persons related to the individual.

➤ Listen calmly and lovingly as you enter into dialogue with them.

➤ Remember that the individual's resistance to you might be steep, but it just may be that he (or she) wants to be convinced that he is wrong.

➤ Keep the lines of communication open. You may have opportunities to talk further.

LAUREN

In the hush of the darkened room, Lauren edged past the other girls to be closer to the Ouija™ board. She felt strange. Part of her was excited: *Can I really make contact with the spirit world? Can I really know what will happen to me tomorrow, next month, next year?*

But part of Lauren was afraid. It was something she heard at a Christian youth rally a month ago. If only she could remember. Her thoughts seemed so confused, and then suddenly the memory came to her. The speaker had told them how Satan would try to influence their thoughts and one way he did that with young people was through music.

Lauren loved music of all kinds. She even had some CDs of groups the speaker was telling them to avoid, like King Diamond, Slayer, Venom, and others. But it was strange how a chorus from AC/DC's "Highway to Hell" came to her mind in French class last week. Lauren pushed the words of the song back into the recesses of her mind that day. But now they were coming back, this time stronger than ever.

Should I use this Ouija™ board or shouldn't I? Suddenly she heard a metallic click and a soft mechanical whir. Was it for effect? Was it a warning? Then the words of Venom in the song "Possessed" filled the darkness.

Lauren hesitated for a moment...

T W O

The Tempter's Tunes

Before today's teenagers graduate from high school, they will have listened to 10,500 hours of rock music—only 500 hours less than the time they will have spent in school over a twelve-year period.[1]

Three hundred professionals attending a first-of-its-kind conference on adolescent psychiatry held in San Diego agreed that adolescents are worse today, more likely to get in trouble with the law, and more likely to have serious mental disorders than adolescents of centuries or decades past. Addressing their concerns, they stated, "There is a readily available supply of drugs like crack cocaine in many schools and on the street, more single-parent families, more reports of child abuse, and an attitude of rebellion glorified in music and pop culture."[2]

Stuart Goodman put it succinctly: "Rock's sheer pervasiveness makes it the most profound value shaper in existence today. Unless you are deaf, it is virtually guaranteed that rock music has affected your view of the world."[3]

Readers of "Dear Abby" complain of having to listen to it as they shop, parents protest the bone-rattling vibrato from expensive car stereo systems, and adults form organizations to combat what they see as disturbing signs that rock music is heavily influenced by the occult.

Even more alarming, some parents do not know what their children are watching and do not care. When my wife, Susan, and I returned from nearly ten years of missionary service in Rio de Janeiro, we were blissfully ignorant of MTV (Music TeleVision) which broadcasts rock music videos twenty-four hours a day.

At that time, our oldest child, Ryan, was twelve and entering the seventh grade. MTV came with the basic cable, so Ryan soon discovered it. After watching a few minutes, I realized that this was not what I wanted my son to be absorbing mentally. Not only was I angry that sensuality and a materialistic lifestyle was so blatant, but I had to pay to get the offending channel, that I had not asked for, removed from the package of other channels!

WHAT'S THE BIG FUSS?

As I speak to adults in seminars, I am still amazed at how many do not understand why MTV is objectionable. I always ask how many have ever watched MTV and few hands go up. When I assign them the task of watching thirty minutes of it, they generally become concerned as well.

It is not easy for parents to stay current on the ever-changing youth subculture, but perhaps the following definitions and listing of groups identified with each type may help:

Heavy Metal: a type of music that developed in England in which the music is loud and powerful, with most of the strength coming from electric guitars. The makeup or facial expressions are either hateful or demonic or have symbols and costumes representing power. Examples are facial painting to look "evil," as in KISS; tattoos of a snarling animal or the Grim Reaper as on Ozzy Osborne's body; black leather chains and motorcycles in Judas Priest; or a demonic caricature (Eddy) in Iron Maiden. Members of the group Motley Crue wear pentagrams.[4]

Death Metal: the genre of metal songs that deal with doom and destruction. Key bands: Slayer, Possessed.[5]

Punk Rock: Violence, aggression, and provocation by being outrageous are key attributes. Anarchistic punkers appear on stage in dirty, torn clothes, sporting orange, purple, and/or green hair, or no hair at all. They exhibit self-abusive practices such as sticking safety pins through their skin and express hostility toward the audience with foul language, vomiting, and spitting.[6]

Hard Core: A musical form owing more to classic themes of punk rock than to classic metal bands. Key groups: The Cro-Mags, the Dead Kennedys.[7]

The Mosh: Male-only dancing in which people slam their bodies into each other like linebackers into tight ends.[8]

Pretty Metal (also known as glitter or glam metal): More mainstream groups whose members are good-looking. Key artists: Bon Jovi and Poison.[9]

Speed Metal (also known as thrash or power metal): It borrows a rapid beat and generally short song time from old-style punk bands like the Sex Pistols. Key groups: Metallica and Megadeath.[10]

Thrashers: the subgroup of fans addicted to speed metal.[11]

Never heard anything about the above? Do you think it is much ado about nothing?

Well, the next time you are in a shopping mall and have a few minutes to spare, drop into a record store and take a look at what they are offering. The chart that follows shows a few of the artists you may find there, and some of the material contained within their recordings. If this information does not bother you, then consider the testimony of some of the "stars" themselves and a few of the major issues they address.

One such artist is Ozzy Osborne. He was *Billboard's* Singer of the Year in 1983 and has distinguished himself in other ways as well. He claimed to have seen the movie *The Exorcist* twenty-six times and once said, "I don't know if I am a medium for some outside source. Whatever it is, frankly, I hope it's not what I think...Satan."[12]

Group	Album	Song
AC/DC	*If You Want Blood*	"Highway to Hell"
Black Sabbath	*Sabbath Bloody Sabbath*	"Killing Yourself to Live"
Blue Oyster Cult	*Career of Evil* (Cross of Confusion– in flames)	"Don't Fear the Reaper," "Hot Rails to Hell"
DIO	*Holy Diver* (A beast is drowning a minister)	"Holy Diver," "Shame on the Night" "Rainbow in the Dark"
Ozzy Osborne	*Blizzard of Oz* (A woman is on floor holding up a cross with a skull and cat next to her)	"Mr. Crowley" (Aliester Crowley is a famous satanist)
Iron Maiden	*The Number of the Beast* (Ghoulish figure manipulates the Devil with one hand–flames come out of the other)	"Children of the Damned," "The Number of the Beast," "Hallowed Be Thy Name"
KISS (Kids in Service to Satan)	*Smashes, Thrashes and Hits*	"Let's Put the X in Sex," "(You make me) Rock Hard"
Motley Crue	*Shout at the Devil*	"Children of the Beast"
Spinal Tap	*Break the Wind* (a skull is on the cover)	"Christmas with the Devil,"
Danzig	*Danzig III–How the Gods Kill* (A snake crawls down a grotesque figure which holds a knife with a demonic face on its handle)	"Wear the Mark," "Heart of the Devil" "When the Dying Calls"
Cannibal Corpse	*Tomb of the Mutilation–Censored Version* (Corpse stands over a crypt)	"The Cryptic Stench," "Beyond the Cemetery"

This is from a man about whom *Time* magazine stated that "the singer's onstage artistry has included such excesses as biting the head off a bat,[13] decapitating doves, dumping about 25 lbs. of calf livers and pig intestines on the audience each night,[14] urinating onstage and trampling little puppies to death."[15] Gratefully, rock stars like Osborne and AC/DC have moved from the occult to more promising avenues of music expression, but clearly the damage has been done in the past and those objectionable albums, cassettes, or CDs are still accessible to new legions of fans.

Predictably, players are quick to defend themselves.

Lars Ulrich, the drummer for the popular heavy metal Metallica challenged parents when he said in a *Parade* magazine interview, "There are so few parents out there that really take the time to sit down with their kids and actually pay attention to the music they like and give it a chance: 'What is it this does for you? What do you get out of it?'"[16]

EVIDENCE OF ITS INFLUENCE

On the other hand, Dr. Paul King, a child psychiatrist who treats disturbed teens at the Charter Lakeside Clinic in Memphis, Tennessee, would just as soon that chance be removed as he believes the music can influence its fans. "The kids I've seen who are violent and into drugs by and large are into heavy music. The music doesn't make them do it, but the lyrics become their philosophy."[17]

But just how influential can heavy metal music become? Can it influence you by sending a message to you without your knowing it, as in subliminal perception? Is it influential enough even to cause someone to commit suicide?

The United States Bureau of Census reports that nearly 5,000 Americans under age twenty-four, committed suicide last year. An additional 10,000 teens attempted suicide with 200,000 to 300,000 contemplating suicide.[18] According to one report, the suicide rate among youth has tripled in the past twenty years.[19] The National Youth Suicide Prevention Center in Washington, D.C. reports that every hour of every day more than 228 teenagers in the United States will attempt to take their lives.[20]

Being an adolescent's parent is not easy, just as it is not a simple matter being an adolescent today. As Gary Collins noted, "adolescents are going through a significant change period, characterized first by the need to adjust to a variety of physical changes, second by the influence of great social pressures, and third by the challenge of making life-determining decisions about values, beliefs, identity, careers, lifestyles, and relationships with others, including those of the opposite sex."[21] It is a critical time in the development of the personality.

No one would question that the primary recipients of heavy metal music are today's adolescents, and certainly no one would dare presume that everyone who likes heavy metal music is a Satanist or involved in the occult, nor will everyone who listens to this type of music commit suicide. Nonetheless, some have.

James Vance and Ray Belknap went to a Sparks, Nevada, playground two days before Christmas chanting "do it, do it, do it," and they did. They placed a shotgun to their heads and pulled the trigger. Eighteen-year-old Ray died instantly. Twenty-year-old James survived for a few years with half his face blown away. But in 1988 his life ended due to complications from his injuries.

In depositions prior to his death, Vance recalled that the two had listened to Judas Priest's 1978 album "Stained Glass" for hours while smoking marijuana, drinking, and discussing the lyrics in the song "Beyond the Realms of Death." Vance said they agreed, "Let's see what's next," as in the next life.

Lawyers for the distraught families attempted to prove that the Judas Priest song "Better by You—Better than Me" contained the subliminal urging, "do it, do it."[22]

Fourteen-year-old Tommy Sullivan attended a Catholic school in Sparta, New Jersey, where he studied Satanism in his eighth grade religion class. Tommy was a typical teenager—loving sports and winning trophies for wrestling. He was no stranger to mischief, yet detective Paul Hart of the Jefferson Township Police Department would recall that on that fateful night "we had never heard of Tommy and his family."[23]

Tommy's interest in the occult apparently grew more serious. His parents paid little attention to books on witchcraft and Satanism he brought home from the public library. His friends thought he was just looking for attention when he invited them to join him in worshiping the devil. They didn't take him seriously.

According to one report,

> Tommy grew more belligerent at home. He shut himself in his room and listened obsessively to the music of Ozzy Osborne, Motley Crue and Metallica on the $1,000 stereo system he had bought with his hard-earned savings. He was especially fascinated by songs about suicide, his father later told the police, and he often played one particular song—about killing one's mother—over and over again. Insisting that the youngster not subject the entire family to "junk" music, Tommy Sr. ordered the boy to wear headphones.[24]

As time passed Tommy's obsession with the occult deepened, culminating in a horrible action between 10:30 P.M. Sunday, January 10, and 10:00 A.M. Monday, January 11. The mutilated body of Tommy's mother was found beside Tommy's barbell. Tommy's frozen shirtless body would be found in the snow covered backyard of a neighbor. Alongside his body was a 3 1/2-inch-long Boy Scout knife used to slash his wrist and cut his throat.[25] A note in Tommy's handwriting addressed to "the greatest demons of hell" pledged to kill his family.

SUBLIMINAL MESSAGES

Did music play a big role in the suicides of Ray Belknap and young Tommy Sullivan? Some authorities think so and attribute these violent self-destructive acts to what has been referred to as subliminal perception and backmasking.

Specifically, subliminal perception is a process involving a response to stimulation that is too weak or too brief to be consciously reported. Subliminal perceptions result from stimuli that cause the sensory receptors to fire (sensory threshold) but are not strong enough to reach conscious awareness (perceptual threshold). They are perceptions, therefore, that are below (*sub*) the threshold (*limen*, Latin) of conscious awareness.[26]

Even the theme for the old "Mr. Ed" series was alleged to be satanic. Seventy-five teenagers participated in a mass burning of

Mr. Ed records in April 1986 after evangelist Jim Brown claimed during a seminar at the First Church of the Nazarene in Irontown, Ohio, that "A Horse Is a Horse," when played in reverse becomes "Someone sung this song for Satan."[27]

Even "Saturday Night Live" has cashed in on the idea by creating a newscaster as well as several skits where the "subliminal" word or words are spoken between phrases to the laughter of the studio audience.

However, there is nothing particularly humorous about the messages that purport to be the result of backward masking, or backmasking as it is also known. In this recording technique, words or messages are reversed and "hidden" within the music. The listener does not hear them audibly as he hears the music but subliminally picks the messages up.

You may remember a story some years ago disclosing that a New Jersey theater flashed on the screen every five seconds for 1/3000th of a second the message "Hungry? Eat popcorn" or "Drink Coca-Cola." Concession sales skyrocketed with popcorn up 57.5 percent and Coke by 18 percent.[28]

However, pertinent questions about the experimental procedures were left unanswered by the experimenters, and the results have not been considered reliable.

Some of the classic examples used as evidence of backmasking are the following:[29]

➤ Electric Light Orchestra's gold certified album allegedly includes the phrase, "Christ, you're the nasty one, you're infernal" (meaning hateful or abominable).

➤ The Eagles LP *Hotel California* in the record of the same name reportedly contains the phrases played backward stating, "Yes, Satan organized his own religion . . . it was delicious . . . he puts it in a vat and fixes it for his son and gives it away."

➤ The Rolling Stones song "Tops" of the successful *Tatoo* LP includes, according to some, a backward masked "love song" which says, "I love you, said the devil."

➤ Black Oak Arkansas's song, "The Day When the Electricity Came to Arkansas," allegedly says, "Satan, Satan, he is god, he is god, he is god." Following that is what supposedly sounds like demonic laughter, then the chanting of prayers similar to those used in satanic worship.

After a definition of backward masking and what messages some report to be in the recordings, you might be wondering, How did these backmasked messages get there in the first place?

I believe there are four possible explanations for backmasking.

First, there may be definite words or phrases, but then it may be an overactive imagination hearing what it wants to hear. John R. Vokey and J. Don Read of the University of Lethbridge, Alberta, Canada, conducted research on backmasking and found no evidence that backward messages had any effect on the listener's behavior. In addition, they concluded that most so-called "backward messages" are non-existent and are instead actually "constructed" by previously conditioned listeners. They noted that in public demonstrations of the backmasking phenomenon, one pastor told his listeners the message they were about to hear, rather than having them listen to the recording and then having the listeners relate what they had heard. By so doing, the pastor shaped his listener's perception of the message in a way that was consistent with his.[30]

In the fine video presentation, "Hell's Bells," Eric Holmberg offers three other possibilities as follows.[31]

Second, the artists or engineers intentionally hide messages in the music. For it to be intentional, the vocalists would have to sing just the right lyrics and in just the right way. This would be extremely difficult, as a number of musicians and producers have testified.

Third, the phenomenon is an accident, a quirk of music. Not only are the mathematical probabilities of this absurd, but the fact that virtually every example of this type conveys a message that is intrinsically demonic even further disproves this hypothesis.

Fourth, the procedure is spiritual. Outside intelligence forces with supernatural powers are occasionally able to play an artist, much like we would play a musical instrument.

So which of the four would you choose? Each seems plausible in its own way. I wonder if it really makes much difference to

Satan? It is he of whom Paul spoke in 1 Corinthians 14:33: "For God is not a God of confusion but of peace" (RSV). Satan is a master at leading people to focus on anything but the main issue.

ROCK AND ROLL OBITUARIES

Jeremiah spoke of man's stubborn and rebellious heart with no fear of the Lord, of men who set traps to catch other men. These trap setters would become great and rich, but they would be punished (Jer. 5:23–28).

Rebellion against God always carries a high price tag. The obituary column of rock stars who led a rebellious lifestyle reads like a "who's who" in rock and rock music.

Consider the following:[32]

John "Bonzo" Bonham (1948–80). Drummer for Led Zeppelin, Bonham was known to be a heavy drinker and to take "speedballs," a mixture of heroin and cocaine, plus sleeping pills mixed with booze. A suspected heart attack in June of 1980 did not slow him down until September 26 of the same year when he was found dead in band member Jimmy Page's home with the equivalent of forty measures of vodka in his system. Bonham had choked on his own vomit at the age of thirty-two.

Jimi Hendrix (1942–70). Guitarist extraordinaire, at one time toured with the Monkees as their opening act, Hendrix was known for his exhibitionistic stage manner simulating copulation with his guitar and amplifier and fondling his guitar as well. Many fans of rock music remember Hendrix's total destruction of his guitar at the end of his performance as he doused it with lighter fluid and set it on fire. On September 17, 1970, at twenty-seven years of age Hendrix drank some wine, smoked pot, and entered into eternity with a handful of Vesperin (sleeping pills). Like Bonham, he too choked on his own vomit.

Brian Jones (1943–69). Known at one time as the drive and musical inspiration of the Rolling Stones, rhythm guitarist Jones' heavy use of LSD diminished his contributions to the group after 1966. His life came to an end in his Sussex, England, mansion, a victim of drug overdose and drowning. According to sources, many of his vital organs suffered from fatty degeneration that would have soon killed him anyway. Keith Richards, the Stone's lead guitarist, said concerning Jones, "Brian burnt out all his fuses a long time ago. He'd lived 26 years too fast. A whole lifetime in 26 years."

Jim Morrison (1943–71). The subject of film director Oliver Stone's movie *The Doors*, Morrison, the lead singer of The Doors, was charged by the Florida state attorney's office for acts in public of a sexual nature[33] so vile and disgusting that I will not reprint them here.

Morrison eventually left The Doors and moved to Paris where he died of drug-related causes on July of 1971 at the age of twenty-seven.

The list could go on and on.

In addition to the above, those who died from suicide include:[34] Donny Hathaway ("The Closer I Get to You"), Pete Ham ("Bad-finger"), Paul Williams of the Temptations, and folk singer Phil Ochs. Drug-related deaths are: Greg Herbert of Blood, Sweat & Tears, Robert McIntosh of Average White Band, Brian Cole of The Association, Al Wilson of Canned Heat, Sid Vicious of Sex Pistols, Keith Moon of The Who, Bon Scott of AC/DC, Gram Parsons of Flying Burrito Brothers, and Janis Joplin.

Next we will examine briefly sex and violence in music and the occult lifestyles of the rich and famous in the rock world.

SEX AND VIOLENCE

Puberty marks a dramatic passage for human beings. Hormones cause physical changes, sexual urges, and emotional upheavals. This instability leaves teenagers lonely, afraid, and often angry. They are easily swayed by the sexual messages in advertising and music as they seek self-esteem and identity with their friends.

Tipper Gore, wife of Vice-President Al Gore, co-founded the Parents Music Resource Center which successfully led a fight to get warning labels placed on certain music. These labels state that the songs contain explicit references to sex and/or violence; lyrics in printed form are often found in the CD or cassette packaging.

The 119-store Hastings chain, the 235 stores in the Camelot chain, and others decided to use these labels. An article in *Billboard* magazine shed light on the decision by stating that store leases in certain mall locations have provisions against selling pornographic material,[35] and some of the music definitely falls into the category of pornography.

The point is the message of the music.

Still PMRC director Jennifer Norwood stated, "There is acceptable heavy metal. Parents shouldn't get caught up in their distaste of the sound. It's the message that counts."[36]

For that matter, we would do well to think about the messages of all secular songs we listen to. Country and western songs can be as bad as any of the above and even "easy listening" music can convey values that are not compatible with the Christian lifestyle.

Rev. Don Kimball, a Catholic priest who heads Cornerstone Media, which publishes a rock 'n' roll newsletter for church people correctly states, "The lyrics have one message: 'I'm not going to take it anymore.' It's a scream of pain. Really, a scream of rage."[37]

People in the world of heavy metal describe it as merely the latest in scare-the-bourgeois music culture, no different in kind from the early shock value of 1950s rock 'n' roll, the 1960s British invasion, and the "art rock" of the 1970s. But Elvis and Led Zeppelin were never like this. Their material did not revel in satanic imagery or expound on effective methods of torture and disembowelment. Nor did their lyrics tend to be unprintable or deliberately disgusting.

Incredible, as some would say, but equally disturbing is what passes for entertainment at rock concerts where parents blissfully leave their teens to have a good time.

In his nationally syndicated column, Cal Thomas wrote about what goes on at some concerts and what one city did to put a stop to it.

Perhaps the most detailed ordinance in the country is St. Louis. Seven pages long, it prohibits acts onstage that simulate or suggest in action or language anal copulation, sex with a corpse, sex with a child, rape, incest and sexually objectional language! That some of these concerts contain such material ought to shock and outrage parents and politicians alike, but most people are blind to what takes place once they drop their kids off at the stadium.[38]

A Picture Worth a Thousand Words?

It isn't just the lyrics nor what happens on stage that is troublesome. Some kids don't understand the lyrics or go to concerts but they still buy tapes and CDs. What they're seeing on the albums ought to trouble you. Let's take a quick look at the sexual references on album covers:

The *Los Angeles Times*, the second largest newspaper in the country, refused to promote and advertise Boz Scagg's *Middleman* LP because of it's cover and content. The letters of the title of James Brown's *Sex Machine* are formed with the bodies of nude women. Inside the jacket of Van Halen's top-10 LP, *Women and Children First*, looms a giant poster of bare-chested David Lee Roth tied up in chains. Explains Roth: "The picture got such an intense reaction that we said, 'That's rock and roll.' Anyway, it's always been one of my sexual fantasies to be tied up."[39]

It should be pointed out that it isn't just heavy metal music that deals with sex. The ever popular Prince's LP *Dirty Mind* was praised in *Rolling Stone* with the following tribute,

> Nothing…could have prepared us for the liberating lewdness of *Dirty Mind*. Here Prince lets it all hang out; the cover photograph depicts our hero, smartly attired in a trench coat and black bikini briefs, staring soberly into the camera. The major themes are paeans to bisexuality, incest and cunnilingual technique, each tucked between such sprightly dance raveups as "Partyup" and the smash single "Uptown."[40]

None would deny the blatant sexual lyrics, imagery, and lifestyle of pop star Madonna. From her premier performance as a fifth-grader in a parish talent show dancing in a minuscule bikini, which not only won the crowd but the talent show as well, to her superstar status in the recording industry and the sale of the erotic photograph book *Sex* (which sold 150,000 copies the first day out of 500,000 printed), some have wondered what is behind her success.

Richard Price in a biographical article explains it this way:

Something had clicked in Madonna. She would never stop grab-
bing attention as she had that night (of the talent show) by being
daring and different, and sexy when it works, and naturally funny,
and by giving people a jolt here and there.

That explains the sixty million albums she's sold worldwide.
Her eighteen top-10 hits, the concert sellouts of her Blond Ambition tour, the whirlwind impact on fashion, music and dance, the
startling videos, the spreads in *Playboy* and *Penthouse* and the
practically banned Pepsi commercials, the amazing fame, and the
sexually tinged fascination that people have for her.[41]

Not surprisingly, Madonna would gain another dubious honor,
that of making what PMRC would say constitutes a list of songs
with vulgar lyrics dubbed "The Filthy Fifteen." Dealing with
everything from blatant occultism to raw sex, the list included the
following:[42]

1. "Eat Me Alive," Judas Priest
2. "Bastard," Motley Crue
3. "Darling Nikki," Prince
4. "Sugar Walls," Sheena Easton
5. "Animal," W.A.S.P.
6. "Into the Coven," Merciful Fate
7. "Strap on Robby Baby," Vanity
8. "High n' Dry," Def Leppard
9. "We're Not Gonna Take It," Twisted Sister
10. "Dress You Up," Madonna
11. "She Bop," Cyndi Lauper
12. "Let Me Put My Love into You" AC/DC
13. "Trashed," Black Sabbath
14. "My House," Mary Jane Girls
15. "Possessed," Venom

Even rap music has cashed in on the controversy…and has a
record to prove it, a criminal record, that is.

On June 6, 1990, U.S. District Court Judge Jose Gonzalez of
Fort Lauderdale, Florida, declared that *As Nasty as They Wanna
Be*, by 2 Live Crew (a Miami-based rap group), was obscene in the
three counties under his jurisdiction, making it the first recording
to be declared obscene by a federal court.

Within days, a record store owner was arrested for continuing to sell the album. Two group members were also arrested for performing a song from the album for an adults only audience.[43]

A cleaner G-rated version of *As Clean as They Wanna Be* did not sell as well. According to one record store manager, the "nasty" version outsold the "clean" version ten to one with many managers saying the purchasers were kids eighteen and younger.[44]

When the group performed the G-rated versions, which lacked the profanities, and stopped short of singing the vulgar lyrics, each time teenagers in the audience gleefully shouted them out.[45]

Small wonder the powerful American Medical Association threw its support behind voluntary record labeling by the music industry and declared its concern about the impact of destructive themes in certain kinds of rock music.[46]

Themes of sex and violence so prolific in music today provide fertile ground for Satan to sow his seeds.

The lyrics promote a life alien to what we hold to be the truth in Jesus Christ. Whether lyrics can be understood or not or whether they are subliminal or not begs the question. What is their value to the born again believer?

Satan also desensitizes us to immorality through repeated exposure to violent, immoral television shows.

The same can be said for repeated exposure to unwholesome lyrics. I could quote any number of studies to bolster the idea that desensitization works well. Many Christians today are no longer bothered by what once offended them deeply. Let me just offer up the old adage which you will remember.

Place a frog in a kettle of boiling water and it will quickly jump out. Place a frog in a kettle full of water at room temperature and slowly increase the water until it is boiling. The frog will remain in the water until it boils to death.

Certainly no one would be so presumptuous as to say that listening to a song with suggestive or blatantly sexual lyrics is going to cause an individual to become involved in the occult, but such lyrics have no place in the Christian's life, period!

Paul reminds us to "have nothing to do with the fruitless deeds of darkness, but rather expose them" (Eph. 5:11).

OCCULT LIFESTYLES OF ROCK'S RICH AND FAMOUS

Jesus reminds us in Matthew 7:16 that we will recognize false prophets by their fruit. Can rock musicians be false prophets preaching worldly false messages through their music?

Earlier in this chapter we looked at four "movers and shakers" in the world of rock music. Each was also involved in the occult.

John "Bonzo" Bonham's group, Led Zeppelin, is considered by many rock historians to be the front runner of a music style known as heavy metal. Unfortunately, that was not the only thing that set the band apart from others.

Fellow band member, founder of the group, and lead guitarist Jimmy Paige became quite enamored with Aliester Crowley (1875–1947). Crowley, a famed occultist and English magician, described himself as the "Beast of the Apocalypse" and was labeled by the media as "The Wickedest Man in the World." Crowley is also considered by some as one of the most brilliant magicians of his time.[47]

So much of a devotee to Crowley was Paige that, according to Stephen Davis, Paige owned "a priceless collection of Crowley artifacts—books, first editions, manuscripts, hats, canes, paintings, even the robe in which Crowley had conducted rituals."[48]

Paige also purchased Crowley's old home, Boleskine House, near the village of Foyers in Inverness, Scotland.[49] He even went so far as to have Charles Pierce, a Satanist of some renown, redecorate it for him.

Former Led Zeppelin lead singer, Robert Plant, shared Paige's interest in the occult for a time. He no longer will visit Boleskine, believing it curses anyone who comes in contact with it.[50]

One might question the validity of a "curse," but few would question the strange circumstances associated with the occultic influence of Boleskine. One of its caretakers committed suicide, another went insane,[51] and Bonham would go from there to meet his maker.

Jimi Hendrix chose his own route in life with the assistance of the dark side. Jimi told *Life* magazine, "Atmospheres are going to come through music, because music is a spiritual thing of its own.

You can hypnotize people with music, and when you get people at the weakest point, you can preach to them into the subconscious what we want to say."[52]

Eric Holmberg points to a darker side of this rock and roll legend in his brief discussion of voodoo and spiritism.

> Jimi Hendrix's interest in spiritism produced not only the song "Voodoo Chile" but the following observation from one Kwasi Dzidzornu, a conga player who often played with Hendrix. Kwasi was from a village in Ghana, West Africa, where his father was a voodoo priest. One of the first things Kwasi asked Jimi was where he got that voodoo rhythm from ... that many of the signature rhythms Jimi played on guitar were very often the same rhythms that Kwasi's father played in voodoo ceremonies. The way Jimi danced to the rhythms of his playing reminded him of the ceremonial dances to the rhythm his father played to Oxun, the god of thunder and lightning. The ceremony is called Voodooshi.[53]

Fame and riches could not give Hendrix the answers to life he sought. His search was cut short, as we saw earlier.

Brian Jones reaped fame and fortune with the Rolling Stones. Like Hendrix, Jones had a fascination with voodoo and spent time in the remote mountains of Morocco with a group known as The Master Musicians of Joujouka. Believing that music is the key that unlocks the supernatural, the Joujoukans allowed Jones not only to record but later to release an album of their music. The Stones' 1989 album *Steel Wheels* includes various samples of this form of Moroccan voodoo.[54]

The year of Jones' tragic death, the Stones were to appear in a Black Arts Festival at Olympia Stadium in Detroit on Halloween. Scheduled to appear along with the Stones was the group The Coven (this is a term which designates a group of Satanists or witches, usually numbering thirteen); famed clairvoyant Timothy Leary; and Anton LaVey (organizer of the Satanic Church), who was supposed to perform a satanic benediction. The event was canceled, fortunately, when the promoters bowed to pressure from the Detroit Council of Churches.[55]

In 1969 underground filmmaker Kenneth Anger released the film, *Invocation of My Demon Brother,* an actual conjuring of Lucifer—a video version of the Black Mass. The musical background was supplied by the lead singer of the Rolling Stones, Mick Jagger, using a Moog™ synthesizer.

The Stones' drummer, Keith Richards, who replaced Jones, along with Jagger's girlfriend and singer Marianne Faithful, would appear in another Anger film entitled *Lucifer Rising*. Marianne Faithful would inspire Jagger to write "Sympathy for the Devil," and Anger would influence Jagger to use the devil from a Tarot card pack designed by Aleister Crowley for the Stone's album cover, *Their Satanic Majesties Request*.[56]

It would certainly come as no surprise that Keith Richards, responding to those who suggested that the Stones had deliberately courted an evil and satanic image, replied, "There are black magicians who think we are acting as unknown agents of Lucifer and others who think we are Lucifer."[57] Six years later Richards would observe that the Stones' songs freely came like inspiration at a seance with tunes arriving en masse as if the Stones were only a willing and open medium.[58]

Newsweek dubbed Jagger "the Lucifer of rock, the unholy roller" and spoke of "his demonic power to affect people."[59] However, Jagger and his charismatic personality would not be the only great influence on impressionable youth.

Ironically, Jim Morrison was influencing thousands of youth, yet he, too, was looking for what life was all about. "It's a search, an opening of doors. We're trying to break through to a cleaner realm," he said. Keyboard specialist Ray Manzarek added, "Hell appears so much more fascinating and bizarre than Heaven."[60]

And so it was that the dark side did have a hold on Morrison. Traveling with his family, he came upon an accident that left several American Indians dead. He observed, "The souls and the ghosts of those dead Indians, maybe one or two of them, were just running around and freaking out and just leaped into my soul. And they're still there." According to Eric Holmberg, possession by these ghosts or spirits led to a life and art obsessed with death, occult imagery, and the rejection of God.[61]

The influence of Aliester Crowley would be felt by The Doors as well. The back of one of their albums showed Morrison and the band huddled around a miniature bust of Crowley. One year prior to Morrison's death, he married a witch in a ritual that involved satanic invocations and the drinking of blood.[62]

Paul addressed those who "have become filled with every kind of wickedness, evil, greed and depravity" and says they are "God-haters, insolent, arrogant and boastful; they invent ways of doing evil...and those who do such things deserve death" (Rom. 1:30–32).

Of course, we also remember Peter's words: "He is patient with you, not wanting anyone to perish, but everyone to come to repentance" (2 Pet. 3:9). Sadly, many choose not to be repentant, and sadder still they lead so many others down the same road to destruction.

WHAT YOU CAN DO

There is much that can be done to counter the influence of harmful music on the Christian, and God's Word provides us with a wealth of guidelines.

➤ Avoid it. Paul advised Timothy (1 Tim. 6:20) to "avoid profane and vain babblings" (KJV) or "godless chatter" (NIV). Clearly there is much in music that would pass for godless.

➤ Destroy it. In Acts 19:19 we read that "they burned them publicly." Though this passage deals with the destruction of occultic written materials, the precedent would be helpful for ridding oneself of this negative influence. Not only would you benefit, but you would also keep your music from getting into someone else's hands.

➤ Know it. A list of recording company addresses to request the printed lyrics of specific heavy metal songs can be obtained by writing PMRC, 1500 Arlington Blvd., Suite 300, Arlington, VA 22209, or by calling (703) 527-9466. Parents might also visit a record store and become acquainted with the current, as well as past, offensive music and cover pictures.

➤ Teach against it. Moses reminded parents of the importance of self-monitoring and teaching spiritual truths to their children and even grandchildren in Deuteronomy 4:9: "Only be careful, and watch yourselves closely so that you do not forget the things your eyes have seen or let them slip from your heart as long as you live. Teach them to your children and to their children after them."

Nothing is worse than for well-meaning Christians to bemoan the evils of the day and then do nothing about them. Concerned persons, both youth and adults, have banded together and successfully countered this growing influence. Artists like Paul McCartney have said that things are getting farther and farther out and people need to be watchful.[63] Also of note is the fact that original funding for the PMRC came in part from a generous contribution by Mike Love of the Beach Boys.[64]

Anyone interested in organizing such an effort would do well to read appendix A of Tipper Gore's book, *Raising PG Kids in an X-Rated Society.*

None of us is above sin's influence. You yourself should not listen to offensive music so that you can teach someone else of its harmful influence. Jesus' admonition "Why do you look at the speck of sawdust in your brother's eye and pay no attention to the plank in your own eye?" (Matt. 7:3) is especially appropriate here.

There is no question but that such a battle will expose you to evil. Will you try to ignore it as it continues to influence countless others, or will you stand up and be counted against it?

LAUREN

Everything is happening so fast—too fast. I need some time to think this through, Lauren reasoned. *There must be some explanation for why I feel so afraid.*

But she also heard another voice. A voice which seemed to whisper, "There's nothing to fear. You dressed up as a ghost one Halloween and a witch the next year. Did that ever hurt you? Remember all the scary stories you used to hear around the campfire or read in your room? Did they harm you?

"How about all those great horror flicks you saw with your friends and dates?" the voice soothingly continued. "Surely you have not forgotten all those scary videos you saw? Why, you even watched some of those at your church youth group fellowships. They may have scared you a little, but it was all in good fun, no harm done.

"This is so harmless," the voice reasoned. "No sacrifices, no blood, nothing but a simple harmless game. Be a good sport. Don't let your friends down. What will they think if you back down?

You'll spoil everything. They may even think you're chicken. Besides, who knows, you might even get a look into your future!"

So Lauren drew closer to the board ...

T H R E E

You said in your heart, "I will ascend to heaven;
I will raise my throne above the stars of God;
I will sit enthroned on the mount of assembly,
on the utmost heights of the sacred mountain."
— Isaiah 14:13

Get the Picture?
Lucifer's Lessons Through the Media

The darkness is all around us, yet we seem to be either too blind to notice it, too ignorant as to its effect upon the minds and personalities of people today, or too apathetic to do anything about it.

Well-known child psychologist Robert Cole made the point well when he said,

> I think that what children in the United States desperately need is a moral purpose, and a lot of our children here aren't getting that. They're getting parents who are very concerned about getting them into the right colleges, buying the best clothing for them, giving them an opportunity to live in neighborhoods where they'll lead fine and affluent lives and where they can be given the best toys, go on interesting vacations and all sorts of things.
>
> Parents work hard these days; and they're acquiring things that they feel are important for their children. And yet they're neglecting vastly more important things. They're not spending time with their children, at least not very much.[1]

A two-year study on the ethics of youth and college students billed as "the most comprehensive survey of American ethical attitudes and behaviors ever undertaken" revealed that, according to 3,630 college students from all regions of the country[2]:

➤ Eleven percent have stolen something from parents or relatives at least once.
➤ One in eight admits to fraud, such as lying on financial aid forms or borrowing money with no intention of paying it back.
➤ One in three are willing to lie to get a job.
➤ Thirty-two percent admit to cheating on a exam at least once.
➤ One in five say they would falsify a report to keep their job or would probably cheat if it helped them compete on the job.

Ironically enough, 71 percent also said that teaching "firm ethical values" to their children was their second most important goal, and 76 percent of high school students and 81 percent of college students list parents as their biggest moral influence!

Obviously there seems to be a vast difference between what many college students do and what they want to teach their children not to do.

According to the author of the study, Michael Josephson, a hole in the moral zone has blinded a generation of youth to the age-old virtues of honesty, trustworthiness, and personal responsibility. We're setting up a kind of backward society where cheaters do prosper and honesty is not always the best policy.[3]

And it doesn't begin and end with adolescents and college students. The feelings of isolation and loneliness are not restricted just to these age groups. The church is not as relevant as it needs to be in reaching the lonely and disenfranchised. Failing to reach out to the lonely within the church only adds to their burden. It often results in them dropping out of the church, possibly never to be reached again. They may even cast an unhealthy influence over others.

Jimi Hendrix said, "I used to go to Sunday School but the only thing I believe in now is music."[4] Ozzy Osborne sang, "Rock and Roll is my religion," and in an interview concluded, "Rock and Roll is a religion in itself."[5]

Madonna came from a background where the church was not relevant in her life and did not dispel her sense of loneliness. "I had nobody, no friends, and I felt lonely...but the idea that I had a dream or a goal made me feel strong, superior, so when people didn't smile at me, I didn't care. I was going to be somebody."[6]

She fought with her dad over religion. Reflecting on her childhood, she states, "I started to think it (religion) was stupid, that it was hypocritical."[7]

Madonna uses religious imagery in her music in many different ways from words to crucifixes, oftentimes around her neck or as earrings. When asked about her use of them, she told an interviewer for *Time* that she thought they were funny[8] and referred to crucifixes as sexy because there was a naked man on them.

Whether you are a superstar or John Q. Public, you need the daily fellowship with Jesus Christ and the inclusion within a body of accepting and loving believers. If you do not have this, you are likely to be lonely with time on your hands to fill.

Research through the years has compiled a list of characteristics of those vulnerable to the occult. Considering what you have just read, the first nine should help you see how loneliness can plant the seeds for involvement in the occult.

➤ Low self-esteem or self-image
➤ Social recluse
➤ Broken homes and split families
➤ Latch-key kids
➤ Deep need for belonging
➤ Susceptible to peer pressure
➤ Impressionable
➤ Little parental care or involvement in their life
➤ Alienated from church
➤ Middle- to upper-class homes
➤ High intelligence
➤ Victim of prior sexual abuse
➤ Very creative, curious
➤ Rebellious and looking for power
➤ Over- or underachievers

What better way to plant seeds in the fertile mind than with media influenced by the master of deception? Let's look specifically at the influence of motion pictures, television, and books.

The Not-So-Silent Screen

The horror films of today are a far cry from the ones I used to watch at the double features on Saturdays. At that time the emphasis was on big, as in gigantic ants, spiders, moths, preying mantis, etc. Not any more. Today's movies in the horror genre are known by many names. To the growing number of adults concerned about their content they are known as "slasher" films and other similar titles; to the younger movie-going audience they are "must sees" and may even be the subject of discussion at church; and to the motion picture industry they are "big business." The movie series *Halloween*, *Friday the 13th*, and *A Nightmare on Elm Street* well illustrate the above. Let's consider each of them briefly.

The film series *Halloween* began in 1978 with the first of what would, as of this writing, total five films. The original film cost $300,000 and has brought in more than $55 million.[9] The "hero" in four movies of this series, Michael Meyers, is a psychotic murderer who embarks on a killing spree which originated on Halloween when he was a child.

The *Friday the 13th* series has been even more successful. Introduced to moviegoers in 1980, it became so popular that it has spawned twelve sequels to date and even a television series.

A Nightmare on Elm Street series has surpassed both the above. Like the other two, it has also produced other films in the series, namely six to date. Like *Friday the 13th*, it also became a television series popular with many young people.

The main character in the film, Freddy Krueger, was a janitor in a small-town high school. He was burned in the school furnace for his part in murdering innocent teenagers. Krueger continues, however, to come back again and again through a host of special effects, continuing his murderous ways and aided by his glove with five-inch knife blades.

The original film cost a mere $1.8 million to produce, in contrast to the $24 million-plus which it has earned to date. The first three films in the series earned a staggering $103 million. When the third in the series was released to theaters across the country, it netted nearly $13 million in the first *week* alone! These huge profits don't stop at the box office. The same first three films account for the sale of more than a half-million videocassettes, while the Freddy masks and bladed gloves have brought in $15 million in spin-off merchandise.[10]

Just how much influence do these films exert upon those who watch them? Of course, one cannot draw the conclusion that every person who watches these films is going to be drawn into the occult or decide to commit a violent crime. Nonetheless, the research thus far points to some disturbing facts.

The experimental research of numerous social scientists, most notably Edward Donnerstein, has shown with some certainty that aggressive violent sexuality, as depicted in the slasher films, has measurable short-term consequences on male attitudes concerning violence toward women. Research on the effects of watching violent pornography, a category into which the slasher films fall, indicate that the material (1) reduces college-age males' sympathy for rape victims, (2) increases their willingness to coerce women sexually, (3) increases levels of anger, and (4) disinhibits its expression toward women generally. When films offer a mix of sex and violence—always from the point of view of a crazed male aggressor—those movies effectively model and advocate aggressive male sexuality.[11]

It doesn't sound very positive, does it?

These three series will come and go, but their influence will continue to be felt through repeated showings of the movies on television, as well as syndicated reruns of their spinoff television series. Other movies and series will, unfortunately, always be there to step in and meet the public demand for such material.

Watching What You See

Films make an impression in many different ways, not the least of which is upon the mind of the viewer. Film combines several separate artistic elements—story, picture and melody—and thus carries a kind of cumulative clout. The total impact on a person can surpass the sum of the ingredients. Ear and eye are fully engaged. Story, movement, and sound combine to provide a total experience that is brighter, larger, and louder than life itself.[12]

And films drawing record numbers to the box office are saturated with sex and violence.

In 1968, a film rating system devised by the Motion Picture Association of America (MPAA) went into effect. Basically the ratings are as follows:[13]

➤ G—intended for all audiences.
➤ PG—parental guidance advised for those seventeen or younger because of some violence or sex and nudity.
➤ PG-13—sex, nudity, drugs, language, or violence that might frighten or otherwise disturb youngsters thirteen or younger.
➤ R—restricted, adult material; children seventeen or younger must be accompanied by an adult.
➤ X—material not to be seen by children, but not restricted to pornography or obscenity. Excessive violence might earn an X rating.

Asked if the ratings system had been an effective guide for the parental supervision of young moviegoers, Jack Valenti, president of MPAA, offered an emphatic yes.[14]

Since 1968, nearly half of the 9,282 films rated (4,602) have been rated R; 2,942, PG; 426, PG–13; 947, G; and 365, rated X.[15]

The MPAA has introduced two categories into the ratings system since it began in 1968. The PG-13 rating was added in 1984 at the insistence of producer-director Steven Spielberg. The NC-17 rating (no children under 17 admitted) was introduced in 1990.

The movie responsible for bringing about the latest change was *Henry and June*. *Movies on TV and Videocassette* calls it a "thoroughly satisfying drama about writer Henry Miller and his darkly sensual wife. This is a movie that isn't afraid of passion, lust and unbridled sexuality. The lovemaking scenes, including one lesbian pairing are genuinely erotic but are not, repeat not, pornographic."[16] The X designation is considered box office poison by the studios because many equate it with pornography and many newspapers refuse to place ads for X-rated films.[17] Valenti in commenting on the new classification said, "This will give parents more useful information so they themselves can decide which films their children can see."[18] Film critics Gene Siskel and Roger Ebert, hosts of a syndicated movie-preview show, joined Valenti in their support for the new classification. "It represents a victory for everyone who cares about truly adult films. I am using adult here in the sense of mature, thoughtful, serious and intelligent—not in the sense of 'dirty movies,'" Ebert said.[19]

It also represents one more victory for the darkness among us. Because many movie theaters are part of a multiplex, the way is now clear for these NC-17 movies to be shown side by side with other movies from G on up. This is precisely where I see the problem arising. How will you keep children and adolescents from gaining admission to "adult films"?

USA Today carried out some interesting research on the above when Arnold Schwarzenegger's violent movie "Total Recall" made its debut. They observed twenty-two kids age eleven to sixteen who tried to buy tickets to the R-rated *Total Recall* in six cities. Only five were turned away.[20]

If children should be refused a ticket to restricted movies, they can buy a ticket to an unrestricted movie and slip into the restricted movie. In a multiplex cinema, one entry line serves several different movies on different screens. Theaters say they try their best to enforce the restriction, but "it's not the easiest thing to administer," says Mark McDonald of the AMC chain of movie theaters. Bill Kartozian, head of the National Association of Theater Owners, maintains, "If a kid is bound and determined to get in, he will find a way to do that."[21]

The average R-rated movie in 1991 included twenty-two "F-words," three fistfights, and one scene of female nudity. Four PG-13 films depicted nude sex.[22] It should come as no shock that, according to Dave Winston, editor of *Entertainment Research Reports*, a bi-monthly newsletter aimed at parents, "The standards seem to be lowering themselves. When you take your child to a PG movie and you hear the F-word, you become a little bit concerned."[23]

Despite Winston's objections, Valenti has no intention of altering the basic philosophy of his ratings system. The general tone
of the movie is more important than the number of F-words or
the nude-body count, he says.[24]

Ryan Murphy, *Knight News Service*, put it succinctly,

> Teenagers who are making films monster hits by returning to see
> them countless times are the ones most affected by the glut of
> screen violence. This is a generation that has grown up on gore.
> The end result: desensitization.
>
> Look around you at any movie that contains scenes of graphic
> violence. It's the adults, not the kids, who cover their eyes. This is
> a group that cheers at death (the decapitation-by-surfboard scene
> in 'Lethal Weapon 2' gets a huge roar of approval), makes the
> body-count-proud 'Friday the 13th' series a film mainstay and
> adopts as its heroes characters such as Freddy Krueger.[25]

James Dobson, Christian psychologist and founder of Focus on
the Family, was astounded that then Los Angeles mayor Tom
Bradley had designated Friday, September 13, 1991, as Freddy
Krueger Day. He stated:

> No kidding, Krueger is the fictional character depicted in six
> horror movies in which he routinely mutilates and murders chil-
> dren. Yes, sir, Mr. Mayor, you have provided our kids with a great
> role model, to be sure! That's just what we needed is a day devoted
> to death and destruction in blood-soaked Los Angeles, where the
> murder rate increased 53 percent in the first half of 1991.[26]

James Dobson isn't the only one concerned. James D. Tagliarini, lieutenant in the Organized Crime Bureau of the Hillsborough (Florida) County Sheriff's Department, writing to Florida's
chiefs of police, pointed out that movies were possible primary
causes for violent acts performed by occult groups and served to
influence teens towards Satanism.[27] He feels that movies become
a medium where satanic heroes such as Freddy Krueger and Jason
(the demonic slasher of the *Friday the 13th* series) are cultivated.[28]

The Dracula Legacy

Perhaps no satanic hero has endured as the subject of more
films than Dracula. To date, more than two hundred films have

been inspired by the vampire tale from the pen of English author Abraham "Bram" Stoker (1847–1912) but none more expensive than the fifty-million-dollar *Bram Stroker's Dracula.*[29]

Not to worry. The first week it opened it grossed $30.5 million at 2,491 locations for an average of $12,253 at each location.[30] Four weeks later it added another $47.6 million for a total of 78.1 million.[31]

The weekend debut, timed to coincide with Friday the 13th, was so successful that the movie became the number 1 opening in Columbia Picture's history and earned it the best opening for any non-summer movie.[32] No less than 100 products licensed directly by the studio tied in to the movie. Sure to produce even more revenue, they include the following:[33]

> Clothing—Fifteen-hundred-dollar bustier by special order from Macy's, shirt inscribed with the word "Beware," man's tie with symbol, red lace underpants with rosebud applique, and boxer shorts.
> Jewelry—bat, bug, and spider brooches; five-hundred-dollar bejeweled-coffin lipstick holder with vampire-red lipstick ($12).
> Books—"Bram Stoker's 'Dracula' The Film and the Sequel," a collection of photographs and essays; "Coppola and Eiko on Bram Stoker's 'Dracula,'" forty-dollar coffee table book.
> Miscellaneous—removable fang-bite tattoos; a thirty-five-dollar hologram of the monster; pewter figurines; a role-playing game; comic book and trading cards from Tapps; promotions with McLlhenny's Tabasco Bloody Mary Mix and Virgin airlines (first prize a trip to Romania).

An Innocent Fantasy? A look at the above will tell you that it isn't just kids who get caught up in the movie. A closer look at two of the driving forces behind the film make you question if there isn't much more to this than just a film.

Screenwriter James V. Hart tells of a quest to bring the vampire story to the screen that began in April of 1977. Hart remembered the time he went to see the Broadway version in which actor Frank Langella interpreted the principal role. As Hart watched he heard the woman seated in front of him whisper quite loudly, "I'd rather spend one night with Dracula, dead, than the rest of my life with my husband, alive."[34] One doesn't need to be a marriage therapist to determine the state of that marriage!

Nor is it necessary to be a minister to be concerned about Hart's personal perspective underlying his persistence to bring the movie to the screen. Referring to the wife's comment, Hart wrote,

> That telling remark convinced me that none of the previous film incarnations had done justice to Stoker's unnerving, sexually charged novel and its tragic hero. For "Dracula" to be done right on the screen, it needed a magnificent production on an epic scale, and a reading that reached to the heart of the character's seductiveness.
>
> Vampires offer a delectable alternative to the drudgery of moral life and the promises of religion. They offer immortality here and now—life after death that you can take to the bank, because you can see it in action right before your eyes. You don't have to take a chance on going to heaven or hell; you can live forever right here on earth.[35]

Francis Ford Coppola's view is also disturbing. Calling the work "an erotic dream,"[36] Coppola was impressed with Hart's script. "I felt immediately that he had written it as a story of passion and eroticism. The brides [Dracula's vampire brides] weren't just standing around; they actually raped Harker [a character in the story]—and that filled my child's heart with enthusiasm."[37]

The critics shared his enthusiasm, and they did not lack for words to describe the sexual content of the film. Mike Clan for *USA Today* gave it three and a half stars out of four, calling it "A Lush, Lustful, Dracula."[38] Eleanor O'Sullivan of *Asbury Park Press* described it as "A Hip, Scary, Sexy Ride,[39] while *Entertainment Weekly* departed only slightly from the *Asbury Park Press* by describing it as "a scary, sexy love story."[40]

The Real Scare in Dracula. Four things really "scare" me about the Dracula phenomenon. Perhaps you should be concerned, too.

First, let's look at the original author. Born in Dublin in 1847, Bram Stoker was a sickly child whose mother entertained him with Irish ghost stories.[41]

Associated Press special correspondent Hugh Mulligan added,

> Serving as the manager of the Lyceum Theater in London for the actor Henry Irving, Stoker would swap grisly stories with the actor and was soon attending seances held by the Hermetic Order of the Golden Dawn [an occultic group established in 1888 in England attracting poet William Butler Yeats, magician Aliester Crowley and others, it was said to possess at its height the greatest repository of Western magical and occult knowledge].[42]

Noted scholars Radu R. Florescu and Raymond T. McNally, authors of four books on the history of Dracula, wrote,

> Stoker's vampire count is indeed a composite creature, in the end the product of Stoker's imagination, his reading and the result of his life experiences. The personage is indeed the quintessential vision of evil, an anti-father figure of great potency. He is seductive, particularly attractive to women, though the sensual and exotic qualities of Stoker's vampire have been even further amplified by movie scriptwriters since. The count craves immortality and wishes to conquer a decadent and materialistic Victorian England in the first instance, but ultimately he wishes to dominate the world. With this in mind, he goes about his task in a systematic, calculating way, much in the manner of his historical counterpart.[43]

Having become something of a fad, vampire folklore was everywhere (the first reference to vampires in the English language was in the book *Travels with Three English Gentlemen*), and Stoker spent the years between 1890 and 1897 compiling and researching sources for his novel, which has never been out of print. Interestingly, among his sources would be two books entitled *Curious Myths of the Middle Ages* and *The Book of Were-Wolves* by Sabine Baring-Gould. If that name is not familiar, look at the hymn "Onward Christian Soldiers." The same man who authored those two books also penned the words to that great hymn![44]

In a 1972 book, *In Search of Dracula*, scholars proved that a fifteenth-century prince of Wallachia (now a part of Romania) named Vlad Tepes (1431–76), or Vlad the Impaler, was actually called Dracula or a variant thereof during his lifetime. *Dracul* means "dragon" or "devil" and so *Dracula* means "son of the

Dragon" or "son of the Devil."[45] Coppola thought of Dracula as a fallen angel, or Satan.[46]

Stoker married and eventually authored sixteen other books. However, it was his novel *Dracula* for which he will be remembered. Stoker died in virtual poverty in 1912.

Second, the message of the film scares me. *Entertainment Weekly* wrote,

> He calls it *Bram Stoker's Dracula*, but Francis Ford Coppola is just being modest. The director of the Godfather Trilogy has revamped the vampire classic, exposing the lust that hides behind Victorian horror to tell a scary, sexy love story: boy meets girl, boy loses girl, boy defies God and refuses to die.[47]

What messages does the average viewer come away with after sitting through 130 minutes of the film? Enough erotic sexuality and violence are communicated to easily earn the film an R rating.

Third, I am scared by the widespread interest in the subject matter of the film. Film as an art form is a powerful medium, with the audience identifying with the actors and actresses as well as the film's contents. We need to ask ourselves: What worthwhile truths can I learn from this film? What does the film project in terms of deviant sexuality? What does this film offer the viewer who is exposed to the influence of such a powerful occult figure for over two hours?

Earlier in the chapter, we saw that films were one of several factors fueling interest in the occult. Like moths drawn to a fire, the occult offers a tantalizing lure. Over and over again one hears a common theme running through the testimonies of those drawn into its destructive web. That word is power.

Fourth, the implications from the film scare me.

New York Times' Frank Rich sounded an alarm when he wrote,

> What was once forbidden and dangerous is now titillating to a mass audience—at least if viewed on screen or in a book. Violent sex, once considered an offbeat taste, is now a common denominator of eroticism, with ripped flesh and bestial rapists by Mr. Coppola in "Bram Stoker's Dracula." No wonder that torn clothes and bondage fashion, with them intimation of rough trade, have become popular.[48]

The violence, the sex, the lives forever altered because of forced or voluntary involvement are trademarks of the occult. You can take the four things that "scare" me about *Bram Stoker's Dracula* and apply them to any occult movie. Certainly I would not imply that seeing a movie with an occult theme is going to make you a candidate for your nearest local coven, but then again, when did gratuitous doses of violence and sexual content ever make anyone a better person?

James told us, "Each one is tempted when, by his own evil desire, he is dragged away and enticed. Then, after desire has conceived, it gives birth to sin; and sin, when it is full-grown, gives birth to death" (Jas. 1:14–15). Does it need to be any clearer?

DID YOU GET THE PICTURE?

It isn't just the motion picture industry that contributes to occult interest and involvement today. Television is doing a pretty good job in its own right.

It has been estimated that between the ages of two and sixty, a person will view TV for approximately 72,000 hours which translates into three thousand days or nine full years of life.[49]

Every day, millions of fans manage to keep up with their daytime soap favorites. Approximately 2.6 million women watch TV at work while 3.1 million college students watch on campus facilities or temporary residences during the school year.[50]

Calling for parents to reduce their children's video-viewing by at least half, the 39,000-member American Academy of Pediatrics reported that too much TV-watching by children can turn them violent, aggressive or overweight—and possibly all three.[51] Approximately 88.6 million U.S. homes (98 percent) now have at least one TV set, and 60 percent of U.S. homes have two or more TV sets. Fifty-three percent of American homes have video cassette recorders.[52]

Parents, doctors, therapists, counselors, ministers, and scores of others have voiced concern over the content of movies and television today. Even the President of the United States, Bill Clinton, told *TV Guide* he is "mortified" by some of what he sees on television and that television and filmmakers "could, without undermining their artistic integrity, have a major new impact on the way people view the world...There's no question the cumulative impact of this banalization of sex and violence in the popular culture is a net negative for America."[53]

Media critic Michael Medved, co-host of "Sneak Previews" on PBS, contends Hollywood has turned its "dream factory into a poison factory," producing films and TV shows many Americans see as a "threat to their basic values and a menace to the raising of their children."[54]

A threat it is indeed!

The People Behind the Threat

We would do well to consider the background of those who have such a influence upon the general public.[55]

First, many of them are indifferent to religion. While 93 percent had a religious upbringing, currently 45 percent of television programmers claim no religious affiliation. Ninety-three percent say they seldom or never attend religious services. Politically, a large majority consider themselves liberals and regularly vote for Democrats.

Second, they want to restructure America. More than two in five of the men and women responsible for television programming (43 percent) endorse a "complete restructuring" of America's "basic institution." Nearly two thirds (65 percent) believe that the very structure of America's society causes people to become alienated from it.

On such issues as abortion, homosexual rights, and extramarital sex, they overwhelmingly reject traditional restrictions. Ninety-seven percent believe that "a woman has the right to decide for herself whether to have an abortion." Four out of five do not regard homosexual relations as wrong. A majority of 51 percent do not regard adultery as wrong.

Third, they want to "educate America." Gary Marshall, creator of "Happy Days" and "Mork and Mindy" describes how the message comes across:

> You take it from Pogo better than from a man in a suit. I deal with what society's negatives images are, and then try to change them

to be positive...The tag on Mork is almost like the sermon of the week. But it doesn't *look* like that. It's very cleverly disguised to look like something else, but that's what it is...Because sitcoms [situation comedies] teach so many people, we might as well try to put some issues in them.[56]

Of course, few would argue with making education fun and entertaining. The problem is when the industry attempts to present issues in a positive light which run counter to our Christian values and principles.

The Issue of Homosexuality

Homosexuality is not a problem in occultic groups. There are exclusive homosexual occult groups and there are groups with homosexual members. The practice of homosexuality is not criticized and is even carried out between members on occasions. Arthur Lyons, tracing the early growth of the Church of Satan, states, "Homosexuals were attracted by Satanic attitudes of sexual tolerance," and they still are today.[57]

A study in the *Journal of Communication* reported that, according to the networks, homosexuals are the most effective and well-organized pressure group lobbying TV. The networks consult regularly with homosexuals on projects they are considering. Further, the networks solicit substantial input from the Gay Media Task Force. They are even paid for their input.[58]

It worked like this for the sitcom "Dear John":

One of the regular characters, Kirk, admitted that his wife left him for a woman. Writers changed Kirk's explanation after the Gay and Lesbian Alliance Against Defamation (GLAAD) protested. In the original, script, Kirk told people that his wife chose an alternative lifestyle. But the people from GLAAD informed NBC that homosexuals do not make a choice, that they are born homosexuals, so NBC changed the script to fit the homosexual agenda.[59]

It hasn't just been verbal dialogue that has changed; so has the action. Gay rights groups praised what was called the "historic smooch" between two female lawyers on "L.A. Law." But they criticized the man-to-man kiss between Ted Danson and another man when it was followed by the other man slugging Danson. "We were disappointed at the idea that there can't be affection between two men without it being followed by violence," said GLAAD spokesman Richard Jennings.[60]

Gay advocates were not, however, disappointed with the growing acceptance by the public. The belief that it would pave the way for more gay or bisexual roles on television has proved correct. Sitcoms such as "Alice" and "Barney Miller" introduced recurring homosexual characters, and *TV Guide* reported that by the mid-1970s, half the sitcoms on television had done a positive gay show that made its point—and garnered laughs—by having a particularly macho character announce his homosexuality.[61]

It's no laughing matter, however, that the issue of homosexuality is becoming more and more acceptable to viewers. And it is but part of an even larger issue—sex on television.

Sex Sells

There is an adage in advertising that says, "Sex sells," and it does—not just within the context of commercial products but much, much more.

Planned Parenthood reports that Americans are exposed to more than nine thousand scenes of suggested sexual intercourse, sexual comment, or innuendo.[62] A Florida State University study reported that a typical prime-time hour contains an average of 1.6 references to intercourse, 1.2 references to prostitution and rape, 4.7 sexual innuendoes, 1.8 kisses, and one suggestive gesture. In all, TV characters talk about sex or display sexual behavior fifteen times an hour, or once every four minutes.[63]

And who watches prime-time television? Not just adults. Studies show that children under twelve watch a great deal of prime-time television. Ten and a half million children watch television after the 7 to 9 P.M. "family viewing" time.[64]

Not all sexual material on television is limited to nightly viewing, as evidenced by the endless parade of talk shows exploring sexual matters in graphic detail or the soaps which have lowered the standards of decency. All viewers are subject to "sneak attacks" with sexual content, while watching television. One viewer was outraged by what her family saw one evening while watching a family-oriented show.

> At a commercial break my husband and I were shocked to see a commercial come on the screen for a new Mel Gibson movie [*Bird on a Wire*] in which one of the characters asks another about "having sex in weird places."
>
> That's just not right to show an adult commercial like that in the middle of a show that is likely to have entire families watching.
>
> That sort of thing happens on the Nickelodeon [cable] channel. That channel is specifically for young children, but I often see commercials for things such as products that will "give you sexy legs." That's not right."

Indeed it is not, and the critic agreed, saying it was known as "ambushing a viewer."[65]

It must be effective. Several first through third grade girls in our neighborhood were chanting, "The boys have the muscles, the teachers have the brains, the girls have the sexy legs so they win the game."

That may seem innocent enough in the minds of some, but evidence points to the formation of disturbing opinions as these children move into junior high and high school.

In 1987, 1,700 seventh to ninth graders in Rhode Island schools were interviewed. The findings, presented one year later at the National Symposium on Child Victimization, revealed the following attitudes:

> ➤ 24 percent of boys and 16 percent of girls said that it was acceptable for a man to force a woman to have sex with him if he has spent money on her.
> ➤ 65 percent of boys and 47 percent of girls said it was acceptable for a man to force a woman to have sex if they had been dating more than six months.
> ➤ 87 percent of boys and 79 percent of girls said rape in marriage is permissible.
> ➤ 31 percent of boys and 32 percent of girls said it would not be improper for a man to rape a woman who has had previous sexual experiences.

➤ 50 percent of all the students said that a woman who walks alone at night and dresses seductively is asking to be raped.[66]

Where did they get these ideas? From people all across the U.S.A. "Television is like a democracy. People vote by turning on their sets. And despite the vocal minority of militant profamily groups, feminists and TV watchdogs, the vast majority of Americans are voting for sex. Television is basically responsive to what the audience wants, and public tastes and standards have shifted," says Timothy Dyk, a Washington attorney who argued against the FCC when it tried to extend its ban on indecency to twenty-four hours a day. "What might have been viewed as inappropriate 25 years ago is now appropriate."[67]

And if this is true, what of the future?

Tom Shales, television critic for the Washington Post, says, "the bare-breast barrier will soon be broken. Breasts now [are] seen [with] about 80 percent revealable. The nipple is the new frontier."[68]

What we dare not imagine may be just around the corner. Who would have thought that sex on television would progress to the point it has?

Taking a Beating—Television Violence

Equally as disturbing is the staggering amount of violence routinely shown on television! In *Rambo*, Stallone's character terminated groups of people in over seventy explosions and forty-four specific killings for an average of one death every 2.1 minutes in this ninety-three-minute film. *Commando* grossed $100 million or as one writer put it, one dollar for every guy the Schwarzenegger character blew away.[69] In *Die Hard II*, 264 people were massacred at the rate of one death every thirty seconds. Arnold dispatched more than seventy evildoers during his vacation to Mars in the movie *Total Recall*, and *Robocop II* chronicled eighty-one deaths.[70]

The media's preoccupation with violence is grim fare for adults; imagine what it does to kids. A steady diet of true-to-life and fantasy/horror induces a kind of "the world is dangerous" paranoia. This loss of innocence can be harmful rather than helpful in alerting them to their environment.[71]

Dr. Glen Sparks is worried about another aspect of TV violence: It scares children.

> Between the ages of seven and eleven, children frequently mention that violent TV scenes frighten and upset them. Children this age realize these scenes could really happen—and happen to them. They're not ready to cope with this yet.
>
> The availability of scary scenes has risen dramatically with the proliferation of cable TV and VCRs. Many children who saw *Friday the 13th* or *Halloween* are afraid robbers will come and chop them up.[72]

In addition to fear, a steady diet of television violence can also teach another lesson. According to Dr. Victor Strasburger of the University of New Mexico School of Medicine, it can lead children to believe that "if you're a good guy, violence can be acceptable" to solve some problems.[73]

Megadoses of watching violence can also produce other distorted attitudes and beliefs. Ten- and eleven-year-olds were asked to share their favorite part of a movie they had seen. Their comments are listed below with the movie title following:

➤ "I liked it when the alien ate the lady's head and kept on burping." *Xtro*

➤ "When the rats eat up the baby." *Rats*

➤ "I like the part where the girl chopped off her dad's head and ate it as a birthday cake." *Friday the 13th*

As frightening as all of this is, it is nothing more than a method in the madness perpetuated by Hollywood.

Jess Moody is pastor of Shepherd of the Hills Church in Chatsworth, California. Shepherd of the Hills is a Southern Baptist congregation that has a number of TV and movie celebrities as members. Dr. Moody states the dilemma quite well. "I sense a hardening of the moral arteries among the motion picture people," Moody said. "Most really don't care what the American people think. Many of them are making bold and rather arrogant statements: 'We don't care what the church thinks. We're going to do what we think is right, and the First Amendment gives us that right,'" Moody noted. "They confuse liberty with license."

Jess Moody, Tom Lester, and Ted Baehr all agree Hollywood largely ignores the enormous market that exists for family films. The average R-rated film grosses $5.5 million, while an average family film takes in $18.8 million, Moody noted. Yet TV and movie producers continue to pour most of their resources into less-profitable, adults-only efforts, ignoring the massive appeal of family films.

"The perfect example is *Home Alone*," Lester said. "All the people who don't usually go to the theater went to see that film, and it grossed $280 million. That's what the potential is if the studios will keep making that kind of film."

With many major studios on the verge of bankruptcy, Moody believes movie and TV producers should turn their attention to more wholesome products that would attract larger audiences. But more profits may not be the bottom line. "If Hollywood continues to make R-rated film and turns its back on family films, then you know the agenda is not money," he said.[74]

Turning It Off

In one sense, we cannot be responsible for another person's actions. In spite of our feelings and efforts, we may not be able to stem the flood of filth and violence that pours from Hollywood, but we can stop it from entering our homes. "The Father of Electronic Television," Vladimir K. Zworykin, at the age of eighty-four confessed that his favorite part of the TV is the "off" switch.[75]

However, turning it off isn't as easy as it may seem in some cases. Authors Duncan and Priscilla Jaenicke recall their experience vividly when they decided not just to turn off the TV but to unplug it entirely!

Like many families they thought they had their TV-viewing pretty much under control. However, warning signs continued to crop up, like large blocks of afternoon time spent watching programs, Priscilla asking for prayer about her near-addiction to the evening soap "Knot's Landing," and finally, the chain-viewing of program after program in the evening.[76] Once they realized the pattern into which they had fallen, the only solution was to quit cold turkey.

Mary Hasty, a clinical social worker for fourteen years, uses the word "addicted" to describe some television viewers. "We use addiction," she explains, "when we talk about substances being used to the point where they become destructive. I think people compulsively watch TV to the point where it is destructive to the family relations."[77]

It isn't just the older family members either who become attached to the television. Noted authority T. Berry Brazelton in his syndicated column "Families Today" aptly describes the effect of television on the younger viewer.

> Think about how a child behaves when he is sitting in front of a blaring set, watching a horror film. He is completely quiet. Nails bitten, face pale, body tense—he is "hooked."
>
> If anyone interrupts the child by tapping him on the shoulder, he will jump with a start and may even break down in angry crying. If led away from the set, he may dissolve into a combative, screaming, wildly thrashing mass.
>
> The intensity of such a reaction is evidence of the energy the child puts into television watching and the shock experienced when his locked attention is broken into. What a powerful medium![78]

Certainly, not all TV is destructive and there are many fine programs suitable for individual or family viewing. The viewer should be as informed as possible about the content of what he or she is to view, whether it is a program or a movie. Usually, the newspaper or *TV Guide* will provide helpful information.

Any number of good organizations also have the best interests of the movie viewer in mind and use various systems to rate each movie.

One such organization is connected with James Dobson's Focus on the Family. For an annual fee parents can subscribe to *Parental Guidance*, which aids them in evaluating not only movies but music and television aimed at teenagers (that toll-free number is 1-800-A-Family). Another organization is "Christian Parent Alert" (1-

800-776-7432), which publishes a monthly newsletter that addresses the media's effect on children today, education issues, and so on. Still another service is the *Entertainment Research Report* (1-800-322-1296) which issues a twice-monthly newsletter counting every dirty word, dead body, and sexy scene. For instance, the movie *Robin Hood* carried a PG-13 rating yet included eight four-letter words and some three dozen deaths (men beheaded: two, killed by sword: twelve, etc.).[79]

There is no substitute for parental involvement. Parents can discuss with their children what their children see on television. I would certainly rather impart my values to my children than to let the television set do this.

Of course, movies and televisions are not the only avenues which influence people today. Another influence is that of books.

THE PEN IS MIGHTIER THAN THE SWORD

Most of us have heard a ghost story somewhere in our lifetime, and many have also read a ghost story from a book. Five examples will illustrate this influence. At least one book has put a bit of a twist on the supernatural stories.

First, *I Shudder At Your Touch: 22 Tales of Sex and Horror* attempts to attract fans of eroticism and horror by combining the two genres and features stories from authors Stephen King, Clive Barker, and others.[80]

Second, fans of fantasy-horror writer H. P. Lovecraft campaigned to erect a hometown memorial to the writer who hailed from Providence, Rhode Island. Lovecraft inspired writers such as Stephen King and Clive Barker, in addition to influencing countless thousands of readers.

Third, writer Stephen King is himself no stranger to success. In addition to having many of his novels and short stories turned into box office films or television programs, he has written so many books that a Stephen King bookclub is devoted entirely to his works and promoted periodically on television.

Fourth, author Anne Rice has written the best-selling *Vampire Chronicles*, *Interview with the Vampire*, *The Vampire Lestat*, and *The Queen of the Damned*. The New Orleans Chamber of Commerce presented her with a garlic cross and the deed to a burial plot in St. Louis Cemetery at a book-signing party.[81]

Fifth, any number of books exist to "educate" interested readers in how to cast spells, place hexes or curses on enemies, attract someone in whom they are interested, or even conjure up a demon. These book weave their way into the lives of the unsuspecting. One of my students once told me that the manager of the bookstore in the mall where she was employed told her to place the occult-related books next to books appealing to children and teenagers.

Former teen satanist Charles Evans accumulated a personal library of occult books before his deliverance and salvation,[82] and we saw earlier how books on occult-related subjects helped to set Sean Sellers on a collision course with the Oklahoma Penitentiary Death Row.

Reading, Writing, and the Occult?

Something far more significant than money is behind the contest for the hearts and minds of children. Nothing short of a great civil war of values is raging today throughout North America. Two opposing sides with vastly differing and incompatible world views are locked in a bitter conflict that permeates every level of society.[83]

What could be more insidious than to introduce children to occult concepts and practices through books and curriculum in school?

What would you think of a workbook used in school that contains an exercise by the name of "Three Spells"? One spell is called "Zap," and the participant is told to imagine that lightning can shoot out of his hand against all creatures who have no magical defenses.[84] This exercise has been taught in the fourth grade!

Even younger children may be taught how to chant so that the thought sinks deep into their minds, influencing their beliefs and behavior. An example of one such chant said to work with children is the following: "Happiness runs in a circular motion. Life is like a little boat upon the sea. Everyone is a part of everything anyway. You can have it all if you let yourself be."[85]

The point is well made: "The occult is far more dangerous than it could ever be entertaining, and the consequences can be eternal. The danger lies in teaching that the occult is not so bad, that some witchcraft can be used for good, and that we don't have to take this stuff very seriously. Yet, if we properly discern, we find that in some cases it is blatantly demonic."[86]

Witchcraft is not off limits in some grade schools. One boy brought home from school a book called *Curses, Hexes and Spells* to his uncle who had formerly been involved in witchcraft. The uncle was shocked when he reviewed the book because it described and encouraged incantations and "everyday curses."[87]

A northern California mother walked into her fifth-grader's room during his school's open house to find the youngsters gathered in a circle playing a "Dungeons and Dragons" style game called "The Wizard." The children cast spells on each other. A bulletin board explained the purpose of the game: to progress from one "spelling power" level to the next. Humans are at the lowest end of the spectrum, having "very limited powers" and "at the mercy of most monsters." Higher level included enchanters, sorcerers, magicians, and the Wizard.[88]

One of the loudest cries concerning curriculum across the United States had to do with a textbook series entitled *Impressions*. Published by Holt, Rinehart and Winston of Canada, the curriculum celebrates witches in poems and encourages students to cast spells and find "familiar spirits." Some stories focus on violent death, while others have a New Age flavor. One story even centers on cannibalism. Artwork in the teacher's edition is consistently dark and gruesome. Teachers are also advised in the guide that, "there are no...universal truths."[89]

Not all of the *Impressions* series is, however, offensive. Some textbooks include works by authors such as C. S. Lewis and Laura Ingalls Wilder, whose stories became the basis for the much loved television series "Little House on the Prairie."

Nonetheless, internationally recognized religion expert, Dr. Carl Raschke described *Impressions* as "a thorough and consistent means of religious advocacy" and "religious indoctrination" for "witchcraft, Wicca and neo-Paganism." He noted that the "unmistakable signature of magical religion—taught normatively rather than descriptively—can be found repeatedly in the *Impressions* curriculum." Former Wiccan high priest and witch William Schnoebelen states that the exercises in *Impressions* "promote the practices, rituals and belief systems of Witchcraft and Neo-Paganism."[90]

The American Family Association Law Center challenged the constitutionality of the *Impressions* elementary school curriculum in federal district court in Sacramento, California. Norman Lear's People for the American Way intervened in the lawsuit against the AFA. The court ruling went against the AFA and is under appeal as I write.

We certainly owe it to our children to know what they are being taught. Countering the influence of the occult is difficult enough with adolescents. We don't need to let our young be exposed to it in elementary school curriculums. However, apathy does reign supreme in the minds of many parents, and teachers know it.

Johanna Michaelsen shares this disturbing story about a weekend seminar entitled "Through Crisis to Transformation." Michaelson heard a high school teacher describe her elective course entitled "Psychology." The teacher brings in special speakers, among them occultists whom she admonishes to "give the kids an experience with these things, not just lecture at them.

"We do some pretty amazing things," the teacher said, "psychic healing, shamanism, crystals, Witchery, [we] hold ceremonies and stuff, we burn candles and hold a full-moon ceremony once a month."[91]

If this bothers you, consider the teacher's closing statement:

I must have a divine light around me, because I've had no flack from anyone. I've never had anything but positive feedback from the parents. One time, though, I was conducting a spring equinox celebration for the kids. I mean I had the altar all set up—flowers, the candles were lit on the altar—and the principal walked in! Fortunately, he was a new principal and he was thrilled with what we were doing. The focus was on self-affirmations. I was lucky. I have to walk a fine line on the religious issue. Some might say I've crossed it.[92]

I would say she has leaped over it! Accounts like this disturb me. Do they disturb you? Where was the communication between high school kids and their parents that would allow something like that to begin, much less continue? Where were the parents that not one single parent protested? Why were the only comments from parents praise?

It would be sad enough if this was only confined to one state but it is not. It has spread across our nation and it is disturbing. So is the newfound interest in serial killers.

Serial Killers—A New Threat

It seems that America's fascination with evil knows no limits. Time-Life books issued a series on serial killers. Trading cards are now available which carry pictures of the likes of Ted Bundy, Jeffrey Dahmer, and other notorious murderers. On the back of each card for the purchaser's edification is a short biography of the criminal and a description of his crimes.[93] Understandably, the families of the victims are appalled.

Those responsible for the cards hasten to assure us that these cards would not be of interest to impressionable young minds. "Kids would have a difficult time reading them," they maintain.[94] I suppose that explains why, in the same article, it was mentioned that a comic book store which caters to kids carried them.

It is hardly surprising that the editor-in-chief of the cards said, "We've never sold anything this well in our lives. The notoriety proved to be best publicity we could have hoped for." The company has sold about $1 million worth of the cards, more than ten times the sale of any of its other cards. In fact, the company can't meet the demands.[95]

As if trading cards are not enough, one publisher even produced a *comic* book chronicling Jeffrey Dahmer's murders.[96] Not to be outdone, the game "Serial Killer" is on the market. The $49.45 game features a giant board with a silk-screened map of the United States criss-crossed by highways. Players—"killers"—travel from one end of the country to the other, picking cards that describe various types of murders. "Outcome" cards tell the player whether he pulled off the crime. A high-risk murder earns three plastic baby tokens; medium-risk, two; and low-risk, one. The object is to amass more such "victims" than anyone else.[97]

Fortunately Canadians are trying to keep this game out of their country. Would be that we were as concerned.

WHAT YOU CAN DO

There are no moral values in the world of the occult. The more exposure we have to valueless material, the less concerned we become with the kingdom's work. For Christ's sake, we must take a stand. It's bad enough when the wrong goes unseen but doubly so when the wrong is brought to our attention and we still do nothing to stop it.

➤ Be informed about what is going on in your schools and communities.

You and I have an obligation to be informed as Christians. We should know what goes on in our public schools. We ought to be aware of what children are being taught whether we hope to have school-age children someday, whether you currently have children who are in school, or whether you will some day have grandchildren in school. You need to be concerned even if none of the above apply to you. Each of us will be affected.

As James Dobson said, "Indeed, a society that is too busy and too preoccupied for its children is just a nation of aging, dying people who feed on their own selfish interests."[98]

We should be alarmed by the onslaught of sexual themes on television as well as at the corner video store and the big screen. It is comforting to know that there are Christians fighting the good fight all across our nation, and I have included a list of organizations in appendix B. The battle is being waged against a financial army. We cannot afford to sit on the sidelines and watch as spectators. One person can make a difference!

When Charles Read, an American Family Association supporter in Davisville, West Virginia, noticed that the largest video rental business in nearby Parkersburg began offering XXX videos, Read wrote a letter to the managers, pointing out that pornography is an attack on the American family, and that he could not support a business that was a resource for supplying such filth to the community.

"I never received a reply," Read told AFA, "but one week later my sister was driving by this business and saw two large signs in the window proclaiming: 'We do NOT rent adult videos.'"

She called the store to thank them and was told the manager had decided that he was not comfortable carrying them.[99]

As Thomas Carlyle once wrote, "Conviction is worthless unless it is converted into conduct."[100]

The apostle Paul reminded us what we are fighting and how we are to fight when he wrote:

> For our struggle is not against flesh and blood, but against the rulers, against the authorities, against the power of this dark world and against the spiritual forces of evil in the heavenly realms. Therefore put on the full armor of God, so that when the day of evil comes, you may be able to stand your ground, and after you have done everything, to stand. Stand firm then, with the belt of truth buckled around your waist, with the breastplate of righteousness in place, and with your feet fitted with the readiness that comes from the gospel of peace. In addition to all this, take up the shield of faith, with which you can extinguish all the flaming arrows of the evil one. Take the helmet of salvation and the sword of the Spirit, which is the word of God. (Eph. 6:12–17)

➤ Monitor media that you and your family watch.

All such films are not equally bad, but a constant preference for such films could be a troublesome sign. Parents should know what their children and teenagers are watching. While parents cannot watch in advance every video brought into the home, they may find a movie handbook helpful. Such a book will at least provide the theme, among other items, and some books provide ratings, although these are not always reliable guides. The safest approach is, of course, to watch it yourself first.

➤ Cultivate other interests.

Parents and adults should be concerned with what children are being taught in school as well as what books they have access to in the school library. Caution, however, should be exercised so as not to go to the extreme. A child's fictional book on ghosts is one matter, but a book which enables children to learn how to conjure up demons or talk with spirits is another matter altogether.

Outings with family and friends, hobbies, helping the under-privileged, church involvement, physical exercises, etc. are all optional activities.

LAUREN

It seemed to Lauren as if everything was happening in slow motion. In the dim light of the flickering candles she could see the faces of her high school friends. What a mixture of emotions they portrayed. Some had looks of fear while others seemed to look sadly at her. Others were smiling but she wasn't sure she shared that feeling.

As she slowly began to extend her hands toward the marker on the Ouija™ board, a memory shot out from the recesses of her mind. She was in church and her pastor was talking about Satan in his sermon.

She remembered when he said, "The devil is cunning and tempts us where we are most vulnerable. We are no match for him on our own." Her pastor continued, "But in Jesus Christ we can resist him. Satan will promise you the world just as he did to Jesus in the wilderness, but he will only deliver heartache." He admonished the congregation, "Don't give him an opportunity to help you fall."

Though her fingers were now only centimeters away from the marker, Lauren knew the space was still sufficient for her to withdraw.

Would she or wouldn't she?

F O U R

*The God of peace
will soon crush Satan under your feet.*
— ROMANS 16:20

Satan in Scripture

One night my wife Susan and I caught part of "The Tonight Show." In this particular segment Jay Leno was showing a videotape made earlier of his visits to various garage sales around Burbank, California. Naturally, he was poking fun at the different items for sale. At one house he picked up a copy of Hal Lindsey's 1972 book, *Satan Is Alive and Well on Planet Earth*. The look on his face was enough to send the studio audience into gales of laughter as he showed the book cover to the camera.

People continue to laugh about the devil today, but he is no laughing matter. There is much about the devil that we do not understand nor does God's Word provide all the answers. I believe God's Word tells us all we need to know. We simply have to trust God for the rest. What then can we know about the devil?

Shakespeare once wrote that a rose by any other name is still a rose; so it is with the devil. Actually there are many different names for him in the Old and New Testaments. Among them are:

> The devil—Not found as such in the Old Testament; this title is used thirty-three times in the New Testament where it is used synonymously with Satan. "Devil" means the accuser and "slanderer." He tries to play both ends against the middle as in slandering man before God (Job 1:7–12) and slandering God before man (Gen. 3:1–5).

> Lucifer—The Latin translation of the Hebrew word for "day star" (Isa. 14:12). The use of this name for Satan is surrounded in controversy. *Holman Bible Dictionary* states that it refers to a title used for the king of Babylon, who had exalted himself as a god. The prophet taunted the king by calling him "son of the dawn" (NIV), a play on the Hebrew term which could refer to a pagan god but normally indicated the light that appeared briefly before dawn. A later tradition associated the word with evil, although the Bible does not use it as such.[1]

Others prefer the translation "light bearer" and refer to Lucifer's once lofty position among the angels prior to the rebellion and fall from heaven. The apostle Paul reminds us that Satan has the ability to disguise himself as "an angel of light" (2 Cor. 11:14).

> Belial—From the Hebrew *Belias*, this title connotes "worthlessness" and is found chiefly in the Old Testament, with one exception being 2 Corinthians 6:15, "What harmony is there between Christ and Belial?" The expression "sons of Belial" designates certain people as worthless persons.

> Beelzebub—This title is found only in the gospels of Matthew, Mark, and Luke and refers to the prince of the demons whom Jesus identifies with Satan.

> Satan—From the Hebrew *Satan*, which translated means "an adversary." In 1 Samuel 29:4 we find that the Philistines were afraid that David might become their "Satan" or "adversary." When used with a definite article, *the* adversary refers to Satan. Thirty-three references to Satan in the New Testament out of sixty-six use the definite article *the* Satan.

> Abaddon (destruction, ruin) and Appolyon (a destroyer)—Referred to in Revelation 9:11, these titles emphasize the ruin Satan can bring about when he has the opportunity.

➤ Dragon—From the Greek *drakon* meaning a serpent, a dragon. In the New Testament the dragon of Revelation 12:9 and 20:2 is the devil who is symbolically portrayed as red in color and having seven heads, ten horns, an enormous tail and a huge mouth, from which he was able to cast forth water like a river after those whom he would destroy (12:3, 4, 15; 16:13).

➤ The Prince of this World (John 12:31; 14:30),
The Ruler of the Kingdom of the Air (Eph. 2:1–2),
The God of this Age (2 Cor. 4:4)—All point to the power Satan has on this earth though it is nothing, of course, in comparison to God's power. These titles also bear witness to the fact that Satan commands a host that do his bidding.

➤ The Tempter—Referred to in Matthew 4:3 when he came to Jesus in the wilderness. Who better to try and entice others to sin than the architect of sin himself?

➤ A Murderer and a Liar—Referred to in John 8:44, he seeks to destroy what God has made in His image with lies being one of his many devices. Jesus condemns him not only for lying but brands him as "the father of lies."

➤ A Roaring Lion—In 1 Peter 5:8 he is described as such by Peter, emphasizing the Christian's need to beware his constant attempts to undermine the believer.

➤ Other names—Satan is also known as the Evil One (1 John 2:13); Lord of Death (Heb. 2:14); and the Accuser (Rev. 12:10).

We can learn much from the descriptive titles which refer to him, but there once was a time when none of these descriptions applied.

SATAN: HIS BEGINNING

...You were the model of perfection, full of wisdom and perfect in beauty.

You were in Eden, the garden of God; every precious stone adorned you: ruby, topaz and emerald, chrysolite, onyx and jasper, sapphire, turquoise and beryl. Your settings and mountings were made of gold; on the day you were created they were prepared.

You were anointed as a guardian cherub, for so I ordained you. You were on the holy mount of God; you walked among the fiery stones. You were blameless in your ways from the day you were created till wickedness was found in you. (Ezek. 28:12–15)

Scholars have interpreted this passage several ways. First, Ezekiel may have employed a primitive prototype of a paradise myth, one of the popular myths of his day concerning Tyre's origin. Second, the entire story may be taken symbolically in that Tyre with all her wealth was like an earthly paradise, just as Eden which was corrupted. Third, Ezekiel may have been comparing Tyre's fate to that of Adam's fall, seeing the sin of Tyre as being similar to that of Adam and Eve but with Tyre far surpassing the pair, who wanted to be like God, by claiming to be a god.[2]

Conservative scholar Ralph H. Alexander believes that no interpretation of this passage is without problems and readily identifies it as the most difficult passage in the book of Ezekiel if not the whole Bible.[3] Alexander says that some have understood the king of Tyre to be Satan. Others have seen ancient mythology as the basis of the passage. However, to interpret the passage as a myth is unwarranted. To understand the king of Tyre to be Satan also has its difficulties. The most natural and seemingly easier position is to take Tyre's king to be the human ruler of that city in Ezekiel's day.[4]

Popular author Hal Lindsey in *The Late Great Planet Earth* takes verses 1 and 2 of Ezekiel 12 to refer to the *prince* of Tyre, a man who was so vain about his riches and intelligence that he claimed to be God. However in the twelfth verse we are introduced to the *king* of Tyre who is the real power behind the prince. Lindsey says verses 11 through 15 leave no doubt that this king referred to is none other than Satan.[5]

W. A. Criswell takes another view as he believes verse 12 defies explanation unless it is applied *both* to the king of Tyrus and Satan. He feels that the king of Tyrus becomes a type of Satan. The king is described as perfect in beauty, living in Eden, the anointed cherub, a created being, yet proud and corrupt because of his arrogance and beauty. Those words can be true of the king of Tyrus only indirectly, but they are a perfect description of Satan.[6]

The Mystery of Satan

Evangelist Billy Graham reflected some of the confusion about Satan when he affirmed, "There is much we cannot understand about Satan and why God permits him to work. Our minds are limited, and many of these questions will only be answered when we get to heaven.[7]

Most of our information about Satan comes from the New Testament with few references to him in the Old Testament.[8]

Earlier, the apostle Paul identifies him as an angel (2 Cor. 11:14). Again we run into difficulties as to available information about angels. As one writer put it, what is perhaps most remarkable is what New Testament texts do *not* say about angels (emphasis mine).[9] Nonetheless, there can be no doubt that they exist.

In Genesis 1:26 the "us" to many scholars is a reference to the presence of angels at the creation. We have no explanation of their origin except that they are created beings.

In Job 1:6 we again see Satan mentioned as being in the company of other "sons of God" (angels).

Revelation 12:7–11 tell us:

> And there was war in heaven. Michael and his angels fought against the dragon, and the dragon and his angels fought back. But he was not strong enough, and they lost their place in heaven. The great dragon was hurled down—that ancient serpent called the devil or Satan, who leads the whole world astray. He was hurled to the earth, and his angels with him. Then I heard a loud voice in heaven say: "Now have come the salvation and the power and the kingdom of our God, and the authority of his Christ. For the accuser of our brothers, who accuses them before our God day and night, has been hurled down. They overcame him by the blood of the Lamb and by the word of their testimony; they did not love their lives so much as to shrink from death.

This passage perhaps more than any other succinctly covers the themes of the accuser, the war in heaven, the fall of Lucifer and his angels, the devil's power on earth, and the dragon, who is Leviathan, a primeval monster with which Yahweh does battle in the Old Testament. The deceiver of Paradise is that ancient serpent.

Jude 1:6 and 2 Peter 2:4 refer to the body of angels who followed Satan with an unknown number imprisoned until the final judgment (1 Cor. 6:3). The remainder actively serve Satan.

Revelation 20:1–3 reveals that Satan will be bound for one thousand years during the Millennium of Christ's reign:

> And I saw an angel coming down out of heaven, having the key to the Abyss and holding in his hand a great chain. He seized the dragon, that ancient serpent, who is the devil, or Satan, and bound him for a thousand years. He threw him into the Abyss, and locked and sealed it over him, to keep him from deceiving the nations any more until the thousand years were ended. After that, he must be set free for a short time.

Satan in the Old Testament

As we have seen earlier, a fully defined doctrine of Satan is not found in the Bible until New Testament times. Nonetheless there are various references scattered throughout the Old Testament.

Most people would normally think of Genesis chapter 3 when they think of Satan in the Old Testament. However, the most extensive discussion of Satan in the Old Testament is found in the book of Job.

A quick rundown of Old Testament passages by books reveals the following about Satan:

➤ Genesis 3—Satan appears to Eve in the form of a serpent and tempts her into sin.

➤ Deuteronomy 34:5–6— "And Moses the servant of the Lord died there in Moab, as the Lord had said. He buried him in Moab, in the valley opposite Beth Peor, but to this day no one knows where his grave is." In Jude, verse 9 mentions the incident: "But even the archangel Michael, when he was disputing with the devil about the body of Moses, did not dare to bring a slanderous accusation against him, but said, 'The Lord rebuke you!'" Why Satan wanted the body of Moses is not explained. Perhaps he was going to use it as an object to tempt man to worship it.

➤ 1 Chronicles 21:1—"Satan rose up against Israel and incited David to take a census of Israel." Satan tempts David to number the Israelites. The parallel passage in 2 Samuel 24:1 demonstrates the control God has over Satan and David's willingness to yield to the tempter.

➤ Psalm 91:13—"You will tread upon the lion and the cobra; you will trample the great lion and the serpent." The believer who places his faith and trust in God will be victorious over Satan.

➤ Psalm 109:6—"Appoint an evil man to oppose him; let an accuser stand at his right hand." It is a calamity to have Satan stand at one's right hand.

➤ Zechariah 3:2—"The Lord said to Satan, 'The Lord rebuke you, Satan! The Lord, who has chosen Jerusalem, rebuke you! Is not this man a burning stick snatched from the fire?'" Satan accuses Joshua before the Lord. The Lord rebukes Satan.

The dilemma of finding few passages in the Old Testament does not trouble us in the New Testament. Why such a difference?

First, the biblical writers as a whole were much more interested in advancing a revelation of God than the powers of darkness. Second, the character and purpose of Satan is a gradual historical progression that only comes to light clearly as contrasted with the redemptive work of Jesus Christ in the New Testament. Third, it would be the New Testament that would not only elaborate upon Satan's purpose and work but, as such, would also set forth his limitations and ultimate defeat.

Satan in the New Testament

In the New Testament Satan continues his adversarial and hostile role in opposition to God. He is always working to overthrow the purposes of God. The New Testament describes a great conflict between the forces of God and of good, on the one hand, and those of evil led by Satan, on the other. This is not just the conception of one writer or another, but common among many of the inspired New Testament writers.[10]

We have already examined his titles in the first part of this chapter. Many of these are found only in the New Testament.

Examining the New Testament we find the following references to Satan:

➤ Matthew 4; Luke 4; Mark 1:13—All refer to the temptation experience where Satan did his best to entice Jesus to sin but failed in each attempt. "And he was in the desert forty days, being tempted by Satan. He was with the wild animals, and angels attended him."

➤ Matthew 13:38–43—Satan's activity in the world: "And the enemy who sows them is the devil. The harvest is the end of the age, and the harvesters are angels."

➤ Matthew 16:23—When Peter urges Jesus not to follow the way of the cross, Jesus rebukes Satan. "Jesus turned and said to Peter, 'Get behind me, Satan! You are a stumbling block to me; you do not have in mind the things of God, but the things of men.'"

➤ Mark 4:15—Satan works at stealing the truth from man: "Some people are like seed along the path, where the word is sown. As soon as they hear it, Satan comes and takes away the word that was sown in them."

➤ Luke 13:16—Satan's activity may produce physical effects. "Then should not this woman, a daughter of Abraham, whom Satan has kept bound for eighteen long years, be set free on the Sabbath day from what bound her?"

➤ Luke 22:31–32—Satan is not through attempting to use Peter and Jesus prays for Peter. "Simon, Simon, Satan has asked to sift you as wheat."

➤ Luke 22:3—Satan tempts Judas and succeeds in leading him to betray Jesus. "Then Satan entered Judas, called Iscariot, one of the Twelve."

➤ John 13:2—"The evening meal was being served, and the devil had already prompted Judas Iscariot, son of Simon, to betray Jesus."

➤ John 14:30—With the cross in mind, Jesus says, "I will not speak with you much longer, for the prince of this world is coming. He has no hold on me."

➤ John 8:44—Jesus accuses his enemies of being under Satan's influence. "You belong to your father, the devil, and you want to carry out your father's desire. He was a murderer from the beginning, not holding to the truth, for there is no truth in him. When he lies, he speaks his native language, for he is a liar and the father of lies."

➤ Acts 5:3—Satan tempts Ananias, a believer (5:3) and Elymas (13:10), an avowed opponent of Christianity. "Then Peter said, 'Ananias, how is it that Satan has so filled your heart that you have lied to the Holy Spirit and have kept for yourself some of the money you received for the land?'"

➤ Acts 13:10—"You are a child of the devil and an enemy of everything that is right! You are full of all kinds of deceit and trickery. Will you never stop perverting the right ways of the Lord?"

➤ 1 Corinthians 7:5—Paul reminds us that Satan continues to tempt man. "Do not deprive each other except by mutual consent and for a time, so that you may devote yourselves to prayer. Then come together again so that Satan will not tempt you because of your lack of self—control."

➤ 1 Thessalonians 2:18—Satan makes the work of missionaries difficult. "For we wanted to come to you—certainly I, Paul, did, again and again—but Satan stopped us."

➤ 1 John 3:8—John makes the correlation between sin and the devil clear. "He who does what is sinful is of the devil, because the devil has been sinning from the beginning. The reason the Son of God appeared was to destroy the devil's work."

➤ 1 John 3:10—Man's willingness to be under Satan's domination is a reality. "This is how we know who the children of God are and who the children of the devil are: Anyone who does not do what is right is not a child of God; nor is anyone who does not love his brother."

The News About Satan

In examining the Old and New Testament passages that refer to Satan, the following characteristics and truths about him become apparent:

➤ His power is derivative (Luke 4:6).
➤ He can exercise his activity only within the limits that God lays down (Job 1:12; 2:6; 1 Cor. 10:13; Rev. 21:2, 7).
➤ He may even be used to set forward the cause of right (1 Cor. 5:5; see also 2 Cor. 12:7).

➤ Jesus thought of "eternal fire" as "prepared for the devil and his angels" (Matt. 25:41) and John sees this come to pass (Rev. 20:10).
➤ The conflict with Satan comes to a head in Gethsemane. There Jesus speaks of him as "driven out" (John 12:31), and as "condemned" (John 16:11).
➤ The victory is explicitly alluded to in Hebrews 2:14 and 1 John 3:8.
➤ The work of preachers is to turn men "from the power of Satan unto God" (Acts 26:18).
➤ Paul can confidently say, "the God of peace will soon crush Satan under your feet" (Rom. 16:20).

Although Satan is a powerful adversary, we must always remember that he is a defeated adversary, defeated by Jesus Christ.

We can find comfort in certain facts:[11] First, he is not omnipotent. He has vast power, but that power is limited. Second, he is not omniscient. This is evident from his blunders in history, as seen in his futile efforts to destroy the child Jesus. Third, he is not omnipresent. He makes his power felt world—wide through the operations of his many minions. Satan acknowledged his limitations in his conversation with Jehovah concerning Job.

Satan's Helpers

Unquestionably, Satan has those who do his bidding. They are known as demons from the Greek *daimon* or *daimonion*. A very successful series of movies, *The Omen, Damien—Omen II*, and *The Final Conflict* utilized the name Damien for the main character, the devil's son.

In the New Testament, along with *daimonion*, adjectives such as "unclean" (*akatharton*, Mark 1:24–27; 5:2–3; 7:25; 4:25; Acts 5:16; 8:7; and Rev. 16:13) and "evil" (*ponera*, Acts 19:12–16) are used.[12]

Demonic Origins

The late Merrill F. Unger, known for his scholarly work in the field of demonology, discusses three different viewpoints in his work *Biblical Demonology*.[13]

One theory holds that their origin can be traced to the inhabitants of the pre—Adamite earth, whose sin caused its destruction, and whose bodies were destroyed in the catastrophe that overwhelmed it, leaving them "disembodied spirits" with a keen desire to re—embody themselves on the earth where they once lived. This theory is based upon interpretations of Genesis 1:1–2; Ezekial 28:14; and Isaiah 14:13–14.

A second theory, which follows an ancient pre—Christian Jewish interpretation of chapter fifteen in *The Book of Enoch*, traces the beginning of demons to the offspring of angels and antediluvian women. This theory is based upon interpretations of Genesis 6:1–4; Jude 6,7; Job 1:6; 2:1; and 38:7.

The third theory, obviously preferable, is that demons are fallen angels. Based upon interpretations of Matthew 12:24; 24:41; Revelation 12:4, 7, 9; Jude 6; and 2 Peter 2:4, Unger cites a host of scholars who join him in this view.

Dr. Lewis Sperry Chafer is of the opinion that, of those fallen spirits who were not incarcerated, "another company became demons."[14] John J. Owen concludes in this view that demons are the evil spirits or wicked angels associated with Satan in his rebellion against God.[15] This is "the generally accepted theory" according to G. Campbell Morgan,[16] A. A. Hodge,[17] Charles Hodge,[18] and A. H. Strong.[19] A. C. Gaebelein says "the fallen angels are demons."[20] Unger fairly concludes that there is little unanimity to be expected on a subject of this sort and great latitude exists for speculation.[21]

DEMONIC CHARACTERISTICS

What more can we know about demons from God's word? Unger lists the following ten characteristics of the enemy.[22]

(1) Demons are personalities—They think, they speak, they act (Acts 19:15–16). In the case of the demon possessed, the domination is almost complete (Mark 5:10; Luke 4:34). In case of demon influence, their control is less complete and direct (1 Tim. 4:1,2 and 1 John 4:1–2).

(2) Demons are invisible—Though not ignoring the laws of nature, God's Word also recognizes the possible transcendence of

natural law in evil supernaturalism (Ex. 7:10–11, 22; 8:7; 2 Thess. 2:8–10; and Rev. 13:15).

(3) Demons have intelligence—Since great wisdom characterizes angels in general (2 Sam. 14:20), it stands to reason that it was corrupted in Satan's followers. Though they confess Jesus as Lord and recognize His authority, they do not submit to Him (Mark 1:24; 5:6–7); they cleverly withhold knowledge of His incarnation and completed redemption (1 John 4:1–6), corrupt sound doctrine (1 Tim. 4:1–3), discern between those who have God's seal and those who do not (Rev. 9:4) and know full well their own tragic destiny and inevitable doom (Matt. 8:29).

(4) Demons have strength—The psalmist celebrates this angelic characteristic in Psalm 103:20, Peter speaks of the power and might of angelic spirits in 2 Peter 2:11, and Jesus Himself indirectly referred to demonic strength in Matthew 12:29.

(5) Demons are depraved—Although demons reveal various degrees of wickedness (Matt. 12:45), they are all depraved and are referred to as morally unclean (Matt. 10:1; Mark 1:27; 3:11; Luke 4:36; Acts 8:7; and Rev. 16:13).

(6) Demons use men to oppose God—The opposition of Satan and his demons is evident in every era of church history. The unseen forces of evil will increase their activity in latter times (1 Tim. 4:1 and Rev. 4:1–21), culminating in the debacle at Armageddon (Rev. 16:13–14). Not until the time Satan and his demons are confined to the abyss, the prison of evil spirits (Zech. 13:2 and Rev. 20:1–3) will the kingdom of righteousness and peace supplant the present satanic world system (1 John 2:17).

(7) Demons can oppress the mind—Our attitudes become the means through which demonic oppression can occur. Paul warns us that unresolved anger can give the devil an opportunity to hinder the believer (Eph. 4:26–27).

(8) Demons can oppress the body—Demons can cause physical ailments such as dumbness (Matt. 9:32–33), blindness (Matt. 12:22), and various other defects and deformities (Luke 13:11–17).

(9) Demons alienate men from God—Involvement in the occult opens one to religious delusions and heresies, being insensitive to the stern warning of God's word against complicity in the occult (Deut. 18:9–10). Opposition to God becomes violent, and complete apostasy inevitably results with "doctrines of demons" and the denial of Christ's deity (1 Tim. 4:1–2 and 1 John 2:1–3).

(10) Demons hinder man's general well being—Demons subject man to temptations (Gen. 3:1–7; Matt. 4:3; John 13:27; Acts 5:3 and 1 Thess. 3:5). Satanic and demonic solicitations are both negative and positive (Matt. 13:38–39).

Having examined these ten characteristics of demons, is it possible that they can be distinguished by single characteristics?

L. M. Sweet reminds us that we are told practically nothing about the nature of demons in the New Testament. No theoretical discussion occurs for the center of interest in the Gospels is the person of Jesus Christ.[23]

Demons and Specific Sins

Historian Jeffrey Burton Russell has studied the history of the devil for twenty years. In response to the question, "How recent is the practice of giving demons the names of particular sins, like the spirit of lust or the demon of pride," he says:

> In the Middle Ages there was certainly a tendency to speak of demons of pride. It is not until perhaps the nineteenth century that you get almost whimsical dictionaries of demons: this demon is responsible for lust and this demon for avarice and so on.
>
> Going back to the church fathers, there is some basis for this in Evagrius of Pontus who had the sophisticated psychological idea that demons are attuned to our sins. For example, as soon as you would open your mind to the sin of avarice, as soon as you would be tempted by some deal that would get you a lot of money, then that action would open a hold in your soul's defenses, and the demons are primed to go in. Sometimes Evagrius does speak as if there were special demons who go after avarice and others with all of the other specialties.[24]

Demons and Specific Territories

Writers such as C. Peter Wagner in his book *Engaging the Enemy* have helped to advance the idea that demons have territories. Wagner makes the statement and raises the question as follows:

> We read in 2 Corinthians 4:4 that Satan has successfully blinded the minds of unbelievers so that they cannot receive the gospel. This undoubtedly refers to individuals, but could it also refer to

territories? Could it mean nations? States? Cities? Cultural groups? Tribes? Social networks? Church growth theory has long ago recognized the phenomenon of resistant peoples. Could it be that at least some of that resistance may be caused by the direct working of demonic forces?[25]

Wagner bases his idea on passages such as Deuteronomy 32; Daniel 10; and Ephesians 6:12 among others.[26] Such a thought would certainly explain resistance to the gospel and why certain sins seem to abound in specific areas.

Russell also explores this question,

A hot topic in some Christian circles today is the idea of praying against territorial spirits—that certain cities or areas have a particular demon. These Christians have prayer marathons to cast it out. Is there a historical precedent for this?

He responds,

Definitely. Interestingly, one must go back centuries in the Christian tradition to find it. The territoriality of angels and demons plays very little if any role in mainstream Christian theology. After the fourth or fifth century, you find it rarely referred to. But in some of the church fathers, Origen particularly, you find the idea that each nation or community has its own angel and its own demon. So there is an angel of the Persian empire and a demon of the Persian empire. There is an angel of the Roman empire and a demon of the Roman empire, and so forth.[27]

Though questions will continue to be raised and various opinions will be expressed citing interpretations of different Scripture passages, all Christendom can certainly be united and rejoice over the fact that we do have victory in Jesus over Satan and his demons. Jesus alone is our King of kings and Lord of lords which every tongue shall confess (Phil. 2:11)!

WHAT YOU CAN DO

You may have heard the old sports maxim that the best offense is a good defense.

➢ Look up the Scriptures mentioned in this chapter in a good study Bible. God's Word speaks clearly about Satan, his characteristics, and his work. To know the enemy is to better protect oneself. Have a pen and paper handy to make notes as God's Holy Spirit reveals truths to you.

➤ Read Christian books on the subject (consult appendix B for a list). The sections on demonology and spiritual warfare may be especially helpful.

➤ Consult your pastor. He should be open to helpful suggestions from the congregation. You might ask him if he would consider preaching a sermon(s) on one of the subjects in this chapter.

➤ Talk with your friends. They could be interested in a Bible study on the topics and Scriptures of this chapter.

Remember, our goal is not to stir up an unhealthy interest in Satan and his work. Rather, our desire should be to glorify the Father in our lives and stand strong against Satan and his army. When God's people dig deep into His Word, you can rest assured that He will not only convict and teach you but will point out things that should be changed. This is what spiritual growth is all about!

LAUREN

In spite of the warnings in her mind, Lauren's fingertips came to rest lightly upon the Ouija™ board marker. Her friend Heather, sitting across from her, rested her fingertips on the other side of the marker.

How odd, thought Lauren. *The marker feels warm, almost hot to the touch. It must be my imagination.*

The girls crowded around the board. "What questions are you going to ask?" they whispered. "Find out what's going to be on our physics test next week," one joked. "Why don't you see who will take you to the junior-senior prom?" another suggested. "Knock it off," Heather said, matter-of-factly. "Let her make up her own mind."

"I know what I want to do," Lauren spoke up quickly. "I want to talk to my grandmother." A deep quiet settled over the room. Lauren's grandmother had been an important figure in the community. Everyone knew her. They also knew that she had died two years ago.

"Are you sure?" questioned Heather. Lauren nodded her head affirmatively. "Okay, everybody. Keep quiet and concentrate while Lauren asks her questions."

Once again the room settled into an unearthly quiet, the dark shadows flickering upon the walls of the room as Lauren whispered her first question. "Grandmother, are you here?" For a few moments nothing happened and then the marker began to move until it came to rest over the response, YES.

"What was my personal favorite nickname I used to call you?" Lauren questioned. Slowly the marker moved from letter to letter four times, spelling N-A-N-A. Lauren gave an audible gasp.

"What's wrong?" Heather asked.

"It's true," said Lauren shakily. "It's true. That's exactly what I used to call her. No one knew that."

A chill crept across the room. "I think we'd better stop," someone said. "I'll get the lights," volunteered another.

"No," Lauren cried out with an intensity that surprised even her. "I have one more question."

No one moved as Lauren and Heather once again placed their fingertips upon the marker.

Again the atmosphere grew deathly quiet as a pall of suspense and anticipation descended upon the room.

"Nana, do you have any advice for me?"

The marker slowly and silently slid across the board seeming to pick up speed from letter to letter until it was practically a blur of activity.

Someone screamed, "It spelled it out." One of the girls sobbed. "What?" asked Lauren, almost in a trancelike state.

"It spelled out 'Be careful!'"

F   I   V   E

When men tell you to consult medium and spiritists,
who whisper and mutter, should not a people inquire of their God?
Why consult the dead on behalf of the living?
— Isaiah 8:19

Seances and Spirits:
Spiritism Today

The dark world of the occult often pulls unsuspecting individuals
into its depths through curiosity. Perhaps no aspect of the occult
has more widely appealed to individuals than communication with
spirits, whether by the Ouija™ board or the seance. This can be
a dangerous and terrifying experience as several students learned.

In a small Iowa town a high school student's interest in the occult
became stimulated by a discussion of ghosts and spirits in one of
his classes. It was reported that the ghost of a little girl had been
seen at the town cemetery.

"Several of the students had already been into spiritism [estab-
lishing communication with the dead]," related the student, "but
it was all new to me. I started to read about it out of curiosity. I
went to the public library and pulled out everything I could find
on spiritism and ghosts. I was really interested, but never thought
I would actually become involved in the occult."

The student was persuaded by a group of fellow students to visit
this graveyard late at night for the purpose of raising the spirit of

98

the young girl. One boy, whose family had a history of involvement with the occult, agreed to be the medium [one who uses his body to establish contact with the spirit world]. The student continued: "Our medium lay down on the grave. We sat around him in absolute silence, and he seemed to go into a trance. At first there was some giggling and laughing, but no spirit appeared." Time passed, and then things happened quickly. According to the student, "We recited several incantations [a special word or words] asking for a sign." And it came. "The medium's body began to rise from the ground," the student explained.

At about that time one of the girls, terrified, screamed and pointed to the tombstone where, approximately fifteen yards behind it and by a tree, stood a small, pale girl, dressed in white.

The students ran in terror from the graveyard. As the youth who was relating the story and another boy looked back, they noticed their friend still lying in a trance on the grave.

"He was never the same again, even after psychological care," continued the student. Even now his friends say that he sometimes goes into a trance and appears to lose touch with reality.[1]

The student wisely concluded that experimenting with the occult is dangerous, and one should not become involved in it. Yet literally thousands today call themselves spiritists both in the United States and abroad.

There are nearly twenty spiritist denominations in existence today, and the Morris Pratt Spiritualist Institute in Whitewater, Wisconsin, which ordains ministers. The oldest and largest of the spiritist denominations is the National Spiritualist Association of Churches.[2] Others, however, cite the Universal Church of the Master (UCM) formed in 1908 and incorporated in 1918 as the oldest. It is credited with three hundred congregations, ten thousand members, and over thirteen hundred ministers.[3]

Frank S. Mead reports that, in addition to the UCM, there are the International General Assembly of Spiritualists (1936) with 164,072 members in 209 churches; the National Spiritual Alliance of the U.S.A. (1913) with over 3,000 members in 34 churches; the National Spiritualist Association of Churches (1893) with over 5,000 members in 164 churches; and the Progressive Spiritual Church (1907) with 11,000 members in 21 churches.[4]

Exactly what is involved in a practice which so many subscribe to today?

SPIRITISM — WHAT IS IT?

Though the heart of spiritism or spiritualism (the British term) is the seance, a practice designed to conjure up spirits of the dead, spiritism has other features as well. Many are under the category of divination, as the following: crystal gazing (looking into a crystal ball or crystal object for purposes of foretelling the future), cartouche (Egyptian method of fortune telling), chiromancy (foretelling a person's character and future by the lines and marks on the fingers and palms, known also as palmistry), metoposcopy (practice of divination by interpreting the lines on the forehead), physiognomy (practice of divination by reading the shape of a person's face), phrenology (reading bumps on the head), runes (runes derive their name from the Viking Rune alphabet. These tiles with the letters on them, like dice, are cast and interpreted. These twenty-four characters are considered to be a magical alphabet), and tarot cards (dating back to ancient Egypt these cards are said to be the forerunner of our modern playing cards and are used to foretell the future of an individual as they are "read" by a knowledgeable person). Other forms of divination include astrology (which we will examine in the next chapter), biorhythms, ESP, I Ching, Ouija™ boards, palm reading, and tea leaf reading.

Another feature of spiritism is psychic healing, which includes psychic surgery (a bloodless procedure in which the surgeon makes a supposed imaginary incision and the diseased tissue is removed through the incision), biofeedback (maintaining control of the heart rate, skin temperature and even brain wave patterns by mentally concentrating), and a host of therapies including peditherapy (massaging specific areas of the foot to produce healing), crystal therapy (use of quartz crystals to induce healing as in wearing them, placing them in certain places, etc.), chromotherapy or color therapy (healing from holding a certain colored object or sitting under a particular colored light), or charms.

Spiritist Terminology

A brief look at some of the more common terms used by spiritists today will aid our understanding of spiritism. Among them are the following:

> Automatic writing—Handwriting independent of the writer's conscious control.
> Channeling—A New Age term also known as trance channeling, it is the Spiritist method of communication with the spirits. Better known channelers today include J. Z. Knight, who claims to channel a 35,000-year-old male spirit called Ramtha; the late Jane Roberts and her master, Seth; and others.
> Ectoplasm—A substance that usually flows from a medium's mouth or nose and which materializes into a spirit.
> Familiar—A demonic spirit that serves a medium.
> Ouija™ board—Invented in 1891 by Elijah J. Bond, it was designed to provide a means for those on earth to contact "the other side." In 1966 Parker Brothers bought all rights and markets it today as entertainment.
> Seance—French for "a sitting," it is a meeting to receive messages from the dead through a medium verbally or by means of a Ouija™ board, automatic writing, trumpet, table movement, etc. Participants are usually seated in a circle and holding hands. The seance is the best known feature of spiritism.

Do the Dead Speak?

Seances create unusual feelings and circumstances, to put it mildly.

Even the Barbie™ doll is connected to "the other side."

Barbara Bell of Marin County, California, charges $3 a call to summon the spirit of the doll to solve problems. Bell told *Life* magazine that Barbie™ "has been forced to be shallow all these years, but underneath, she's a profound person."[5]

The Associated Press reported that "nine women dressed in black pulled stockings over their faces in court and began chanting, claiming to invoke the spirit of a murder victim at an arraignment hearing. The women pointed at Alan Jose Reyes who is charged with the stabbing death of his girlfriend, Virginia Fer-rer."[6]

Hotel officials in the quaint, scenic town of Eureka Springs, Arkansas, brought in a California psychic to conduct a seance in order to gain more information about four ghosts rumored to haunt the hotel. About 150 people, some from as far away as Dallas, Chicago, and Kansas, gathered in a dimly lit room to hear the psychic "identify" the presence of two people who had pre-viously lost their lives in the hotel. Relying on her spirit guide Zyra, Olivia, the psychic, permitted two prearranged individuals to ask questions concerning the whys of the haunting and after the seance opened the floor to inquiries from the audience, many who were skeptical.[7]

The successful movies *Ghostbusters I* and *II* even owe their success in part to the seance, as Dan Akroyd tells it. "My family was fascinated with the paranormal," he said. "I grew up with tales of seances, and was even told the spirits of my dead grandparents appeared smiling at the foot of my mother's bed after I was born. One day I saw this article about applying quantum mechanics to ghost hunting. And bang! I had the plot idea for Ghostbusters!"[8]

Even Abraham Lincoln attended a number of seances following the death of his son, Willie. Several of the seances were conducted by a teenage medium, Nettie Colburn.[9] Thomas A. Edison and Guglielmo Marconi, inventors of the radio, both are known as pioneers in communication, but not with the dead! Nonetheless, they had hoped to establish some form of electronic contact with the next world.[10]

Perhaps one of the strangest facts is this contact with "the other side" has been admitted as evidence in a court trial. In 1980 José Nunes was charged with killing his best friend Mauricio Henri-que, at Goiania in Brazil.

The police refused to believe José's claim that the shooting was an accident, so his mother decided to contact Chico Xavier, Brazil's most famous medium. Xavier was so famous that he was featured on a series of Brazilian postage stamps. José's mother asked this famed medium to contact the deceased. Xavier did, and he attended José's trial to read the spirit message he had received by automatic writing. "José is not to blame," the dead friend reportedly declared. When the handwriting of the automatic writing script was compared with Mauricio's, they were found to be the same.

As he gave the verdict on the case, Judge Orimar de Bastos told the hushed court that Chico Xavier was highly regarded for his honesty and would not make up such messages. "I am not a spiritualist," said the judge, "but I feel I have to give some credibility to this message—even though it is unprecedented for the victim after his death, to give an account of his death. Mauricio's message backs up what José has told us" and with that, the judge pronounced José Nunes, "not guilty."[11]

SPIRITISM—A BRIEF HISTORY

In 1871 anthropologist Sir Edward Taylor first suggested in his study of *Primitive Culture* that a belief in spirits is a universal feature of human societies.[12]

Several personalities helped to introduce spiritism to the United States.

Emmanuel Swedenborg (1688–1774) was a dynamic figure, an important Swedish intellectual and religious force who influenced the poet William Blake. Philosopher Immanuel Kant was so fascinated by Swendborg's psychic abilities that he devoted a small treatise to him.[13] Among Swedenborg's reported gifts were clairvoyance, remote viewing (in 1759 he witnessed a fire in Stockholm from a location three hundred miles away), and communication with the dead. Following Swedenborg's death his followers established the Church of the New Jerusalem in England in 1778 and in the United States in 1792.

Interest in spiritism within the United States is said to have begun in 1843 when Andrew Jackson Davis, a New York cobbler, claimed that he could contact the spirit world as a medium.

The Fox sisters—Margaretta (Maggie), fourteen, and Catherine (Katie), eleven—are credited with actually beginning spiritism in the United States in 1848. At their home in Hydesville, New York, the two young sisters heard strange rapping noises and subsequently claimed to be able to communicate with the source of the noises, the spirit of a murdered peddler by the name of Charles Rosa.

Their fame spread rapidly with generous help from the media, especially Horace Greely, editor of the *New York Tribune*, and P. T. Barnum. Others impressed with the sisters were William Cullen Bryant, James Fenimore Cooper, George Ripley, James Greenleaf Whittier, Henry Wadsworth Longfellow, William Lloyd Garrison, Harriet Beecher Stowe, Elizabeth Barrett Browning, and Arthur Conan Doyle. Both sisters, though, fell under the influence of alcohol.

In 1888 both appeared in New York, where Maggie revealed that they had deceived the public by causing the rapping sounds. They were produced, she said, by "popping" their knee joints in an effort to trick their mother. One year later Maggie retracted her statement, saying she was bribed into making it earlier.

Nothing seemed to dampen the spiritist movement, and it spread rapidly during the mid-1800s. Physician Thomas Nelson wrote that "nothing within my memory has had so great an influence. It has broken up hundreds of churches and changed the religious belief of hundreds of thousands."[14]

In 1854, author Orestes Brownson counted three hundred spiritist clubs in Philadelphia alone and complained that "the injection seizes all classes, ministers of religion, lawyers, physicians, judges, comedians, rich and poor, learned and unlearned."[15]

SPIRITIST BELIEFS

Spiritism today cuts across racial and occupational lines as it did in the 1800s. That many believe deeply in spiritism is a foregone conclusion, but just what do they believe? Let's look briefly at their beliefs about God, Jesus Christ, the Holy Spirit, sin, redemption, salvation, and retribution.

➤ God—God is impersonal. He is creator and sustainer. To assert that God inspired the writers of the Bible to make known His divine will is a gross outrage and misleading to the public.

➤ Jesus Christ—Christ Himself was nothing more than a medium of high order. The teaching of spirits supersedes and is an advance upon the teachings of Christianity. Jesus Christ was not divine. He is now an advanced spirit in the sixth sphere. He never claimed to be God manifest in the flesh and does not at present. Jesus did not claim for Himself more than He held out for others. His identification with the Father was the oneness of mediumship. He was a medium or "mediator."

➤ The Holy Spirit—Denies the personality of the Holy Spirit. The Holy Spirit from God is the spirit of some holy person who has once been in the flesh.

➤ Sin—Man never had a fall. Whatever is, is right. Evil does not exist. Evil is good. No matter what man's path may be, good or bad, it is the path of divine ordination and destiny. A lie is the truth intrinsically; it holds a lawful place in creation; it is a necessity.

➤ Redemption—There is no atoning value in the death of Jesus Christ. Jesus was a Jewish enthusiast and came to an untimely death. Salvation by a vicarious atonement is a wicked and soul-destroying delusion.

➤ Salvation—Man becomes his own savior. Man is made better in this life by intercourse with spirits. We affirm the moral responsibility of the individual, and that he makes his own happiness or unhappiness as he obeys or disobeys nature's physical and spiritual laws. Man becomes a spirit after death, doing both evil and good, but he may be saved as he progresses from one spirit level to the next. We affirm that the doorway to reformation is never closed against any human soul, here or hereafter.

➤ Retribution—Hell does not exist and never will. All spirit people of wisdom, knowledge, and love know there is no hell and no devil. No resurrection and no judgment. When you believe in spiritual manifestations, you will feel far happier than you do now. You will not fear the threats of damnation and hell. Such doctrine is wrong.

The Chaplain's Handbook supplement carries ten principles which are an expansion of The Seven Principles of Spiritualism. They are as follows:

(1) "We" believe in the fatherhood of God and the brotherhood of man.

(2) "We" believe that all phenomena that occur within the realms of nature, both physical and spiritual, are manifestations of infinite intelligence.

(3) "We" believe that true religion is discovered by understanding the laws of nature and of God, and by living in harmony therein.

(4) "We" believe that individual existence, personal identity, and memory continue after the transitional period called death.

(5) "We" believe that communication with those in the unseen or etheric world is a scientific fact, fully proven under test conditions by the phenomena of psychical research.

(6) "We" believe that the Golden Rule, "Whatsoever ye would that others should do unto you, do ye also unto them," is the essence of morality.

(7) "We" believe that every individual is morally self-responsible. Happiness flows from obedience of the laws of nature and of God and unhappiness and misery follow their disobedience.

(8) "We" believe that genuine improvement and reformation of the human soul are always possible in this world and the next.

(9) "We" believe that prophecy exists in our times as in biblical days.

(10) "We" believe that the universe, as a spiritual system expressing divine wisdom, makes possible the eternal progress of the aspiring soul who loves truth and goodness.[16]

THE BIBLE SPEAKS ON SPIRITISM

Of course, that truth is fully revealed in the person of Jesus Christ, and God's Word sets forth the truth clearly for us to see from the first words of Genesis through the last word of Revelation.

Our desire should be to speak directly with God through prayer, yet many attempt to speak to departed loved ones when in reality they may well be speaking with lying, seducing spirits.

Perhaps one of the best known accounts of communication between the living and the dead is the encounter between King Saul and the witch, or better, the Medium of Endor, found in

1 Samuel 28:1–25. It has been called "the most prominent and detailed case of necromancy (communication with the spirits of the dead) in Scripture.[17] Koch called the account "the subject of much debate."[18]

King Saul was afraid of an impending attack by the Philistine army whom David had joined earlier. Camping at Mt. Gilboa with his army, he sought and desperately tried to get a word from the Lord by means of dreams, prophets, or Urim (holy instruments used as lots in determining God's will; see Ex. 28:30), according to verse 6. Although he had "expelled" the mediums and spiritists, he must have known they were still around for he told his attendants to find one. They immediately knew of one in Endor, a town of the tribe of Manasseh six miles southeast of Nazareth.

Saul disguised himself and requested that she bring up the prophet Samuel who had died earlier (1 Sam. 25:1) while David was a fugitive from Saul. Samuel had anointed Saul king and had been the chief religious authority in the land.

After brief resistance on her part, she agreed to do so. It is here that we encounter the debate. Did she or didn't she conjure up Samuel? Was it the Samuel who died? Did the medium have control over Samuel?

Theologians Augustine and Tertullian believed that a spirit was conjured up but it wasn't Samuel but rather the devil. Reginald Scott, a sixteenth-century English writer who disbelieved in witchcraft, disagreed with this idea, believing that the devil would have been banished by the realization five times of the name of God or Jehovah and the devil would not rebuke or punish someone for evil but rather would encourage them to do more evil. According to Scott, there was no spirit, only a woman who was a ventriloquist.[19]

Merrill F. Unger sees it in a different light. Samuel did appear and in so doing exposed her for the charlatan she was. Why else would she cry out? Wouldn't a true medium be accustomed to such appearances? In reality, she was surprised that it truly was Samuel back from the dead.

She did not bring Samuel back. God did. Unger says this is the only example in all Scripture where God permitted a deceased person to come back, as a *spirit*, to hold communication with the living. Others came back (Jairus's daughter, Lazarus of Bethany) but not as spirits. Jesus and others who "came out of the tombs" after His resurrection (Matt. 27:52–53) were resurrected persons, not spirits.[20]

The medium's role in all of this was passive. She did nothing except show compassion for Saul following Samuel's dire prophesy of Saul's death the next day. The conversation with Samuel did not take place *through* her but rather *between* Saul and Samuel.

A broader examination of God's Word will reveal that Saul's encounter at Endor was not the only occasion for God to warn His people against involvement in spiritism. We see numerous Scripture references relating to spiritism as we come to the same conclusion which Unger and occult scholar Kurt Koch came to, and that is that many passages (Ex. 22:18; 1 Sam. 28; 1 Chron. 10:13; Gal. 5:19–21) should be treated not as witchcraft but as sorcery-spiritism.

Further, Koch broadens spiritism to include visions, prophesy, communication with spirits, materialization (production of phantom figures by mediums), aggressive and defensive magic, healing, etc.[21]

God's Word is not silent in regard to the exercise of occult powers regardless of the form they take.

➤ Daniel 2:2—King Nebuchadnezzar linked sorcerers, astrologers, magicians, and enchanters all together to discover the meaning of his dream.

➤ Isaiah 47:9—These wizards practicing witchcraft were the equivalent of mediums or consulters of the dead in spiritualism and were regarded as an evil influence in Israel.

➤ Leviticus 19:31; 20:6, 27—God speaking through Moses warns the Israelites not to seek out mediums or spiritists as the Israelites will become defiled.

➤ 2 Kings 23:24—In the great revival under Josiah, mediums, spiritist, household gods, idols, etc. were all put away.

➤ 1 Chronicles 10:13–14—Saul's consultation with a medium is stated as sin contributing to his downfall.

> Isaiah 8:19—The folly of listening to man's suggestion to consult with spiritist instead of seeking God's guidance.
> Isaiah 19:3—Isaiah's prophecy about Egypt and the futility of their consultation with idols and spirits of the dead.
> Malachi 3:5, 2 Thessalonians 2:9–11; Revelation 21:8, 22:15; 1 Samuel 15:23, 18:3–20—Sorcerers abound with lying wonders and will be judged and punished when Christ returns.

The highly regarded Bible scholar and teacher Herbert Lockyer also includes these passages as denouncing the practice of sorcery (Deut. 18:10; 2 Kings 21:6; 2 Chron. 33:6; Isa. 8:19–20; Jer. 27:9; Gal. 5:20; Rev. 9:21; and 21:8).[22] You surely see that this was a serious problem. The sheer volume of references throughout God's Word is ample evidence of this truth.

Just as we have seen modern day occult figures, so were there also these personalities in the Bible. Simon Magus was renowned for his sorcery (Acts 8:9–11).

Elymas (Bar-Jesus) was a sorcerer who Paul challenged and rebuked (Acts 13:6–11).

The deception of the spiritist followers in biblical times occurs today just as then. Dr. W. A. Criswell addresses this in Exodus 22:18 (also vv. 19–20) — The practices of these abominations, according to Criswell, "so distort the mind of the participant as to render it almost impossible for him properly to perceive the things of God. Note almost the exact parallel to this in Romans 1:18–32.[23]

It is precisely this mind distortion which prevents many from seeing the fraudulent side of spiritism.

FACT OR FRAUD?

The famous magician Harry Houdini was one of the greatest critics of spiritism, yet he hoped that it might be proven true.

When Lady Conan Doyle produced a message from Houdini's deceased mother via automatic writing, Houdini broke his friendship with Arthur Conan Doyle as well, claiming that the message was the sort any mother might write and that it showed a great command of English that his mother never possessed.[24]

One professor of psychology at York University in Toronto wrote an interesting article "Spirits Cannot Speak Through Human Beings" and quoted Graham Reed as saying,

> Much has been made of the sagacity and profound insights communicated by [channelers'] messages. These alleged qualities have been regarded as clear proof of the messages' supernatural origins because, it is argued, the channelers themselves have neither the erudition nor the intellectual power to produce such material without help. But in actual fact, if the messages are examined objectively, ignoring their assumed origins, they prove to be simplistic, repetitive, and extremely vague. They quite lack the clarity, the tightness of argument, and the succinctness of expression that characterize productive thinking. On the contrary, they seem to consist solely of strings of loosely associated gobbets of naive ideas and verbal formulae. They are well within the intellectual capacity of channelers of even moderate education.[25]

As in other areas of life, no amount of explanation or denial will convince the believer that he is actually being duped. One such fake who came clean after many years told in a book how he did it. He was a pastor of a spiritualist church in Tampa, Florida. On one occasion he wanted to impress his congregation with the ability of departed spirits to protect folks on earth from harm.

He took a glass of water that was sitting on the pulpit and poured it on some flowers. After wrapping the glass in a handkerchief, he smashed it against the side of the pulpit. The congregation gasped at the sound of glass shattering. The minister opened the handkerchief to show the jagged pieces of glass, popped a piece into his mouth, munched on it, and then swallowed it.

The people in the audience groaned. One woman fainted. "Spirit protection is a wonderful reality," claimed the spiritualist pastor. After the service, the incredulous church members crowded around the pulpit to examine the leftover jagged glass. They went away shaking their heads.

What the people didn't know was that before the service, the minister had placed a dish containing ice inside the pulpit. What he was munching on during his "amazing demonstration" was not glass, but a piece of ice.

There were other spiritualist tricks. An accomplice, for example, would pick the pockets of a member of the congregation.
Several weeks were allowed to elapse—enough time for the victim
to miss the lifted item. Later, during a seance, the "spirits" would
return the stolen object to the grateful and dumbfounded person.[26]

It would be convenient if we could list every occurrence of
spiritist phenomena and state unequivocally that each is fraudulent. Certainly many are, but some defy explanation. Consider
Mrs. Leonona E. Piper, who began as a medium in 1885 and was
never found by the scientific community to be fraudulent.

> Mrs. Piper gave some 88 sittings, for example, carefully observed
> at all times by members of the British Society for Physical Re-
> search. Professor Oliver Lodge, later Sir Oliver Lodge, one of
> England's most brilliant scientists and a careful psychic investiga-
> tor, compiled a checklist of some 41 specific incidents wherein
> Mrs. Piper stated facts and general information concerning those
> who attended her SEANCES, facts that were unknown to those
> persons at the very time the seances were in session! This is
> carefully verified and is beyond refutation. Mrs. Piper convinced
> Sir Oliver Lodge, Sir William Crooks, Dr. William James, Dr.
> Hodgson and Dr. Hyslop...that she was indeed possessed of
> supernatural capacities.[27]

How Do You Explain Spiritism?

Essentially five theories could account for what transpires in
spiritism. They are fraud, educated guesses, actual communication with a spirit of the dead, ESP, and demonic deception.

As we have already examined the fraudulent aspect, let's look
briefly at the remaining four.

First, educated guesses. This theory has the medium using
educated guesses and ambiguous statements until he has gathered
information from the people in attendance.

Second, actual communication with the dead. It is not possible
to receive a message from the deceased. One may receive a
message from a spirit posing as the loved one, but it simply is not
possible for the deceased to communicate with the living.

Third, ESP. As John Newport explained it,

The genuine medium is a person of such telepathic sensitiveness that he gathers information from the conscious and subconscious parts of the sitter's mind. Mrs. Eileen Garrett admitted that she used ESP in seances. Kerr calls this the "super-ESP" theory. Two women filled their mind with the characteristics of a fictitious person in an unpublished novel for two weeks. They then went to a reputable medium. The medium proceeded to describe accurately their imaginary friend as a loved one beyond the grave and delivered messages from him.[28]

He continued, "Closely connected with ESP is the idea of a cosmic consciousness. According to this theory, every event leaves a psychic tracing. The medium can pick up the information from the cosmic mind. There is no loved one sending messages from the 'other side.'"[29]

Fourth, demonic deception. Perhaps we will never see this quite as clearly as in the tragic case of Episcopalian bishop James A. Pike, called "one of the brightest stars in the psychic firmament."[30]

When Pike's twenty-year-old son Jim, Jr., committed suicide, his death impacted his father in ways no one would imagine. Postcards Jim, Jr., had bought but never mailed began to appear, objects associated with Jim changed location in his apartment without human assistance, a woman who assisted with the church secretarial work and whose bangs Jim, Jr., had never liked awoke on three successive mornings to find a portion of her bangs gone until all had been removed. She could not explain their disappearance. The clock hands swung and stopped at the hour of Jim's death and the thermostat of the apartment kept itself at the temperature Jim, Jr., preferred, regardless of attempts to set the temperature at different degrees!

Bishop Pike, at the close of his own book *The Other Side*, emphatically believed that he was actually in touch with his son. Asking himself that question in place of the reader, "Do you believe you have been in touch with your son?" he answered "Yes, I do."[31]

Unger saw it differently, not as a fantasy or hoax or actual spirit contact between father and son.

Bishop Pike, seen in the light of scriptural revelation, became the victim of demon imposture and delusion when he dared to challenge them in his own strength. Demonic forces won their first round with the bishop when he departed from biblical faith, opening his mind to the teachings of demons (1 Tim. 4:1).

The second round was won when demonic forces [led] him through psychic phenomena to seek contact with his son.

The knockout blow landed in the Judean desert where Pike succumbed to heat and weakness. Diane, his wife, would see him welcomed into the spirit world by his old friends but there was no sign of Jesus.[32]

WHAT YOU CAN DO

As I write this closing portion of the chapter, it is 4:30 A.M. and all is totally black outside. Surely the death of loved ones is akin to the blackness of night. Though we know that they, as Christians, have their joy complete as they are united for eternity with their Lord and loved ones they have missed, we still feel the loss here.

Soon, however, the darkness of this night will give way to the dawning of a new day. So it is with life as believers. We do not need to communicate with our loved ones through seances or other occultic means. King David was right when he said about his infant son who died, "I will go to him, but he will not return to me" (2 Sam. 12:23).

How comforting and exciting we find Paul's words, "Where, O death, is your sting?" (1 Cor. 15:55). Truly as Christians "we have the best of both worlds." Life with Christ here and the promise of that continued relationship in "a land that is fairer than day."

Accept the fact that you are going to be continually exposed to many of the concepts of spiritism in New Age teachings. You might want to refer to chapter 4 again, in addition to the Scriptures you will find within this chapter. God's Word is clear that the Christian must have no part in spiritist activities.

➤ Avoid talk shows, television programs, or movies with spiritist themes, i.e. seances, divination, etc., which might create a desire to know more about it. Certainly, as much as possible, we ought to try to protect our children from watching or reading about these same things.

➤ Pray for those involved in spiritism and by all means share God's Word with them. You may want to do so with the assistance of a good Christian friend.

➤ Do not let anyone convince you to attend spiritist meetings so that you may better understand spiritism. Christians who have done so have become confused and have compromised their faith. We do not need to give Satan "an open door" into our minds and hearts.

LAUREN

Lauren was careful, very careful. She did not want her parents to suspect what she was doing. She began researching witchcraft on her own time privately, checking out books from both the school and public libraries. She never expected her school library to have so much information on the subject of witchcraft.

One day during study hall, Lauren went to the school library to check out eight different books on witchcraft.

"Going out tonight with your broom?" Mr. Sims, the librarian, joked.

"Yes, sir. I'm going to have a devil of a time!" Lauren came back with a laugh.

Mr. Sims watched Lauren walk away with her stack of books cradled between her arms. *Funny*, he thought. *I've seen students check out one or two books on witchcraft, but never that many. Could it be a term paper? Come to think of it, I haven't seen Lauren in the library like I used to. Hmm, I'll have to check on that.* But Mr. Sims quickly forgot about it; he had other things on his mind. In the meantime,

Lauren retreated to her room to pour over her new books. Months later, Mr. Sims would regret his forgetfulness.

Her parents noticed a gradual change in Lauren. They passed it off, however, as the typical mood swings of adolescents. However, one of Lauren's friends from church, Heather, had taken note of her changes in behavior. She had noticed her talking with two new girls in the cafeteria, Caroline and Pam. The three girls would sit huddled together, talking in whispered tones. Whenever she approached them, they would quit talking altogether.

"Lauren, you have been acting so strangely lately. I'm worried about you," Heather finally broke the silence. "Some of the gang said you had gone overboard with books on witchcraft."

"There's nothing wrong with books on witchcraft. They're educational," one of the girls shot out before Lauren could say anything.

"You really should read some of them," the other girl chimed in. "You might even learn something."

Heather did not waste a second as she quietly, but firmly responded, "I have read a book that tells me all I need to know about witchcraft."

"Which one?" Lauren's new friends inquired in chorus.

"The Bible," Heather said, to their surprise. Lauren felt troubled...

S I X

The acts of the sinful nature are obvious:
sexual immorality, impurity and debauchery;
idolatry and witchcraft...I warn you, as I did before,
that those who live like this will not inherit the kingdom of God.
— GALATIANS 5:19–21

On the Road to Endor: Witchcraft in the United States

Mention the words "witch" or "witchcraft" and what images come to mind? Do you think of the television comedy series "Bewitched" that portrayed a witch married to a mortal?

Perhaps you think of the wicked witch that tricked Snow White into eating the apple and falling into a deep sleep, or maybe the witch of Hansel and Gretel. Children's stories are filled with them.

The words may bring to mind Halloween. Did you ever dress up as a witch in your younger years? You may simply associate black clothes, a pointed hat, a broom, a black cat, and a smoking caldron with witches and witchcraft.

Most people likely do not take witchcraft too seriously. God's Word is an exception.

WHAT THE BIBLE SAYS ABOUT WITCHCRAFT

Let's examine God's Word as it speaks to the subject of witchcraft in both the Old and New Testaments. We will clear up some of the confusion that exists today over the term as used in the Bible and then look at a few vignettes of witchcraft today.

In Exodus, the second of the books of the Law, we read, "Thou shalt not suffer a witch to live" (22:18, KJV); both the NIV and RSV substitute "sorceress" for "witch."

Rosemary Guiley states, "The distinction between sorcery and witchcraft is at best murky. In many cases, the terms sorcery and witchcraft have been used interchangeably."[1] From a spiritual point of view, Herbert Lockyer talks about "wizards practicing witchcraft,"[2] and cites the aforementioned passage under the heading "The Sorcerer."

Other passages that some feel deal with witchcraft but which do not are Deuteronomy 18:9–15; 1 Samuel 15:23; 1 Samuel 28:3–25 and 1 Chronicles 10:13; 2 Kings 9:22; 21:6; 2 Chronicles 33:6; Micah 5:12; Nahum 3:4; and Galatians 5:19–21. In all these passages only five actually use the word witchcraft in the NIV.

Biblical scholar Merrill Unger offers a word of explanation to clarify the confusion. The term "witch" occurs twice in the authorized version, and in both cases it has been correctly rendered by "sorcerer" and "sorceress" by the Revisers of 1884.[3]

Unger prefers "sorcerer" as a better translation than "witch," as he feels it encompasses the entire field of divinatory occultism while at the same time avoids the superstition time has attached to the designation "witch."[4]

But what of the five passages (1 Kings 9:22; 2 Chron. 33:6; Micah 5:12; Nahum 3:4 and Gal. 5:19–21) where witchcraft is mentioned? Unger states,

> The Revisers partially recognized the inappropriateness of the terms "witch" and "witchcraft" in the English Bible, and remedied the situation by eliminating the term "witch" entirely. However, for some incomprehensible reason, they strangely clung to the expression "witchcraft" (*Keshaphim*) in 2 Kings 9:22; Micah 5:12; and Nahum 3:4 but in all these instances, a proper rendering would be "sorcerers" or "magical arts" and not "witchcrafts" which term is inaccurate and misleading. The translation "sin of witchcraft" in 1 Samuel 15:23 is correctly "the sin of divination" (*gesem*). The phrase "used witchcraft" Manasseh, is correctly translated by the Revisers "practiced sorcery" (2 Chron. 33:6) as the word denotes

"to practice magic," and is the same verb from which the participles translated "sorceress, sorcerer" in Exodus 22:18 and Deuteronomy 18:10 are denied.[5]

To sum it up, "witchcraft" is more appropriate than the word "sorcery," which was still a major concern to the biblical writers and which we will address in this chapter. For the moment, though, let's turn our attention to the modern-day problem.

WITCHCRAFT — SERIOUS BUSINESS

Consider the testimony of Kaytee, a sixteen-year-old witch:[6]

> When I was younger, me and my older sister started bringing home books and we were really interested. And then three years ago the whole family started getting into it. My parents...are first-degree witches. I'm not initiated yet; I'm practicing still. I'm learning basically how to go into alpha, about the gods and the goddesses and the magic circle...My friends say, "Oh wow, that's so cool."

Kaytee will soon do her first spell because she wants to get the part of Peter Pan in the school play. "It's like a prayer," she says. "I will project that I will get this part of Peter Pan in the musical"—then adding a Wiccan amen—"harm me none and for the good of all."

Her mom added: "She will ask the god and goddess to protect and do what is best for her and hopefully her creativity and her skills will come forward."

It isn't easy being a witch these days.

Harassed Witches

Karlyn Straganana and Ken Stanley-Rogers, self-proclaimed witches, asked the Mount Diablo District School Board in Concord, California, to ban the 1812 Grimm's fairy tale "Hansel and Gretel" because it degrades witches as well as suggesting that it is all right to burn them and steal their property.[7]

"To show witches as bad people is a horribly wrong stereotype" said Stanley-Rogers, thirty-eight. "We want peace, we love nature."[8] Echoing the above, Morgane Sojourner, fifty, a high priestess, asserted, "We definitely don't eat children. That's just another example of an excuse used by early Christians to get rid of us."[9]

The goal of their request is to get teachers to present witches "accurately" to their students.

Evicted Witches

The Associated Press reported that a buyer agreed to purchase a half-empty shopping center, with one condition: the witches must go. "The Gypsy Heaven" was at the end of the shopping center and sold herbs, incense, candles, and oils for use in the practice of Wicca, or witchcraft. It also sold New Age books and jewelry. The owner described business as "brisk."

About thirty witches, some carrying infants, demonstrated outside the store. Some were dressed in their red or white robes. One forty-year-old woman, who refused to give her name, blamed the negative portrayal of witches in movies for the discrimination faced by followers of Wicca.

"We are not green-skinned evil people and we do not kidnap babies," she said. "In 24 years I've never ridden a broom. It just doesn't happen."[10]

Witches' Rights to Rites

Even the military cannot defend itself against the movement.

Witches in the U.S. military in Germany have tried to keep a low profile, but they are getting publicity because of a fuss over whether they can use a troop recreation center for their meetings.

"We do not conduct sacrifices, animal or human," Spc. 2nd Nelson, 34, of El Paso, Texas, wrote in a letter to the military *Stars and Stripes* newspaper. She also pointed out that they were not devil worshippers and that 30 Americans met regularly in Kaiserslautern to practice WICCA, the religion of witches.

Air Force Staff Sgt. Ethan Crisp, himself a Wiccan, stated that "harassment is part of being a witch, so they prefer to keep to themselves."[11]

Witness the Witches for World Peace

In Chicago, Illinois, six thousand religious leaders gathered to hold the 1993 Parliament of the World's Religions. The theme of the nine-day conference was World Peace, as religion is said to be at the core of more than two-thirds of the world's conflicts.

According to the report, "During the processional, Jewish and American Islamic leaders marched side by side down three aisles of the opening session in a packed ballroom at the Palmer House Hotel. Adding to the color of the processional were Wiccans, or witches, with ornate headgear."[12]

Witches Work Office Magic

Are things going poorly at work? Here's what two "office witches" offer as a solution.

Whether it's a talisman to keep that cranky copier running or tips on the best day to schedule the big meeting, office witches Zsuzsanna Budapest and Laurel Olson say if you believe, you can wish yourself a spell of good luck. Olson has even written a book called *The Goddess in the Office* published by Harper San Francisco.

Olson, who noted that the best of spells can't replace regular maintenance, has another spell for recalcitrant copiers. Cut four strips of black construction paper and put it behind the machine for better operation. "On some weird level it works," she said.

Budapest, on the other hand, has the days figured out.

She recommends taking it easy Monday, making a nest of work on the desk for reassurance. Tuesday, one should be aggressive and give orders. Wednesday is for communication—and a good day to do that load of wash. Thursday is for money and Friday is for such ego-massaging activities as the power lunch.[13]

She didn't say what Saturday or Sunday were good for.

Witch Star On and Off Camera

In *USA Weekend* beside a picture of an attractive young redhead teasingly posed, was a reader's question, "I'm really impressed by Robey on 'Friday the 13th, the Series.' Who is she? The answer,

This is a bit spooky. The show, one of the top three syndicated TV dramas, is based on the occult, and its story dabbles in the super-natural.

"I go to a church of witches," says Robey, 27, "sort of like taking witch lessons. I'm not an ordained witch. That takes years." As if to add impetus to her actions, this caption appeared under her picture: "Sexy Sleuth: TV star Robey says she's wilder and more sensuous than her character Micki."[14]

Witches Practice Witchcraft Religiously

From Providence, Rhode Island, the Associated Press reported,

Witchcraft is a legitimate religion and its churches, or covens, are entitled to the same tax breaks as those of more established religions, the state division of taxation ruled.

The ruling announced by Tax Administrator R. Gary Cleek overturned an earlier decision that said the coven did not meet criteria for being a church. The coven, also known as Our Lady of the Roses Wiccan Church, will no longer have to pay 6 percent state sales tax for supplies.[15]

The fact of the matter is that witchcraft is taken seriously by its practitioners, according to one adherent.

Witchcraft is a participatory religion. This isn't a religion where you go sometime and sit and listen to a sermon.

This attracts the young person because he or she is sick of the organized and recognized religions. They [youth] want to be active, to take part. Witchcraft is actually a return to nature, a worship of the natural gods as opposed to the chrome and glass gods you find in society. We're more interested in finding powers within ourselves, in broadening our minds. The chants, music, color and things are sort of a way of turning on without drugs.

There are among us some who are perfectly good christians, but they believe this is the way to go because they're disenchanted with the Christian religion. They feel their religion has gotten away from the people.[16]

A BRIEF HISTORY OF WITCHCRAFT

If estimates are correct, the number of practitioners of witchcraft is increasing. Estimates range from thirty thousand to over two million in the United States.[17]

Many scholars trace witchcraft's origins back to paleolithic times. Because of this, practitioners call witchcraft the "Old Religion" or simply "the Craft." Ancient man attributed a god to every aspect of nature, even the lightning, the water, the sky. Today, we call this belief animism.

Along with the god of hunting was a goddess. She was associated with fertility in a total sense: fertility of the animals so there would be an abundance, fertility of man, and fertility of the crops. The goddess became the great provider and comforter: Mother Nature or Mother Earth. As beliefs and numbers of believers evolved, so did the need for organization. Priests and priestesses began to direct the rituals. They came to be known as the Wicca or "Wise Ones," also spelled Wica or Wita.

The practice of witchcraft in various forms extended throughout Canaan, Egypt, and Mesopotamia. The Israelites were forbidden to have contact with those involved in occultic practices of any type. The New Testament is just as specific.

The church was blamed for misunderstanding witchcraft and labeling non-Christians as pagans, meaning "people who live in the country" or heathens, meaning "one who dwells on the hearth." An example of "the misunderstanding" is the idea of witches riding broomsticks.

> An old ritual act for fertility was for the villagers to go to the fields in the light of the full moon and to dance around the field astride pitchforks, poles and broomsticks; riding them like hobby horses. They would leap high in the air as they danced to show the crops how high to grow. A harmless enough form of sympathetic magick. But the church claimed not only that they were working against the crops, but that they actually flew through the air on their poles.[18]

The sparks of misunderstanding would eventually be fanned into a raging fire of persecution that would sweep across Europe and eventually reach the United States. Estimates of the number of people burned, hung, or tortured to death on the charge of witchcraft is nine million.[19] Not until 1951 in England were the last laws against witchcraft repealed.

"WHO'S WHO" OF WITCHES

Gerald Gardner

Known as the man chiefly responsible for reviving witchcraft in the modern West, Gerald Brousseau Gardner was born into a wealthy home in Blundellsands near Liverpool, England, on Friday, June 13, 1884. Gardner's family was no stranger to witchcraft. His family roots could be traced to Grissell Gardner, who was burned as a witch in 1610.

Gardner suffered severely from asthma, so his nurse convinced Gardner's parents to let him travel with her to more suitable climates. They eventually went to Ceylon because his nurse married a man who was a native of that country. There Gardner studied the spiritual beliefs of the natives in the Far East and was fascinated by them, more so than Christianity.

In 1927, Gardner married an Englishwoman, Donna, and continued his travels to places about which he had dreamed. He interpreted those dreams to mean he had lived there in a previous life. Gardner was introduced to witchcraft in England. Here he also was introduced to Aleister Crowley, who had been involved in witchcraft himself. Gardner admired Crowley and was influenced by him.

Gardner promoted witchcraft in every way possible. He served as a "resident witch" at the Museum of Magic and Witchcraft in Castletown on the Isle of Man and made numerous public appearances. He became so well known that he was given the title "Britain's Chief Witch."

He wrote books including *Kris and Other Malay Weapons* (1939), *A Goddess Arrives* (1939), *High Magic's Aid* (1949) under the pseudonym Scire, *Witchcraft Today* (1954), and *The Meaning of Witchcraft* (1959).

Gardner was honored at Buckingham Palace in 1960 for his work in the Far East. Three years later he met Raymond Buckland, who introduced the Gardnerian tradition to the United States.

Gardner died of heart failure on February 12, 1964.

Raymond Buckland

Raymond Buckland claims to be the first witch to be recognized in America. Buckland's uncle played a formidable role in Buckland's introduction to the occult. He interested young Buckland in spiritism at age twelve.

Buckland's interest did not stop with spiritism, but also included the occult in general magic and witchcraft. Two books greatly influenced his decision to accept witchcraft, *The Witch-Cult in Western Europe* by Margaret Murray and *Witchcraft Today* by Gerald Gardner.

Buckland spread the Gardnerian tradition slowly in America but eventually left that tradition to form seax-Wicca, a new tradition based on a Saxon background. Buckland has assumed a high profile, appearing on talk shows, lecturing at conventions, and writing eleven books.

Alexander Sanders

Known as the self-proclaimed "King of the Witches," Alexander Sanders established the tradition that bears his name, Alexandrian. He was born in Manchester, England, to an alcoholic father. According to Sanders, he discovered his grandmother standing in the middle of a drawn circle in the kitchen. Revealing herself to be a witch, she initiated him.

Although Sanders did much to advance witchcraft, his claims were often doubted, and he died in seclusion in 1988 from lung cancer.

WHAT WITCHES BELIEVE

Part of the difficulty in understanding what witches believe is knowing which tradition a person subscribes to—Gardnerian, Celtic (various forms), Druidic, Irish, Scottish, Alexandrian, Norse, etc.

Basically there are five major witchcraft groups in the United States.[20] These groups, their founders, and a sampling of their publications are listed on the following page.

In spite of the diversity, at least seven beliefs are held in common today, these being derived from Gardnerian Wicca:[21]

First, all share belief in the Great Mother Goddess. Throughout history she has been manifested in numerous forms: Artemis, Astarte, Aphrodite, Diana, Kore, Hecate, etc. The consort Pan (the Horned God) is the male principal of Wicca. He too possesses a varied nomenclature, including such names as Adonis, Apollo,

Name	Location	Founders	Publications
Circle, Inc.	Mount Horeb, WA	Selena Fox Jim Alan	*Circle Network News* *Circle Guide to Wicca Pagan Resources*
Covenant of the Goddess	Berkeley, CA	No one person	*Covenant of the Goddess Newsletter*
Feminist Wicca	Nationwide	Numerous personalities	*The Wise Woman*
Gardnerian Wicca	Long Island, NY	Gerald Gardner Rosemary & Raymond Buckland	*The Hidden Wicca Path*
Saxon Witchcraft	Charlottesville, VA	Raymond Buckland	*The Tree* 1974 (book)

Baphomet, Cernunos, Dionysius, Lucifer, Osiris, Thor, etc. The symbolism is rich. The Mother Goddess is represented by the moon and the Horned God by the sun. Each year Pan dies and is brought back to life in a ceremony called "drawing down the sun." The ceremony associated with the Mother Goddess is called "drawing down the moon," however ceremonial details vary in each coven.

Second, Wiccans practice certain rites that are believed to harmonize with the rhythm of nature. Esbats also are held regularly. They may be on the full moon, new moon or weekly and vary as to where they are held, inside or outside the homes of coven members. Worship, healing, magic, and business matters are part of these meetings. Food and drink are shared at the close of the esbat. The term "circle" is generally preferred by witches today in place of the formal esbat.

Third, witches and pagans practice various forms of magic, including clairvoyance, divination, astral projection, and spells.

Fourth, Wiccans follow a principle known as the Wiccan Rede: "That ye harm none, do what ye will." In other words, do what you will, but don't do anything that would harm anyone else.

Fifth, religion is generally viewed as being synonymous with the practice of magic. Magic is able to develop and nurture the higher planes of the mind, "the collective unconscious," or the spirit world.

Sixth, the very belief in gods (plural) and goddesses (plural), whether symbolic or not, advances the point that Wiccan groups embrace a polytheistic conceptualization of the universe.

Seventh, witches in many covens pass through three distinct stages or degrees of initiation. The neophyte becomes a member. The training of the member is the second stage, which must be completed before the third stage, which is initiation as high priest/priestess of the coven.

The third degree—or Great Rite—is a ceremony which has the initiate participating "symbolically" or literally in sexual intercourse with the high priest/priestess of the opposite sex. Practices vary with different covens. The preferred way to conduct the sabbat, esbat, and other ceremonies is skyclad, or nude.

Setting the Record Straight

Myths concerning witchcraft are numerous. Among them are the following:

First, witches and Satanism are synonymous. Practitioners of both have been persecuted through the years and were lumped together as worshipping the devil. Many witches, however, deny the reality of Satan or even the concept of evil.

Second, witches practice black magic. Many disavow the use of black magic, which is the use of magic to bring harm to an individual. Most witches prefer white magic, or the use of supernatural powers for good goals such as healing and so on.

Third, witches are female. Many males are involved in witchcraft today but do not use the term warlock as commonly heard. Most male practitioners prefer to be known as witches or Wiccans.

Symbols of Witchcraft

As might be expected, witchcraft is steeped in symbols that figure into the practice of the religion. These include the amulet, talisman, ankh, athame (sword), circle, pentagram, cup or chalice, pentacle, nine, sigil, tarot, wand, cauldron, and altar.

WHAT YOU CAN DO

➤ You will want to be as informed as you can be on witchcraft in general. Major denominations print information to enable Christians to understand cults, as well as to better witness to them.

➤ Children need to be protected from "legitimizing" witchcraft. It has long been popular to dress children as witches at Halloween. If your children participate in trick-or-treating, you may want to dress them as something else. Be prepared to explain why pretending to be a witch is not consistent with being a Christian.

➤ Witches appear frequently in cartoons, syndicated television reruns such as "Bewitched," books, and films. Parental discretion should be exercised as to what children are allowed to see. Children are impressionable.

➤ Attention should be given to the type of books in the school library available to children. The presence of books on witches is inevitable, but there is no need for children or any one else to have books teaching them how to cast spells or participate in other activities associated with witchcraft.

➤ New Age bookstores carry books on witchcraft, but these stores should be avoided unless you feel led of the Holy Spirit to witness there and even then it would be prudent to take someone else with you.

➤ You should remain strong in your efforts to pray for those involved in witchcraft. You should love them as well. You might even be invited to observe a coven in its practices, but you must not become involved. Even to observe could be to open yourself up to severe problems.

➤ You can rest assured that you will hear much more from those proclaiming to be witches in the days ahead. We need to be sure that the "good news" is proclaimed more loudly and with more fervor than those being used by the deceiver.

LAUREN

Lauren nursed her troubled spirit. She felt as confused as she had that night at the slumber party.

My old friends don't understand me, she sighed. *And I don't totally understand my new friends. My parents wouldn't understand if I asked them. But Heather seems sincere. Her locker is close to mine. Maybe I can catch her before gym class if I go now.*

Lauren set out at breakneck speed and as she rounded the corner of the hall, she ran headlong into her new friends, Caroline and Pam. Lauren's books flew in all directions.

"I'm so sorry," Lauren apologized. "I was on my way to talk to Heather."

"Oh, that's okay," Caroline replied, glancing over at Pam. "We'll help you pick up your books."

It seemed like an eternity for Caroline and Pam to pick up her books. The bell was going to ring soon, and Lauren really wanted to talk to Heather now more than ever. She didn't want to be rude, either. After all, they were being helpful.

"Oh, Lauren, do you have any plans for Halloween?" Pam asked, handing Lauren her notebook.

"You mean like trick-or-treating?" Lauren responded. Pam laughed.

"Not exactly," Caroline replied. "We're getting together with some other kids out at the old Darkins place."

"What are you going to do out there?" Lauren questioned. "That house in the woods has been vacant for years."

"Halloween is a special night," Pam said mischievously.

"Very special," Caroline joined in. "We might even bring up the devil."

All three girls laughed, but Lauren had a strange feeling about the whole thing. That should have been a warning to Lauren, but she ignored those inner warnings. She should have said, "No, I'm not interested," but she found herself saying, "Okay, I'll come."

"Good, we'll pick you up Halloween night around ten o'clock," they decided...

S E V E N

The Devil You Say?
The Spread of Satanism Today

How does the average "churchgoer" today feel about Satanism?

In 1993, *Christianity Today*'s June 21 cover story was devoted to Satanic Ritual Abuse (SRA). That article cited a survey and a study that you will find interesting. A study presented at the 1990 annual meeting of the Society for the Scientific Study of Religions revealed that Satanism is spreading rapidly, that it is becoming increasingly organized, and that it is a serious threat to society.[1] A 1989 survey conducted by the Public Policy Laboratory of Texas A&M University also reported that 80 percent of Texans believe that Satanism is getting worse and that it is something to worry about.[2]

In November 1992, James Dobson's Focus on the Family released, upon request, a twelve-page fact sheet devoted to Satanism. In April 1993, the publication *Christian Counseling Today*, which reaches professional, pastoral, and lay counselors, contained an article entitled, "SRA: One Counselor's Response."

We have examined previously the origin of Satan, his names, and his work, as well as that of his army of darkness. We will now look at worship sites favored by Satanists and the dates which are significant to their worship. We will trace the history of Halloween and learn where many present day practices of this holiday originated. We will examine four of the personalities important to the followers of this movement and their influence, the nine Satanic beliefs, and then discuss why Satanism is so difficult to prosecute.

THE WHERE AND THE WHEN OF SATANISM

Places to Remember

Quite often students and adults will tell me of confirmed or suspected places where occult-related activities take place.

Areas frequented by Satanists include the following:

➤ Abandoned churches (a favorite for obvious reasons)
➤ Cemeteries
➤ Mountainous areas
➤ Desert areas
➤ Beaches
➤ Abandoned buildings
➤ Wooded areas
➤ Basements
➤ Under bridges
➤ Parks
➤ Business locations after hours

It may be a strong temptation to explore some of these places in "the safety of daylight." But there *are* no safe times for such explorations. Just as those involved in the drug trade grow marijuana in secluded, remote areas like forests, so also the Satanist wants to practice his beliefs in areas where he will have total privacy. Some Satanists have been known to booby trap their worship sites so that an unsuspecting person may be seriously injured. One site in the Ft. Worth, Texas, area was discovered to have a trip-wire connected to a shotgun!

Experts who pinpoint locations of cult activity in a county or a community use a widely practiced procedure to locate the center of the activity. They take a map of the county or community and place an inverted star over it. The center point will likely be where the cult activity is occurring.

Dates to Remember

Just as there are places to remember, there are dates as well. Occultic activity may occur at various times, but serious practitioners hold these dates to be very important:

Date	Celebration
Jan. 7	St. Winebald Day
Jan. 17	Satanic Revels
Feb. 2	Satanic Revels
Feb. 25	St. Walpurgis Day
Mar. 1	St. Eichatadt
Mar. 20	Feast Day (Spring Equinox)
Apr. 21-26	Preparation for the Sacrifice
May 1-June 26	Grand Climax
June 21	Feast Day (Summer Solstice)
July 1	Demon Revels
Aug. 3	Satanic Revels
Sept. 7	Marriage to the Beast Satan
Sept. 20	Midnight Host
Sept. 22	Feast Day (Fall Equinox)
Oct. 29-Nov. 1	All Hallows Eve (Halloween)
Nov. 4	Satanic Revels
Dec. 22	Feast Day
Dec. 24	Demon Revels

The more important holidays are those of February 2, May 1–June 26, and August 3. The cult member's birthday is also of prime importance.

According to Anton LaVey, the organizer and founder of the Church of Satan and author of *The Satanic Bible*, "The highest of all holidays in the Satanic religion is the date of one's own birth...The Satanist feels: 'Why not really be honest and if you

are going to create a god in your own image, why not create that
god as yourself.'"[3]

In addition to the above, eight sabbats are observed throughout
the year. A sabbat is a meeting held to observe or celebrate the
Black Mass which ridicules Christianity and blasphemes God.

Date   Sabbat

Date	Sabbat
February 2	Candlemas
March 21	Spring Equinox
April 30	Beltane
June 22	Midsummer Solstice
August 1	Lammas
September 21	Autumn Equinox
October 31	Halloween
December 22	Winter Solstice

Of course, the best known holiday is the age-old one we have
commemorated since anyone can remember—Halloween!

Halloween—A Trick?

Probably few realize that the evening of October 31 marked
the transition between the long days of summer and the darkness
of winter to the ancient Celts and their priests, the Druids. This
day, known as Samhain (the lord of the dead), was regarded by the
Celts as a time when "spirits" and "dead souls" could roam free
and harm the living. A "treat" of food was offered in hopes that
these spirits would not wreak mischief by destroying crops, killing
cattle, turning milk sour, and generally making life miserable with
their "tricks."

Chosen villagers, according to one account, disguised themselves as these "spirits" and "dead souls" and "assumed" their
attributes, going from house to house to collect the treats. Following this, they led the ghosts right out of town.[4]

Bob Larson in his book *Satanism: The Seduction of America's
Youth*, points to other associations of Halloween with the occult:[5]

First, the jack-o-lantern came from the tale of a notorious man
named Jack, who was turned away from both heaven and hell.
Condemned to roam the earth as a spirit, Jack put a glowing coal

into a carved-out turnip to light his way through the night. This forerunner of the pumpkin symbolized a condemned soul.

Second, the colors orange and black can be connected to commemorative masses for the dead. Unbleached beeswax candles used in the ceremony were orange, and the ceremonial caskets were covered by black cloths.

Third, dunking for apples came from the practice of divining the future. The participant who successfully clenched an apple between his teeth could count on a fulfilling romance with the lover of his choice.

The name Halloween is a form of the designation "All Hallows' Eve," a holy evening instituted by the church to honor all the saints of church history.[6] All Saint's Day, or All-Hallow's Day as it was originally known, was celebrated May 13 but was shifted to its present date by Gregory III in the eighth century. This holiday, which according to pagan custom begins as the sun sets on October 31, was originally a festival of the dead, in which sacrifices both human and animal were offered. It was, however, made into a celebration of all the known and unknown saints and martyrs of the Catholic Church by Pope Boniface IV in the seventh century.[7]

We are used to seeing children dress up in costumes and try to "frighten" us during Halloween. Though they do their best, we do not panic. There are, however, any number of personalities whose involvement in the occult is frightening and sad. We will look at four of the better known in the pages ahead. As you look at them you will see a number of common factors emerge.

WHO'S WHO IN THE OCCULT

It would not be difficult to compile a who's who in the gallery of the occult, but it would be difficult to find one who could attain the heights of evil which our first personality reached. So influential was he that he has been referred to as the spiritual ancestor of contemporary Satanism.

Aleister Crowley

Edward Alexander Crowley was born on October 12, 1875, in Leamington Spa, Warwickshire, a small peaceful town. His father made his fortune from Crowley's Ales and retired to preach the doctrines of the Plymouth Brethren. Some scholars refer to his upbringing as repressed due to the conservativeness of the Plymouth Brethren. Crowley's autobiography does not support this view. Quite the contrary, Crowley describes his parents as affectionate and indulgent to the point that he referred to himself as "a spoilt little boy."

A turning point in Crowley's life seemed to occur at eleven years of age when his father passed away. Deprived of his father and bitter because of his father's death, Crowley "grew to detest the faith in which he had been brought up and, without knowing why, went over to the side of Satan."[8] So rebellious did his life become that he entered and departed from several schools, the last being Trinity College, Cambridge. He never graduated but rather devoted his time to writing poetry and becoming more deeply involved in the occult.

Crowley's dark studies eventually led him to join others who shared his interest in the occult. On November 18, 1898, he joined the Hermetic Order of the Golden Dawn in London where he rapidly advanced to its highest degree. The Golden Dawn, which had about one hundred members spread among several lodges, taught the use of magical weapons, how to consecrate talismans, set up magic circles, travel astrally and so on. It also gave instruction in the use of that ground plan of western magic, the Cabala.[9] Also spelled Kabbala, this text attempted to interpret the Torah according to secret or hidden knowledge. In addition to Crowley, Yeats, and Stoker, other notable members included Algernon Blackwood and Sax Rohmer. Crowley was eventually expelled from this organization after quarreling with one of its members.

Crowley then joined another organization, the Ordo Templi Orientus (OTO), a German secret sexual magic group. Such was his stature and knowledge that he was made "the Supreme and Holy King of Ireland, Iona, and all the Britains that are in the Sanctuary of the Gnosis."[10] Ultimately Crowley founded his own organization—The Order of the Silver Star, also known as A.A.

From 1915 to 1919, Crowley lived in the United States, but due to his degenerating physical condition, he eventually looked elsewhere. While driving through Italy, he had a vision of a hillside villa which turned out to be in Sicily. Crowley acquired the villa, decorated it with obscene paintings, and renamed it the Sacred Abbey of the Thelenic Mysteries. His vision was to make this villa a colony, where magic would be practiced in addition to vile, indescribable sexual practices.

Fascinated by blood, torture, and sexual degradation, Crowley freely used drugs, prostitutes, and visitors in his sexual practices at the Abbey. Those practices led to Crowley's expulsion from Italy in May 1923 by Benito Mussolini.

When Crowley sued the author of an unauthorized biography, which charged him with using black magic and human sacrifices, the testimony was so repugnant that the trial was stopped. The jury ruled against Crowley, in favor of the biographer.

Among Crowley's beliefs were the following:

1. Do what thou wilt.
2. Good is evil, and evil is good.
3. Thou hast no right but to do thy will.
4. Man has the right to live by his own will...eat what he will... think what he will...love as he will. Man has the right to kill those who thwart these rights.
5. There is no god but man.

Aleister Crowley was known for many things, none particularly good. Some considered him one of the most brilliant magicians of all time (he spelled magic with a k—magick or occult magic as distinguished from magic which Crowley considered as "weaklings seeking an escape from reality").

To say his influence upon others was unhealthy would be an understatement. Crowley was married twice and his second wife went insane, as did Crowley's nineteen-year-old mistress.

He wrote a number of books, including *The Book of the Law* which he dictated while in a trance after contacting the spirit messenger Aiwass, *Diary of a Drug Fiend* (1922), and *The Book of Troth* (1944) which was his interpretation of the Tarot.

One author who does not share the enthusiasm of many for Crowley is John Godwin. To him Crowley was nothing more than a fake and a charlatan. He said, "Crowley was a fine mountaineer, and a pretty good chess player, but as a Satanist he was a crashing bore. You see, everything about him was second hand. Even his motto, "Do what thou wilt shall be the whole of the law," he lifted from Francois Rabelais.[11]

On December 5, 1947, Crowley died a poverty-stricken heroin addict unable to communicate coherently. His influence, unfortunately, lives on.

Aleister Crowley, christened by his own mother as "the Beast" after the Antichrist, inspired Ozzy Osborne to sing a song entitled, "Mr. Crowley," David Bowie to record "Quicksand," a song about Crowley's cult, and led the Stiff Kittens as well as the Beatles to feature Crowley on their album covers. John Lennon was known to have books on Crowley in his personal library.[12]

Not to be forgotten is his influence upon David Berkowitz, better known as "the Son of Sam" who murdered six people and wounded seven. Berkowitz wrote a minister friend that Berkowitz's Satanic group followed the philosophy of Crowley and practiced ancient magick.[13]

Still another whom Crowley's legacy continues to influence is the founder of the Church of Satan, Anton LaVey,[14] as well as such groups today as Ancient Mystical Order, Rosae Crucis, Ordo Templi Orientis in New York City, the Society of Ordo Templi Oriento in America in Nashville, Tennessee, and Ordo Templi Astarte in Pasadena, California.[15]

Anton LaVey

Perhaps few have had the impact on Satanism today as has Anton LaVey.

LaVey's life has certainly been out of the ordinary and, as we shall see, some of the people with whom his life crossed paths became well known in their own right though not necessarily for good.

Howard Anton "Tony" LaVey was born in Chicago on April 11, 1930, to Joe LaVey, a liquor distributor, and his wife, Augusta. A descendent of Georgian, Romanian, and Alsatian grandparents, including a gypsy grandmother, LaVey heard scores of legends of vampires and witches from her, a native of Transylvania.[16] In his early adolescence LaVey became fascinated with the occult, particularly Aleister Crowley.

Unhappy at home, LaVey ran away to join the circus at sixteen years of age to become a cage boy and gradually an assistant lion tamer. He later claimed his experience taming lions taught him force of will.

He left the circus at eighteen to work at a carnival where he became involved in a number of jobs ranging from mentalist to hypnotist. While he was in the carnival business he learned to play the organ, a skill he utilized in burlesque houses. It was there that he met a young woman working on stage by the name of Marilyn Monroe. LaVey claimed to have had a "close" relationship with her in both the figurative and literal sense of the word.[17]

Undeniably LaVey saw a sordid side of human nature from his work in the carnival, burlesque houses, and his work as a photographer for the San Francisco Police Department.

LaVey once said,

> On Saturday night I would see men lusting after half-naked girls dancing at the carnival, and on Sunday morning when I was playing the organ for tent-show evangelists at the other end of the carnival lot, I would see these same men sitting in the pews asking God to forgive them and purge them of all carnal desires. And the next Saturday night they'd be back at the carnival or some other place of indulgence.[18]

Only too happy to oblige man's desires and promote his organization at the same time, LaVey organized such things as a "topless witches Sabbath" in San Francisco. One of the women he enlisted went by the name "Sharon King." In reality she was Susan Atkins, later part of the Charles Manson family which brutally murdered actress Sharon Tate and four others in 1969.

LaVey's interest in the occult grew to the point that he began holding Friday night lectures in his home on vampires, sex, magic, witchcraft, and werewolves, among other things. Writer Arthur Lyons reports that "during one such lecture on cannibalism, a severed human leg was brought from East San Francisco Bay

Hospital by a physician member, basted in Triple Sec, and served to the less queasy in the group.[19]

These study and lecture sessions attracted capacity crowds. Among them were novelist Steven Schreck and filmmaker Kenneth Anger, who produced the films *Invocation of My Demon Brother* and *Lucifer Rising.*

These three—LaVey, Anger, and Schneck—became the basis of "The Magic Circle" which on Walpurgisnacht (April 30) of 1966 became the Church of Satan, with LaVey as the High Priest and self-christened "Black Pope" and his second wife Diane as the High Priestess.

LaVey was a man with a mission, albeit an unholy mission. In his own words he claimed he had both a "mission" and a "legacy" to fulfill. He envisioned a time, which he called the formation of the Age of Satan, when satanic emblems rather than crosses would rise from church roofs. He would make hatred and defiance of authority not only respectable but a socially powerful force.[20]

Numerous events gave LaVey's new organization much needed publicity, ranging from a Satanic wedding between a socialite and a journalist, to the Satanic baptism of his then three-year-old daughter Zeena, to the Satanic burial at sea of a sailor who was a member.

It did not hurt that celebrities from Hollywood embraced him and his cause. According to Arthur Lyons, the late Sammy Davis, Jr., even served as a liaison between LaVey and the Hollywood community. Actor Keenan Wynn was "honored" with an honorary priesthood and actress Jane Mansfield became a devotee, inviting LaVey into her home for private rituals.[21]

Daughter Zeena LaVey claims that even today several well-known entertainers are affiliated with the Church of Satan but declines to release their names.

His Hollywood contact does not begin or end with the stars. LaVey played the part of the devil in the film *Rosemary's Baby* and called the financially successful film, "the best paid commercial for Satanism since the Inquisition."[22]

Is Anton LaVey all he claims to be? Does he truly believe what he writes? Researcher Carl Raschke states, "In 1971 *Newsweek*

magazine dismissed LaVey as a man unworthy of the devil's trust."
Denounced as a con artist and posing no danger, the consensus
was that he was a slightly successful scalawag or buffoon.[23] Nonetheless, Raschke concludes that LaVey is far more powerful within
the occult underworld than his cultivated reputation as a buffoon
or a cynical P. T. Barnum-style huckster would suggest.[24]

The Criminal Satanists

Earlier we saw how individuals may be drawn into the occult,
becoming involved in the fringe- or thrill-seeking category, or the
dabbler category. Unfortunately, their experiences do not always
stop there.

One couple shared a heart-rending story of the abuse of their
three-year-old son in a day care center. He saw animals killed, was
photographed naked, playing with other children, who were also
naked, given strange things to drink, taken to different locations,
where he described people dressed in robes and told of other
incredibly vile and perverted things. Such activity falls into what
is labeled as the third category of Satanism, the criminal level.

Child abuse is a serious issue in dealing with the criminal
Satanist. The listings in appendix A should prove helpful to you
if you need more information on victim abuse or need to know
where to go for help, but child abuse is not the only criminal
element.

Satan worship may involve nudity and sex (homosexual and/or
heterosexual), drugs, torture of animals and humans, sacrifices of
animals and humans, self-mutilation, ingestion of blood and other
fluids, and every type of self-degradation and debasement imag-
inable (and many you would not want to imagine) including
urinating and/or defecating upon someone or being the recipient
of the same.

It should be noted that the fourth category of Satanist, the
orthodox or religious Satanist, does not claim to be a part of such
activity. LaVey's Church of Satan "disavows any connection with
any other Satanic group, either in philosophy or practice within
or without the United States. The sadistic excesses and puerile
ritualistic practices indulged in by many of the other cults are

described by church members as 'nonsense, perpetrated by a few individuals on their own.'"[25]

The only time police have been called to raid the Church of Satan was when the neighbors called the police to complain about LaVey's four-hundred-pound lion, which he kept as a pet. The neighbors complained that the lion was on dope, roared in the middle of the night, and kept them awake. LaVey ultimately donated his lion to the San Francisco Zoo.[26]

It bears pointing out that Satanism is a constitutionally protected religion just as any other minority religion. It is recognized as a legitimate religion by the Army and is described as such in the chaplain's handbook by historical roots, current world leader, number of adherents in the U.S., organizational structure, leadership and role of priest, who may conduct a ritual, workshop guidelines, (requirements, facilities, etc.), special religious holidays, funeral and burial requirements, basic teachings and beliefs, recruitment, and so on.[27]

BELIEFS OF SATANISTS

When you look at "The Nine Satanic Statements" you can better understand what the spiritual battle is all about.

1. Satan represents indulgence instead of abstinence.

2. Satan represents vital existence, instead of spiritual pipe dreams.

3. Satan represents undefiled wisdom, instead of hypocritical self-deceit.

4. Satan represents kindness to those who deserve it, instead of love wasted on ingrates.

5. Satan represents vengeance instead of turning the other cheek.

6. Satan represents responsibility to the responsible instead of concern for psychic vampires.

7. Satan represents man as just another animal sometimes better, sometimes worse than those that walk on all fours, who because of his "divine spiritual and intellectual development," has become the most vicious animal of all.

8. Satan represents all of the so-called sins, as they all lead to physical, mental or emotional gratification.

9. Satan has been the best friend the church has ever had, as he has kept it in business all these years.[28]

Perhaps this statement from the *Handbook for Chaplains* sums it up best. "The Church of Satan stands as a gathering point for all those who believe in what the Christian Church opposes, and members [Satanists] are generally hostile to its teachings and resultant behavior patterns."[29]

One of the strangest telephone conversations I had while researching this manuscript was with an occult apologist in New York City. When he found out I was writing a book and that I was a Christian, he warmed to the subject quickly. The bottom line to him was that I give those involved in the occult "a fair shake." "We are all not abusing or sacrificing children," he claimed. He even sent me articles to bolster his point of view.

True, there may be some who commit no crimes in pursuit of their beliefs regardless of how strange or unusual they might seem to us. Nonetheless, there is ample evidence to bolster the other side of the coin that illegal acts are carried out in the name of Satan.

WHERE IS THE EVIDENCE?

Any confrontation—whether with someone involved in the occult or with the skeptic—always comes around to the question, where is the evidence? This is a bona fide question, in my opinion. The answer is five-fold.

First, there is the difficulty of investigation by the police. One former FBI agent explained that there is a problem of disbelief. Many police officers do not accept occult crime nor do many in the general public. A second problem from an investigative standpoint is that it must be handled as an undercover operation. If you proceed on this basis, you have undercover officers involving themselves in terrible crimes. In addition to the above, you are talking about massive amounts of time and manpower devoted to the investigation. Some law enforcement officers appear to be apathetic and don't desire to be involved.

Deputy Probation Officer Darlyne Pettinicchio addressed the dilemma in part when she stated, "It's not an area that police know. I've run into cops who tell me that their chief doesn't even want them mentioning the word Satanism. I get a lot of that."[30]

Second, Satanists generally do not leave any evidence of their crimes...especially murder. Testimony of those formerly involved say that incriminating evidence is difficult to come by because the bodies are disposed of in any number of manners including burning, dismembering the body and dumping it in the ocean, pouring concrete over them, and even consuming them and making tools from their bones.

Offficer Pettinicchio says, "I've seen kids who carry body parts, like fingers, around with them for the power they're supposed to contain. Yeah, it's nuts, but the kids believe in it."[31] Of course it isn't just the kids but adults as well.

Third, Satanists work at discrediting eyewitness sources. Psychologist and minister James Friesen reports,

> They take the children along to watch them bury the remains. It is a great way to come up with a water-tight cover up. If the perpetrators really wanted to hide the sacrificial remains, they certainly would not take the children along to watch. They would do it in secret. The perfect way to discredit the children's testimony is to exhume the remains later, after the children have watched them buried. Who would believe a child's story when he says he knows exactly where the baby is buried, and no baby is found at the site?[32]

Fourth, Satanists are adept at making evidence disappear. Friesen spoke with a law enforcement friend who shared the following chilling account of evidence obtained in the planned prosecution of SRA (Satanic Ritual Abuse) in California.

The evidence was disappearing from the police department as quickly as it came in. The children's accounts were compelling and consistent, and there was no question in the officer's mind about what had happened—a ring of SRA perpetrators had been discovered. The officer knew one of the investigators very well, and that he was baffled about how the evidence disappeared. That investigator said he simply didn't want to get involved. The evil of the perpetrators was too much for him, and he didn't want to get his family in trouble with them. He wasn't going to say anything about how the evidence, which doubtless would have convicted the perpetrators, had vanished. He had to conclude that somebody in the department unit was on the cult side, but he was not about to go public with it. The cover-up was very successful.[33]

Fifth, investigations stop short of making a Satanic connection because of unfavorable publicity. In spite of attempts at secrecy, evidence is found from time to time. Usually it is one of three types: mutilated animals, ritual sites, and robbed graves. Detective Pat Metoyer of the Los Angeles Police Department Criminal Conspiracy Division addressed the fifth reason in part, using the Hollywood Memorial Cemetery as an example. An individual was apprehended trying to remove the head from a corpse and causing $6,500 worth of damage. Why were no charges were filed? Detective Metoyer answered, "Do you want somebody to know that your loved one is placed in a cemetery that they can't control?" That's the bottom line. That's why so many cemetery desecrations go unreported or misreported.[34]

In the grisly account above the individual wanted to use the head in his rituals! It isn't just one body part that may be prized for ritual use. It is not uncommon that hands are often valued, namely the left hand called "the hand of glory," so called because it is believed to be the path of the devil while the right hand is the path to righteousness. Satanists will dry the hand and then light the fingers on an altar.

The right index finger is also considered to be very powerful as power is felt to enter the left side of the body, continue through the heart and on to the brain and eventually exit through the right index finger. If you possess that finger, you possess that power.

Law enforcement officials know that not only are these and other body parts valued by Satanists but a network exists to sell these parts to other groups for use in their rituals.

WHAT YOU CAN DO

To be sure, a certain amount of hysteria exists and wide-eyed claims have been made about how many practicing Satanists exist today, what they do, and so on. I have tried to use credible sources in my documentation. Nonetheless, I feel quite certain you may simply find some of this too much to swallow.

It does happen and it will continue to happen. God's Word warns us of troubled time as the end draws near, and the darkness grows ever denser. Are you ready?

➢ Be as informed as you can be as to the beliefs and practices of Satanism today. Though this chapter has attempted to provide you with an overview, other books have more of an in-depth examination of Satanic practices and beliefs. You may find the resources on Satanism in the recommended reading of the appendix B helpful.

➢ Should you suspect that there may be Satanic activity in your community, check with your local law enforcement officials to determine if they have someone who could speak to a group of concerned citizens, parents, and/or youth.

➢ Check with the Ministerial Alliance (an organization of ministers from all denominations) for the purposes of inviting someone with expertise in this area to speak to your group. Mental health professionals might also be consulted with the same purpose in mind.

➢ Be aware that direct confrontation with Satanic groups, regardless of what category they fall in, may place you and your family in a precarious position. This is certainly not to say do not get involved, but rather to make your involvement a matter of prayer and procedure as directed by the Holy Spirit.

➢ Remember that Satan's influence is everywhere and as Christians, we must fight the spiritual battle on every front, including forms of amusement and education.

➢ Be certain that your interest in knowing more about Satanism does not spring from an unhealthy curiosity. Satan can "dress up" Satanism to look "civilized" or "attractive." As you pray daily, God's Holy Spirit will help you honestly determine the extent of your interest.

➢ Be ready for demonic oppression which we will discuss more fully in chapter 10, as well as certain inexplainable circumstances to occur. Satan is like a snake. Generally speaking, snakes will not bother you if you don't bother them. Of course, daily he bothers the Christian, but when you actively war against him, he responds in kind. Just remember, the battle is not yours, but the Lord's, and He will always take care of you.

LAUREN

There were other aspects of the occult to which Lauren should have said no. She became very careful to do many of the things her friends were doing. One of those things was astrology. Several talked about their "signs" and some actually would avoid dating someone if their signs were not "compatible." She started reading her horoscope every day. She wasn't really sure that she believed it, but it had been amazingly accurate at times. Besides, it was fun. She was also surprised to learn about the prophecies of Nostradamus, Edgar Cayce, and others whose names were unknown to her prior to that night at the slumber party.

Lauren was spending less and less time with her old friends and more and more time with Caroline and Pam. They were so different from many of Lauren's friends and seemed to know all about things that Lauren had never considered. "Sure, you can know your future, and not just through your horoscope," they told her, "We have a good friend who can tell you everything. You will be amazed at what she tells you about yourself and your future."

Who wouldn't like to be sure of tomorrow? Lauren reasoned silently in her mind. "Okay," she replied aloud, "when can I meet her?"

"We'll make all the arrangements," Caroline said.

"She'll be at the gathering Halloween night," Pam joined in.

Pam whispered into Caroline's ear, "'Step into my parlor,' said the spider to the fly." They laughed knowingly.

"What's so funny?" questioned Lauren.

"It's kind of a private joke," responded Caroline, "but we'll let you in on it soon. You probably wouldn't understand it right now."

That much was true. Lauren could not see that she was being drawn into the dark world of the occult one step at a time. Had she heard Pam's whisper, she would have been forewarned of what was to take place Halloween night...

E I G H T

The ruler of the kingdom of the air,
the spirit who is now at work in those who are disobedient.
— EPHESIANS 2:2

The Prince of Power of the Air:
Prophecy and Astrology

Have you ever wondered how something would turn out? A
sporting event? A relationship? Something in which you were
deeply involved? Of course! But to what lengths would you go to
be "sure"?

In this chapter we will examine prophecy and astrology. God's
Word thoroughly addresses both subjects, which we shall place in
the category of divination. Biblical scholar Merrill Unger states:

> The underlying thought of all forms of this forbidden art is that
> by resorting to certain means, at variance with an infinitely wise
> and holy God, men may obtain desired knowledge otherwise
> beyond their grasp. But since the religion of Israel made Jehovah
> the sole legitimate source of that information, and the prophet the
> constituted medium through which it came to men, all recourse
> to illegitimate methods, or appeal to spiritual beings other than
> God, or search for forbidden or illicit knowledge which would not
> pass the divine scrutiny, is taboo.[1]

Prophets who did pass divine scrutiny, in addition to the four major prophets (Isaiah, Jeremiah, Ezekiel and Daniel) and the twelve minor prophets (Hosea, Joel, Amos, Obadiah, Jonah, Micah, Nahum, Habakkuk, Zephaniah, Haggai, Zechariah, and Malachi) were Moses, Samuel, Elijah, Elisha, and Nathan, among others of the Old Testament.

New Testament prophets include Zacharias, Simeon, John the Baptist, John the Apostle, and even the apostle Paul, Judas, and Silas (Acts 13:1) and others.

The female counterpart, the prophetess, includes Miriam (Ex. 15:20); Deborah (Judg. 2:18; 4:4); Huldah (2 Kings 22:14; 2 Chron. 24:22); Noadiah (Neh. 6:14); and Isaiah's wife (Isa. 8:3) of the Old Testament; and Anna (Luke 2:36); Philip's daughters (Acts 21:8–9) and Jezebel (Rev. 2:20) of the New Testament.

One of the Old Testament words for prophet, *nav*, means "to well up, to gush forth." God's Holy Spirit was their inspiration. As Augustine said, "The prophet of God is nothing else but the teller forth of the words of God to men."[2]

One problem with prophecy in biblical times lay with the pagan prophets of the Old Testament, such as the 450 prophets of Baal, and the false prophets of the New Testament, such as those referred to by Jesus in Matthew 7:15 and Mark 13:22. And so it was that the true prophet would be recognized by a threefold test: First, by signs (Ex. 4:8; Isa. 7:11, 14); second, by fulfillment of his predictions (Deut. 18:21–22); and third, by his teaching (Deut. 13:1–5 and Isa. 8:20).

This threefold test is still valid today and, when applied through the principles in God's Word, eliminates the Islam prophet Mohammad, Sidhartha Gautama (Buddha), the Mormon prophet Joseph Smith, Jr., Nostradamus, Edgar Cayce, and Jean Dixon.

Just as the false prophets created confusion for God's people in biblical days, so do they continue to do so today, and not just in a religious sense. Consider the following stories. During Ronald Reagan's second term as President of the United States, quite a furor was raised when the media reported that he and First Lady Nancy Reagan had consulted regularly with Joan Quigley, better known as the "White House Astrologer."

In her book *What Does Joan Say?* Quigley writes,

> The President had asked Nancy to ask me about going to Reykjavik; he and Shultz followed my advice to negotiate there as long and hard as possible, and following my advice they stayed later than planned. Ronnie asked Nancy, "What does Joan say?" when he wanted to know when the Irangate ordeal would be over. And he phoned to thank me personally for a letter written at the end of Irangate, in which I described myself as his astrologer, addressing him as "Dear Ronnie" and signing it "Dear Joan."
>
> There is no doubt whatsoever in my mind that the President was fully aware of the contribution I made: the scheduling, my ideas, the problems solved and the advice I gave.[3]

In the second story, a prediction attributed to Nostradamus created quite a stir in New England. According to an Associated Press report, "A ghoulish rumor about an impending mass murder sent chills down the spines of students last week as the tale wound its way around New England campuses." The rumor was heard in several versions, each seemingly designed to frighten students on a specific campus. According to one version, the killings were predicted in the writings of the sixteenth-century mystic Nostradamus.

At the University of Massachusetts at Amherst, the murders were supposed to take place on a campus with a pond and a building named for President Kennedy. The University has both.

About one hundred women living in the University's dormitories were so frightened they met with the campus police chief to ask how they could protect themselves.[4]

As frightened as the women above, if not more so, was a young woman who thought she received a very disturbing "glimpse into the future" and wrote "Dear Abby" for advice.

> DEAR ABBY: I am a happily married woman who just turned 25. I have two small children and I'm living in fear that I will not live to see them grow up.
>
> When I was 13, I was fooling around with a Ouija™ board, when I got a message from my dead grandmother saying she would see me in heaven on my 26th birthday, meaning I was going to die on that day in an accident.

I told my husband about my fears, telling him to marry again soon after I die so my children won't be without a mother, and he said, "That Ouija™ board stuff is a lot of bunk, so forget it."

Abby, for some reason, I can't forget it. I am not afraid to die. If God wants me, I'm ready to go, but I only have 11 months to prepare myself if the Ouija™ board was right.

Have you or any of your readers ever had any experiences with a Ouija™ board? I'm terribly confused and very frightened.

— W.VA. READER

DEAR READER: I agree with your husband. While I respect the rights of others to believe as they wish, I have yet to find a shred of convincing evidence to support the theory that the living can communicate with the dead.

I urge you to put those frightening thoughts of impending death out of your head, dear.[5]

THE FALSE PROPHETS

Unfortunately, many do not heed God's word, Dear Abby, or anyone else. What may continue to confuse the believer is the fact that the false prophet may claim that his word is from God. Such an individual was Nostradamus.

Nostradamus (1503–66)

Born Michel de Nostredame into a Jewish home, he was the oldest of five boys. He was exposed to the occult knowledge contained in the Kabbalah and, as his parents converted to Catholicism, the prophecies of the Bible.

Known for his healing powers and clairvoyance, his predictions have caused no mild stir. He predicted the reign of three Antichrists; two of these were believed to be Napoleon and Hitler. The third, supposedly, will hail from the Middle East and, with the aid of the Soviet Union, start a nuclear war (World War III) between 1994 and 1999 by destroying New York City. The war will continue for twenty-seven years resulting in the eventual defeat and death of the Antichrist and a thousand-year reign of peace.

He believed the world would end in 3797 and prophesied one thousand predictions, half of which scholars say have come true. Among them are the American Revolutionary War, Civil War, assassinations of Lincoln, John and Robert Kennedy, the rise of Khomeni in Iran, air and space travel, and the development of the atomic bomb.

Edgar Cayce (1877–1945)

No less interesting than Nostradamus is the man known as "The Prophets' Prophet," Edgar Cayce. Also known as the "Sleeping Prophet," Cayce gave thousands of "medical readings" while in a trance-like state, and people all over the world sought his help. He was said to be accurate in more than 92 percent of his cases, though he never studied medicine.

Raised in a Christian home, Cayce was a Sunday School teacher at one time and claimed to have read the Bible through every year from age twenty-two until the day he died at sixty-seven years of age. He also demonstrated clairvoyance at age seven and claimed to be able to see nonphysical beings whom he welcomed as his childhood playmates.

At thirteen a woman appeared to him offering the fulfillment of any request. He chose healing. He also believed in reincarnation, and that in an earlier life, he was the nephew of Luke, the gospel writer. Among his prophecies are the second coming of Christ in 1998 accompanied by cataclysmic changes in the earth.

BIBLICAL FORMS OF DIVINATION

Just as there are means and ways of prophesying today, so were there also various forms in the Bible. Prophecies in Biblical times were often made through the following means:

➤ Cup — Genesis 44:5
➤ Wand — Hosea 4:12
➤ Arrows — Ezekiel 21:21
➤ Lot — Numbers 26:55; Leviticus 16:8
➤ Liver — Ezekiel 21:21
➤ Dreams — Jeremiah 29:8f; Zechariah 10:2
➤ Days of ill omen — Micah 3:6

Divination is not always viewed positively in God's Word, and those who engaged in it, for the most part, did so without divine approval. On the other hand, prophets who foretold the future received their messages directly from God.

As Patrick Fairbairn stated it:

> Divination differs from prophecy, in that the one is human device, while the other is a divine gift; the one an unwarranted prying into the future by means of magical arts, superstitious incantations, or natural signs, arbitrarily interpreted; the other a partially disclosed insight into the future by the supernatural and of Him who sees the end from the beginning.

In Scripture language, the diviners were false prophets and divination was allied to witchcraft and idolatry.[6]

Many people today want to know what days of ill omen or bad days await them so that they might be avoided.

Perhaps the most widely accepted means of seeking to know the future is astrology.

ASTRONOMY OR ASTROLOGY?

Astronomy and astrology are two different matters altogether.

Astrology comes from the two Greek words, *astra* meaning "stars" and *logos* which means "word, logic or reason." Combine the two and you have "word of the stars." Two of the more familiar terms in astrology have to do with the horoscope and the zodiac.

A horoscope is essentially a blueprint of your personality and characteristics. It is more appropriately known as a vitasphere, from *vita*, life and *sphere*, globe. The vitasphere is usually represented as a flat surface, though it actually is a globe, with the earth at the center and the planets and stars completely surrounding it, exactly as they were at the moment of your birth. This is why specifics such as exact time and place of birth, even the location within the city become very important. Due to the fact that the positions of the planets are constantly changing, the entire chart changes every four minutes.

Once an astrologer has this essential information he can consult a book known as an ephemesis to determine the precise position of the moon, the sun, and the stars at the time of your birth. The position of the sun at your birth is known as your sun sign.

Horoscopes come in different forms as evidenced by the following:

➤ Natal horoscope—Charts the planets' positions at your time of birth.
➤ Mundane horoscope—Charts the position of the planets at the time of certain events in the world.
➤ Business or financial horoscopes—Charts the position of the planets at the time something relative to the business is occurring, i.e., signing of important papers, beginning or expansion of business, etc.
➤ Horary horoscope—Charts the planets' positions for the hour or movement in which the consumer asks the astrologer a question.

The word *zodiac*, comes from the Greek *zodiakos* referring to animals or "circle of animals." The twelve signs of the zodiac make up the path or course the sun travels during the course of a year and are supposed to have an important bearing upon the evolution of an individual throughout his lifetime. His disposition or character is determined by his sign.

The chart on the following page may be of some value in understanding the above in terms of the constellation or sign, the date, the animal representation and characteristics.

The twelve signs may be further subdivided into active sun signs (Cancer, Aries, Libra, Capricorn) which characterizes people as active, creative, and able to conceive plans well; and stable or fixed signs (Taurus, Leo, Scorpio, Aquarius) characterizing positive and sustaining personalities. The remaining signs are mutable and variable.[7]

You could define astrology as the art of predicting or determining the influence of the planets and stars upon human affairs. Astronomy, on the other hand, is altogether a different matter. The main difference can be summed up in the word *science*. Astronomy is the science of the heavenly bodies.

Just as people might confuse the two terms, research into the origin of astrology is just as confusing. Pulitzer Prize winner Carl Sagan maintains that Claudius Ptolemaeus, or Ptolemy, was both

ZODIAC SIGN	DATE	ANIMAL	CHARACTERISTICS
Cancer	June 22–July 22	Crab	clinging, protective exterior shell
Leo	July 23–Aug. 22	Lion	proud, forceful, born leader
Virgo	Aug. 23–Sept. 22	the Virgin	reticent, modest
Libra	Sept. 23–Oct. 23	Scales	just, harmonious, balanced
Scorpio	Oct. 24–Nov. 21	Scorpion	secretive, troublesome, aggressive
Sagittarius	Nov. 22–Dec. 21	the Archer/Horse	active, aims for target
Capricorn	Dec. 22–Jan. 19	Goat/Fish	tenacious
Aquarius	Jan. 20–Feb. 18	Water carrier	humanitarian, serving mankind
Pisces	Feb. 19–Mar. 20	Fish	attracted to sex and alcohol
Aires	Mar. 21–Apr. 19	Ram	headstrong, impulsive, quick-tempered
Taurus	Apr. 20–May 20	Bull	plodding, patient, stubborn
Gemini	May 21–June 21	the Twins	vacillating, split personality

an astrologer *and* an astronomer. Sagan calls astrology a pseudo-science (false science). He maintains that in Ptolemy's time the distinction between the two was unclear, but today it is.[8]

Consider, for example, the Italian astronomer Galileo. His area of expertise was in the scientific realm, but the Grand Duchess of Tuscany asked him to chart a horoscope for her ailing husband. Not having any choice in the matter, Galileo obliged, made his calculations, and forecast positively that her husband would live several more years. Imagine her surprise when he died three weeks later! Don't, however, tell that to the general public. They aren't going to buy it. Astrology has never been more popular. Nearly two-thirds of adults in the United States read astrology material periodically and some twenty-six million read them regularly. At present, five thousand professional astrologers practice in the U.S. and dial-a-horoscope services are available. New York Telephone alone receives one million calls a month.[9]

But how do you know that you are dealing with a genuine astrologer and not a "charlatan?" Atlanta, Georgia, and Las Vegas, Nevada, are the only two cities who screen astrologers. Las Vegas requires a background check with approval by the mayor and City Council. Atlanta, however, has a formal three-member Board of Astrology Examiners, the only one in the nation.[10]

Jayj Jacobs, legal committee chairman for the Association for Astrological Networking in San Francisco, said more boards may be needed to distinguish legitimate astrologers from charlatans. She said, "It's the spell-casters and curse-lifters that are a problem. Those are the people the public needs to be protected from."[11]

CHRISTIANS, ASTROLOGY, AND THE NEW AGE

Evidently astrology wrapped up in New Age beliefs is finding fertile ground among citizens of the United States. It is like a "good news" and "bad news" situation.

The "good news" is that about half of Americans familiar with the New Age movement don't take its teachings seriously and a third of them say New Age runs counter to Judeo-Christian teaching. The "bad news" is that the number of Americans who adhere to New Age practices is alarmingly high, even among those professing to be Christians. "Many who consider themselves good Christians nonetheless have engaged in practices that seemingly are counter to the teachings of their church," according to a poll conducted by the Princeton Religious Research Center.[12]

Roughly half of all Americans say they believe in extrasensory perception. Thirty percent of Roman Catholics and 22 percent of Protestants say they believe in clairvoyance, while 48 percent of Roman Catholics and 44 percent of Protestants say they believe in psychic healing. The poll indicates that 25 percent of both groups believe the movement of the stars may help govern the affairs of men and women.[13]

Certainly it is disturbing to see the inroads which occultic practices have made into Christianity and it is alarming how early it begins. David Burnett cites an occult survey taken in Great Britain in 1989 which revealed that: 67 percent of the English occultists becoming involved before eighteen years of age.[14]

The allure of the occult to teenagers in the United States is no less disturbing. Bill Gordon relates a case in point as he talks about reaching out to those in cults. Serving as a national interfaith witness missionary for the Home Mission Board of the Southern Baptist Convention, Gordon goes to New Age meetings where he attempts to establish an evangelical witness. At a Tampa exposition, eighteen former Southern Baptists came by a booth Gordon had set up. One was a witch, one a New Ager, and another a psychic.[15]

The Ancient Appeal of Astrology

Astrology has appealed to people for thousands of years. Scholars differ in their opinions as to whether it was the Babylonians or the Chaldeans who formalized the zodiac in 3000 B.C. Ezekiel 21:21 confirms the fact that magical arts were widely practiced in Babylon, and star worship spread from Babylon to the nations that surrounded ancient Israel.[16]

In Genesis 2, we read about the Tower of Babel which is thought by some to have been patterned after the ziggurat or temple built to worship as gods the stars and planets as well as the sun and moon.[17]

The Chinese as early as 2000 B.C. utilized astrology as did the Romans and the Greeks. Ptolemy the astronomer authored the book *Tetrabiblios* (or *Four Books on the Influence of the Stars*) which established the foundation upon which astrology rests today.

A Help or a Hindrance?

Beatrice Wernick, the daughter of a prominent New York astrologer, says the astrologer is able to help a client in three main areas:

1. Basic character analysis, i.e. a breakdown of the individual's personality and what makes him tick, based on exact birth dates.

2. Problem-solving, the casting of a horoscope to answer a specific question.

3. Comparisons, the relationship between two or more charts.[18]

A nationally-known syndicated astrologist whose readings helped motion picture executives plan successful movie openings including *Star Wars* and *Chariots of Fire* is Joyce Jilson.

"I use it," she said, "but I believe that astrology gives you an edge. It's not that you should use 100 percent astrology and use it by rote." The knowledge of your stars' positions can clue you in to the world trends and your personal forecast, she explains, "but doing well on a test means knowing [the information on] the test. Horoscopes help by letting you know how to schedule the test on a day when your performance level is highest."[19]

Jilson stressed that astrology is not mind-reading but rather an analytical technique which, she says, uses "lots of logarithms and correlations between different planets or between the sun and the moon." She now spends most of her time working on her syndicated daily horoscopes. "I get up at six in the morning and write about four or four and a half days a week for the column. I do all the math in one day and transpose it when I get to the typewriter."[20]

JEAN DIXON: PROPHETESS OR PHONY?

The best known of all astrologers is perhaps Jeane Dixon, the subject of the best seller, *A Gift of Prophecy*.

According to the book,

> Sometimes she merely "tips the fingers" of a person and seems instantly to know what the future holds for him. She can often pinpoint events in the past and future for people she has never seen, merely by learning the date of their birth. Her most frequent revelations come through perusal of the crystal ball, but the forecasts to which she herself attaches the greatest significance have come through unsought visions.[21]

From where did she receive this "gift"? The origin and development have some most unusual events. Biographer Jean Montgomery states that Jean Dixon was born Jean Pinckert in the Wisconsin lumbering village of Medford in 1918. As a child she moved with her parents Herr Pinckert and Emma von Graffee to California. Jean's father was fascinated by Indians and gypsies and suggested that his wife take Jean to visit an old gypsy woman camped nearby. That visit changed Jean's life.

The gypsy was a fortune-teller and was using cards to tell a woman's future when Jean arrived with her mother. She took Jean's hands, examined them and exclaimed that she had never seen such lines and that this eight-year-old girl must be protected as she would be famous, would foresee worldwide changes and events, and had the gift of prophecy. So impressed was the gypsy that she disappeared into her covered wagon and returned with a crystal ball for Jean to keep.[22]

And see things she did. Immediately she saw surroundings of a country far away and realizing it to be the homelands of the gypsy woman, Jean described them perfectly. She also warned the gypsy not to scald herself after seeing the gypsy woman in the crystal ball bending over a boiling pot. Sure enough, a later return found the gypsy woman with bandaged hands due to a severe scalding from a cooking accident.

Her mother encouraged her to make predictions for family and friends which she did, acquiring a neighborhood reputation as a "seeress."[23] Eventually she married a divorcee, moved to Washington, D.C., where she handled real estate for the government and gave readings to serviceman, politicians, and diplomats.

Dixon has made several predictions which have come true, including the deaths of Martin Luther King, the three astronauts tragically killed on the launching pad at Cape Kennedy, and Robert Kennedy. Her most famous prediction to date has been the assassination of President John Kennedy.

She has also had more than her share of errors, including predictions of mishaps and misunderstandings to befall President Nixon on his trip to Peking (which was a success) and the prediction of a presidential election battle between Nixon and Walter Reuter in 1964 with Reuter representing the Democrats (neither man ran). Fortunately World War III did not break out in 1958, though Dixon predicted it would.

Judging the accuracy of Dixon's gift becomes relatively simple as the short-term predictions happen as she said they would or they do not. It is another matter to hear her thoughts on the subject of astrology and her visions. To the unaware, the uncritical, and the Christian who does not know God's Word, Dixon's words may be confusing. Consider her definition of astrology.

At a Hollywood, California, Chamber of Commerce dinner in November 1971, she defined astrology as a science. "It is also a glorious key to the pattern energy of the Infinite," she explained, "and this cosmic force is God's expression of His divine plan that can be seen in the various stars and planets that comprise our universe. And this energy, this pattern of cosmos is for everlasting to everlasting. Astrology takes the stars from our eyes and puts them into our lives."[24]

Her experience with visions is no less accurate when compared with God's word:

A vision fills you! I can only describe it by saying, "My cup runneth over." During this experience I'm so filled with the glory of God that I want to give everything to everyone. I feel that I will never be tired again, because I'm so full of strength. At such a time I feel there is nothing in this world that I will ever want for myself. You know what it is to truly worship God. You yearn to develop the talent that He has assigned you; to do His work on earth.[25]

Is this a talent from God? How do you explain it? Is there truth in prophecy and astrology? Let's look at two sources of explanation for prophecy and astrology.

AND NOTHING BUT THE TRUTH

Truth from a Human Standpoint

➤ Many of Dixon's prophecies cannot yet be verified because they are long term.

➤ Admittedly, Dixon moves in knowledgeable circles in Washington and has access to information as few others.

➤ "Astrologers know what their clients want and they dish it out," says psychologist Joyce Brothers. "This feeling is further reinforced by what psychologists call the 'self-fulfilling prophecy'—the likelihood that saying a thing is going to happen will actually bring it about."[26]

➤ Attributing characteristics of the personality, physique, or diagnosis of illness on the basis of sun-sign astrology is without factual basis.

R. B. Culver and P. A. Ilanna in *The Gemini Syndrome: A Scientific Evaluation of Astrology* examined the claims of astrology in detail. According to one astrologer, people born under the sign of Aries are supposed to have red hair, among other characteristics. Of course, that eliminates all blacks, Orientals, and most Hispanics. When Culver and Ilanna surveyed three hundred redheads to find out what sign they were born under, they found that (1) only twenty-seven of them were born under Aries, (2) no one sign showed a predominance of red hair. Natural red hair, which is a genetic trait, is not determined at the moment of birth.[27]

Another case of point was an experiment utilizing the horoscope of a person born on January 17, 1898, at 3:00 A.M. in Auxerre, France. The horoscope for this individual read in part:

As he is Virgo-Jovian, instinctive warmth of power is allied with the resources of the intellect, lucidity, wit...He may appear as someone who submits himself to social norms, fond of property, and endowed with a moral sense which is comforting—that of a worthy, right-thinking, middle-class citizen. The subject tends to belong wholeheartedly to the Venusian side. His emotional life is in the forefront—his affection towards others, his family ties, his home, his intimate circle . . . sentiments . . . which usually find their expression in total devotion to others, redeeming love or altruistic sacrifices...a tendency to be more pleasant in one's own home, to love one's house, to enjoy having a charming home.

An advertisement was placed in a French newspaper by Michel Gauquelin inviting people to send in their name, address, birthday, and birthplace. About 150 replied; each person was sent the same full, ten-page horoscope from which the quotation above is taken, a return envelope, and a questionnaire. Of those who answered the questionnaire, 94 percent said they were accurately portrayed in the horoscope and 90 percent said that this judgment was shared by friends and relatives. In fact, the horoscope was of Dr. Marcel Petoit, a mass murderer. Dr. Petoit posed as an underground agent who would help refugees fleeing from the Nazis. Instead, he lured them to his home, robbed them, and dissolved their bodies in quicklime. Indicted for twenty-seven murders, he cynically boasted of sixty-three.[28]

Similar studies by the same two authors failed to produce significant correlations between personality characteristics or diagnosis of illness and the sun-sign of the individual. These next two truths attest to that:

➤ Astrology dispenses predictions so general that they could be applied to anyone.

➤ Astrology gives "meaning" and "explanation" to the individual's desires and aspirations.

Truth from a Scriptural Standpoint

Passages in the Bible dealing with astrology include:

➤ Isaiah 47:13–14—Isaiah mocks the futility of astrologers and the usefulness of their predictions.

➤ Jeremiah 10:2,7—Jeremiah encourages the Israelites not to be afraid of signs in the sky as are the unbelievers, but neither should the Israelites follow the counsel of "wise men" who believe in these signs.

➤ Daniel 2:1–49; 4:1-37—It is God who gives to Daniel the ability to interpret the meaning of Nebuchadnezzar's dreams.
➤ Daniel 5:7–15—God enables Daniel to correctly interpret the writing on the wall which the King's astrologers failed to do.
➤ Acts 7:41–43—Steven reminds the Sanhedrin that "God turned away and gave them (the Israelites under Aaron's care–Ex. 32) over to the worship of the heavenly bodies" (v. 42).

The Christian's Response

As Christians we marvel at God's creation and are grateful to Him for it. We worship the Creator, not His creation. The psalmist reminds us of the following, "The heavens declare the glory of God; the skies proclaim the work of his hands" (Ps. 19:1). Though the stars long were thought to have an influence on the fortunes of men including biblical times (Judg. 5:20 and Job 38:33) up to today, it is God who gives us guidance. As the writer of Proverbs reminds us, "In all your ways acknowledge Him, and he will make your paths straight" (Prov. 3:6).

The Scripture cited from both the Old and New Testaments should remind the Christian to have nothing to do with astrology. The apostle Paul also urged us, "Do not conform any longer to the pattern of this world, but be transformed by the renewing of your mind. Then you will be able to test and approve what God's will is—his good, pleasing and perfect will" (Rom. 12:2).

The individual who has believed in astrology in the past would do well to follow the example of the Christian believers at Ephesus who burned their astrological books. Not only would that separate you from them, but it would guarantee that they could not influence anyone else!

A Final Word on the Star

There is a star that has had an influence unrivaled upon humankind. This star was prophesied in Numbers 24:17 and prophecy fulfilled as it shone above the manger in Bethlehem when Jesus was born.

The stars as worshiped in astrology enslave humans, but Jesus, who is the truth, sets us free!

WHAT YOU CAN DO

➤ Do not read your horoscope. There is no value in it, and it could compromise your walk with the Lord. Your time would be better spent reading the comics!

➤ Have no contact with psychics of any kind, unless it is to witness to them and win them to the Lord. "Christian" psychics can mislead and severely compromise other Christians.

➤ Do not patronize the innumerable psychic hotlines which are advertised extensively on television, no matter how popular they appear. If your child is utilizing this service, talk with your local telephone company about placing a block on 900 numbers so they cannot be accessed from your home.

➤ Destroy any such materials (books, charts, and so on) in your possession which deal with astrology.

You must know that your life is not controlled by the stars, but by Him who created the stars. Your daily walk with Him through acceptance of His Son, Jesus Christ, as your Lord and Savior will provide you with the guidance and direction you need in your life.

LAUREN

And step Lauren did, slowly but surely. It was strange how her involvement just naturally seemed to move from one step to the next, and it all appeared so innocent. Take for example, what happened in Lauren's world geography class.

Caroline and Pam had suggested that Lauren might find the book *Strange Happenings Around the World* to be of interest. Lauren really couldn't believe what she was reading: there were stories of dead people coming back to life in Haiti, priests in Tibet who could levitate, UFO abductions in France and Brazil, death spells in New Guinea, and many other unusual events.

Lauren found herself reading this book more and more. Several times she thought, *I'll have to remember to ask Caroline and Pam about this. I'm sure they can explain it to me.*

And so it was that one afternoon in her world geography class, the subject focused on islands in the Caribbean.

"Mrs. Carter?" Lauren raised her hand, with a serious look on her face. "What is your opinion of voodoo?"

You could have heard a pin drop. Lauren's friends wondered where she had ever had the idea to ask that question and why. Mrs. Carter was totally taken aback. She wondered what had come over Lauren as she noted the seriousness with which Lauren asked the question. She was not trying to get attention, of that much Mrs. Carter was certain.

"I really don't know, Lauren," she responded rather weakly, "Class, let's move on."

Mrs. Carter missed a warning sign, but not Caroline and Pam. They intuitively knew that Lauren was progressing nicely. *It won't be long now*, they both thought...

N I N E

Where on Earth
Is the Prince of the World?

In the previous eight chapters, we have examined occultic influence through the Bible, through history, through rock music, the media, and astrology. Now we will see that this force must be reckoned with on the foreign mission field as well.

God's Word very clearly acknowledges that Satan is the "ruler of this world," "the prince of this world," "the god of this age" and "the prince of the power of the air." The people of the Old and New Testament believed in the existence of evil spirits. Many miracles of Jesus concerned themselves with the demonic and the activity of Satan, who provides his dark leadership to his army.

Scripture assumes some kind of hierarchy within the realm of the hostile supernatural powers, but it never gives any delineation of the chain of command. Satan is the ruler of the kingdom of the air (Eph. 2:2), and he has within his sphere of authority a vast group of powers, dominions, thrones, angels, demons, unclean spirits, elemental spirits, and rulers.[1]

The apostle Paul was no stranger to battling Satan and his forces throughout his ministry. He encountered the slave girl at Philippi (Acts 16:16–21) possessed by a spirit of divination in his second missionary journey. It was Paul who stripped away the deceitful cover under which Satan's servants operated. In 2 Corinthians 11:13–15 he denounces those servants as "false apostles... masquerading as apostles of Christ" and brands Satan as "an angel of light." Paul admonishes the Christians in 2 Corinthians 6:14–15 to refrain from uniting with unbelievers by asking the question, "What harmony is there between Christ and Belial [Satan]?" In his letter to the Galatians, Paul addressed the acts of the sinful nature and included witchcraft among them (Gal. 5:20). In his second letter to the Thessalonians, he warned them of the coming of "the lawless one" which "will be in accordance with the work of Satan displayed in all kinds of counterfeit miracles, signs and wonders, and in every sort of evil that deceives those who are perishing" (2 Thess. 2:9–10).

Paul referred to Old Testament history naming Jannes and Jambres, Egyptian court magicians who opposed Moses according to Jewish tradition, as examples of men who oppose God (2 Tim. 3:8). Paul reminded the Colossians that Jesus had conquered and disarmed the evil angels (powers and authorities) who entice people to follow asceticism and false teachings about Christ (Col. 2:15).

It is precisely the victorious Christ that missionaries proclaim today throughout the world, but the opposition is strong.

The Demonic Influence in the Mission Field

Upon learning that I was writing a book on the occult, the wife of a minister remarked how sad it was that Christians can sit around and talk about the Holy Spirit and other matters, but no one wants to confront the activity of Satan and the demonic. "How will we ever be able to defeat the enemy if we refuse to try and understand his ways?" she questioned.

She makes a good point. Applied to the mission field, how can we pray effectively for our missionaries if we are oblivious to the work of the adversary or, worse yet, refuse to admit it? Missiologist

Timothy Warner echoes the latter when he says, "Our world view says that spirits are not real."[2]

J. Dudley Woodberry, professor of Islamic studies at Fuller Theological Seminary, stated, "Exorcism seems to be a significant part of conversions from Islam, particularly from the people we would call folk Muslims, where they are already in many cases involved in some kind of demonization, be it real or imagined."[3]

Samuel Olson, pastor of the nondenominational Las Acacias Church in Caracas, Venezuela, experienced his first "power encounter" (evangelism seen as a battle between the forces of light and the forces of darkness) while working in a drug rehabilitation center. While praying for a fifteen-year-old addict, Olson watched the boy curl up in a ball and crawl around the floor, all the while talking to Satan. The boy claimed he had given his life to the devil a couple of years before and could not give up this allegiance.[4]

Fetish Sacrifices in Western Africa

One missionary shared that the country to which she was appointed in Western Africa underwent a strike sponsored by the opposition government. The missionary awakened one night to acrid, bad odors in the air. When she mentioned this to a native of that country, the friend confirmed the presence of the foul smell in the night air and explained that both sides were performing fetish sacrifices against each other as political tension mounted.

Protected by Amulets in Thailand

Another missionary related that in Thailand, opposition to the gospel comes in the form of "animism, spirit houses, home altars, temples with images of Buddha, Chinese spirit money, demon worship, curses, and witch doctors who consult spirits, demons, and others. He continued:

> In addition to this, there is the wearing of amulets by all ages and cords blessed by monks tied around wrists and ankles of children and even adults. These are supposed to protect the wearer from the power of evil spirits and demons.
>
> A certain policeman, working in a remote, dangerous area wore over 200 amulets in the belief that they protected him from danger

(bullets, knives, etc.) and from the power of evil spirits enlisted by his enemies to destroy him.

Demonic Rappings in Guyana

Mary Love, a missionary with more than twenty-seven years of service, tells a disturbing story that happened to her and her husband Charlie. They had traveled to initiate a new work in a Hindu-Muslim village. As there were no Christian churches in the village, they spent the night in a home of a young Christian woman who had originally come from a Hindu background. Her father, still a Hindu, lived with her.

Everyone settled down for the night. Soon the house was quiet and sleep enveloped the occupants. During that quiet, from out of nowhere, came a loud noise against the side of the bedroom wall. So intense it was that it awakened Mary, who first thought that cows had wandered into the house from the yard and collided with the walls. But then the noises increased in intensity until they were coming from the ceiling as well as the walls.

The room was in total darkness. There was no lantern to brighten the room, and all the batteries in their flashlights had run down. In addition, the two doors from the room were both padlocked, one from the outside and the other from the inside. There was no escape except through prayer.

Mary realized that these sounds had no earthly origin, so she prayed aloud and bound Satan in Jesus' name. Adding to the unusual situation was the fact that Charlie slept right through it until he woke up in the middle of the night to leave the bed and get a drink of water.

The sounds stopped the moment he awoke. Mary did not want him to venture outside the room, but he did and returned unharmed and immediately went back to sleep.

Mary told how the noises continued through the night as she alternately prayed and dozed until, finally, the only noises she heard were those of breakfast being prepared.

"No one else heard the noises," Mary told a colleague. "Satan would have been crazy to not try to frighten you away," replied her friend.

Today there is an established evangelical ministry in the village, and a missionary couple is to be transferred there to continue the work. As to the noises, Love reports that they have made subsequent trips to the village and have stayed in that same home praying for Satan's power to be bound and praying for the protection of Jesus. The noises have never occurred since that night!

Satan's Influence

One young missionary sounded a familiar refrain when she shared that two missionary deaths since 1987 had caused many people of the country where she served to believe that the mission was "jinxed" or that God had not been blessing them. She felt it to definitely be Satan's influence through the old "health and wealth idea" that God blesses through these two attributes and the lack of one or the other is a sign of God's disfavor.

Another missionary in Ethiopia ran headlong into a confrontation with Satan's blinding influence when he felt a deep conviction to share the good news with the Guji people of Southern Ethiopia, who actively worship Satan. The people of this tribe were not only involved in worshiping Satan; one of the requirements for manhood in the tribe included murder and dismemberment of the victim as proof.

It was in this climate that one missionary had lost his life, and God had called another to go and take his place. The new missionary was uneasy due to the lack of opposition that he encountered during his first year of work. His sense of uneasiness grew as the days passed until one day it happened.

On his way into town with an Ethiopian, the road through the mountains collapsed under his land rover, causing it to fall one hundred yards to the valley below. The Ethiopian was killed and the missionary seriously injured. His wife, a nurse, was summoned by a runner. She provided what medical aid she could, then drove him to a hospital three hours away. The Gujis were amazed, not only that he lived, but that he continued his ministry among them.

It wasn't until later that the missionary received two items of information that helped to put this incident into perspective. One came from another missionary who worked with the Guji people somewhat distant on the other side of the mountain. He told the missionary that a man in a position somewhat akin to a witch doctor told of a dream where Satan came riding a hyena and wanting to know why the Guji people were permitting these missionaries to work among them. A second item was the Guji belief itself that Satan was not going to allow this missionary to continue his work and his accident was Satan's way of dealing with him.

The fact that he continued his work among them led them to conclude that his God was stronger than Satan and many trusted in Jesus Christ.

Stories such as the above can be told by missionaries around the world. The reason why we don't hear them more often is that missionaries know all too well that many people stateside simply can't accept it or don't want to.

I have long since known that the North American believer underestimates drastically the power of Satan. In our "sophistication" we have simply written off those who share such unusual experiences as unusual themselves and we put little, if any, stock in their stories.

Small wonder that missiologist C. Peter Wagner has written, "Many Southern Baptist missionaries are seeing tremendous acts of God out on the mission field, but say they can't talk about it here (in North America)."[5]

Missionaries Acknowledge Satan's Reality

Missionaries have become believers themselves through personal experience on the mission field. When I asked missionaries the question, "Could you relate how your perspective of Satan's influence has changed since coming to the mission field," missionaries from three different continents with experience ranging from five years to over twenty-eight years on the field shared the following:

➤ "Stateside I didn't think much about it but in my country one faces the opposition to Satan daily. Also many of the people have mentioned that we need to pray for God's protection and guidance. Therefore I'd say that my perception of Satan's influence differs greatly. Now I realize the power of prayer so much more."

➤ "Demon possession is a real phenomenon at least to those who fear it. Satan uses all means available to him to prevent and hinder the witness of the Gospel. When I came to the field I doubted the existence of the hordes of evil spirits, though I did believe in Satan and his power."

➤ "We have sensed a strong spiritual oppression in our everyday living and we must assume that it is related to the strong spiritist influence that dominates our area."

➤ "I have seen how every detail of the everyday life of the African is tied to his religion. Thus Satan controls his whole life. I understand better how Satan counterfeits Christian practices and even heavenly actions."

➤ "My perspective has changed in that I see Satan's influence more overtly—not as subtle as manifest in the USA. It is not so much that Satan is stronger but that he is more 'recognizable.' I do take his influence more seriously and this has made me more aware of how much stronger the power of the Lord is in overcoming the worldly power."[6]

VOODOO INFLUENCES

Satan influences this worldly power that confronts missionaries throughout the world though it is much stronger in some countries than others. The practice of voodoo began in Africa and is extremely strong in the Caribbean. The word "voodoo" comes from the West African *vodun* meaning god, spirit, or sacred object. Followers of voodoo see the world as filled with demons, gods, and spirits of the dead. Therefore, charms and spells take on a special importance, and believers used them to protect or cause harm to another.

During the ten years we were under appointment to Rio de Janiero, Brazil, by the Southern Baptist Foreign Mission Board, Susan and I saw the devil at work in ways we could scarcely imagine. Voodoo's influence is felt through the cults of Macumba, known also as Comdomble and Umbanda. Worship centers and stores that that sell statues of their gods, good luck charms, and so on abound throughout the city of Rio and all over Brazil.

Evidence of the worship was everywhere as followers would leave coins, a plate of food, flowers, cigarettes, and other items under the trees and on street corners in every neighborhood. Even the dogs won't touch this food because it is sacred, I was told. Someone, however, neglected to pass along that information to our boxer.

Still, over and over through our years in Rio we saw individuals destroy all items related to their involvement in Macumba and come out of the bondage of worship to other gods and demonic possession to find freedom in Jesus Christ.

Interest in voodoo has spread to the U.S. through various means, including immigration and popular movies such as *The Serpent and the Rainbow* and *Angel Heart*. It has seemingly touched every segment of society from consumerism to politics.

In Houston, Texas, the Texas Alcoholic Beverage Commission decided to rescind its original order and allow the sale of Dixie Blackened Voodoo Lager beer. It wasn't the beer to which the commission objected. It was the label. The can depicts a swamp scene in Cajun country, with small animal eyes peering out of the dark blue dusk. The Texas commission, in a somber letter addressed January 11 to the New Orleans brewery, had linked the label and design to witchcraft and other cult organizations.[7]

Even politics does not escape the influence of voodoo. In a rather bizarre sequence of events, a former impeached mayor of Florala, Alabama, ran for office with a strange promise: no more voodoo. This campaign promise resulted from events during his former term. Then-Mayor H. T. Mathis accused his police chief of being a witch. Mayor Mathis was labeled the "voodoo mayor" by the press for his act in sprinkling "voodoo powder" around City Hall. Witches can't stand this, he was advised. As if that wasn't enough, Mayor Mathis summoned the press for a midnight news conference, and he dressed for the occasion in a red bathrobe with a white turban on his head and a rubber snake around his neck. The purpose of the midnight conference? He wanted to proclaim "National Voodoo Week."[8]

Even the American Civil Liberties Union has gotten into the act. When the suburban New Orleans St. Tammary Parish School Board decided to ban *Voodoo and Hoodoo* from its school libraries because it contained "recipes" for casting spells and was a "how-to manual for sexual perversion and killing," the ACLU stepped in and sued the school board for banning it![9]

Even the use of animals in religious sacrifices has been called into question. The scope of religious freedom in America was tested in the nation's highest court by an Afro-Caribbean sect whose four thousand-year-old ritual of sacrificing animals is forbidden by South Florida laws.[10]

Attorney Richard Garrett said the laws were necessary because Hialeah, Florida, faced "human health hazards" created by the sacrifice of "tens of thousands" of chickens, goats, turtles, sheep, and other animals by practitioners of an Afro-Caribbean religion known as Santeria. He told of fifty-two animals being sacrificed in a ceremony in a residential neighborhood, of "blood put in pots" and heads of goats being left on a public beach.[11]

There are an estimated sixty thousand Santerians in South Florida alone; most of these are refugees from Castro's Cuba. Even mainstream denominations joined forces with the Santerians, believing that outlawing animal sacrifices was government interference or discrimination. On June 11, 1993, their efforts were rewarded as the Supreme Court ruled that animal sacrifices were a legitimate aspect of Santerian worship.

SANTERIA: ORIGIN, BELIEFS, AND PRACTICES

"Santeria" comes from the Spanish word *santo* for "saint." The santeros are the priests, though practitioners may also be known as santeros and santeras. In the eighteenth century, when the Spaniards captured large numbers of African slaves to work in the Cuban sugar plantations, they took their slaves out of southern Nigeria from the Yoruba tribe. The slaves were forced to convert to Catholicism but continued to practice their religion by blending it with Catholicism and giving the names of Catholic saints to their gods. Slave owners became so fascinated with Santeria that many began to practice it themselves.

The Yoruba *orishas* or gods are worshipped in rituals which make use of lighted candles, herbs, bead necklaces, statues of Catholic saints, and offering food and water to the gods. The ceremonies include spirit possession, speaking in tongues, and magical healings. The seven major orishas are believed to control four hundred gods in the Santeria pantheon.[12]

Sacrifices bring good fortune to the believer. Healing and solving problems are mainstays of this cult. When one considers that Santeria is found in cities with large Hispanic populations and that Hispanics are projected to be the ethnic majority in the two thousands, it is a force for the Christian to reckon with.

The branch of Santeria which practices black magic is known as Palo Mayombe Kimbrisa. Palo Mayombe is best known for the deaths of thirteen people in Matamoros, Mexico, in April 1989. So gruesome were the murders that this massacre has been referred to as "the killing fields" of Mexico.[13] Major wire services, network news, and magazines kept the public informed daily of developments in the case. The discussion which follows is based upon those reports in addition to two books written about the tragic circumstances.

This cult reemphasizes the basic principles that we have seen repeated in occult involvement and help us answer the question, "How does something like this happen?" A look at the leadership, the recruitment, the rituals, and the rewards should prove helpful.

The Leadership

One cannot read the following and fail to see what happens when the family structure is not strong and vibrant. Adolfo de Jesus Constanzo, the leader of the cult was a Cuban American, twenty-six years of age, who grew up in Miami, Florida.

He was born November 1, 1962, to a teen-aged mother. His father left within the year. His mother remarried, but her husband died of cancer when Adolfo was ten. Adolfo's mother married a third time, but like the first marriage it ended in divorce.

His friends were afraid of him and even more so of his mother because of the strange religion she allegedly practiced. Constanzo's mother claimed her son possessed psychic powers and could predict the future, which he did for Mexico's biggest celebrities as he grew older.[14]

Second in leadership was Sara Maria Aldrete, twenty-four, a 6-foot-1 brunette described by Texas Attorney General Jim Mattox as the "witch of the operation." A wanted poster described Aldrete as "extremely dangerous. Use caution."[15]

She was a resident alien from Mexico, the oldest of three sisters. Her father, Israel Aldrete, retired as a clerk with the Mexican Federal Electricity Commission. Sara had been married but was divorced as she became involved in the cult. A physical education major, she was one of thirty-three students listed in the Texas Southmost College Who's Who (which required nomination by the faculty and at least a 3.0 grade average), president of the college's soccer booster club, and recipient of the "Outstanding Physical Education Student" award.[16] Sara Aldrete's college records were impressive but even more so was the note which U.S. Customs Service investigator Oran Neck found attached to Aldrete's records.

The Recruitment

Adolph Constanzo's involvement in the occult evolved to the point that he truly believed that human sacrifice would put a magic shield around him and his followers, protecting them from bullets or any other harm. These beliefs helped to lure the curious into his cult.

The fact that he had such a charismatic personality did not hurt his appeal to the right people. So strong was the devotion of his followers that he was known as El Padrino, the Godfather. It was not difficult for him to keep his followers in line once they had been recruited. If he had to, he could resort to threats.

One cult member, a forty-three-year-old former model, helped recruit in Mexico City. She herself was recruited after going to Costanzo for help since she was having a run of bad luck.

Adolfo made some marks on her back and killed some chickens to turn her life around. You might say Maria went from the frying pan into the fire as she turned her life over to Adolfo and later told police that she helped him because she was afraid of what he might do to her children. Sara Aldrete added, "He would get the spirits or something to kill you. He was a strong personality. If he told you to do something, you would do it. We were his servants...I didn't love him, but I followed him."[17]

It was precisely her following Constanzo which concerned the administration of Southmost College. A note attached to her college records warned that she should be kept under observation because she was known to recruit fellow students to join the cult.[18]

And an effective recruiter she was. She told one young man who later became a member of the cult that she could introduce him to someone who would protect him, make him a millionaire, and bring him to heights he hadn't known before.[19]

Four of the suspects confirmed that Sara Aldrete recruited men to join the cult by showing them the 1986 film starring Martin Sheen, *The Believers*.[20] Leonard Maltin reviewed the film as a "gripping, genuinely frightening story of a widower and son who move to New York City and became involved (in more ways than one) with the cultish religion of Santeria, which believes in the sacrifice of children. The well crafted film knows how to manipulate its audience."[21]

The film would make a definite statement about how powerful a cult can become and therefore make an excellent soapbox from which Sara could make new converts.[22]

The Rituals

According to one source, the cult had been involved in human sacrifices for about nine months. Authorities searching for twenty-one-year-old Mark Kilroy, a University of Texas senior who had been missing for a month, came to the end of their search at a cattle ranch twenty miles outside of Matamoros, Mexico.

In a shack 15 x 25 ft. they found candles and kettles full of body parts, animal bones, and a caldron containing brains, hearts, and other organs of victims. During the ritual killings, victim's brains were cut out and put on a fire, mixed with blood, herbs, rooster's feet, goat's heads, and turtles.[23]

Officers found the bodies of thirteen males, one as young as fourteen. Several of the victims had been slashed with knives, others bludgeoned. One had been hanged, another apparently set afire, and at least two pumped with bullets. Some had been tortured with razor blades or had their hearts ripped out. Nearly all had been mutilated: ears, nipples, and testicles removed. The eyes had been gouged from one victim, the head was missing from another.[24] Cult member Sergio Salinas, who kidnapped Mark Kilroy, confessed and said simply, "It was the thing to do."[25]

His followers acknowledged that Costanzo had an unnatural hold over them. His power was the occult. Once they murdered in the name of Palo Mayombe, the cultists were even more bound to Costanzo, who convinced them that the victims became "spirit walkers" who would report directly to him so that nothing his drug cult members did would go unknown.[26]

The Rewards

Adolfo Constanzo masterminded a cult of drug smugglers who moved two thousand pounds of marijuana a week into the United States. Business was good and the rewards were evident.

According to George Gavito, a lawman involved in the investigation, Constanzo "had a wealthy lifestyle." He paid cash for a 1989 Mercedes. Constanzo wore fur coats.[27] He wore rubies and diamonds on every finger and twice went on ten-thousand-dollar spending sprees in Brownsville to clothe a boyfriend.[28] Sara Aldrete didn't do badly either. She showed up at college driving a brand new 1988 Ford Taurus equipped with a cellular phone. Police later learned that Aldrete, who earned $3.35/hr. on a work study program, paid $12,000 cash for the car and spent as much as $250 to $300 a month on the car phone bill.[29]

The rewards, however, carried a price tag far more costly than the members might have imagined. For Adolfo Constanzo, the discovery by Mexican police and U.S. Customs Service personnel of their drug operation and cult murders brought about an end to his leadership and his life.

Mexico City police surrounded his apartment, and a forty-five-minute gun battle ensued. Constanzo threw money and gold coins from a fourth-story window and burned thousands of dollars on the stove, declaring, "If I can't have it, no one can." His last act was to embrace his homosexual lover and order a subordinate to kill them both. When the subordinate refused, Constanzo slapped him in the face and said, "Do it, or it will go bad for you in hell."[30]

This time the follower obeyed, spraying both men with machine gun fire, ending both their lives before they could stand trial for the earthly consequences of their actions.

The remainder of those taken into custody were charged with a battery of crimes, ranging from murder in the first degree to the carrying of firearms without a proper license, and are currently serving their prison sentences.

The Regrets

Regrets are held not only held by cult members, but also by the families. The Kilroy family will live with regret over the loss of their son Mark as will the families and loved ones of the other twelve victims.

The body of Adolfo Constanzo was sent home to Miami. His brother, Fausto, said that funeral dates would not be released as he did not want the press or public intruding into the family's grieving.[31]

Sara Aldrete's father maintains his daughter's goodness and innocence. "She's the best daughter that a man ever had." He affirmed that "she never gave us a moment of worry."[32]

Robert Kahn, a reporter for the *Brownsville Herald*, spoke to Sara's father and confirmed that her parents knew nothing of Sara's cult activities. "I believed her father. The man was crying. It was obvious he was in shock over the whole thing," said Kahn.[33]

Sara Aldrete no doubt spoke for every individual who has ever been drawn deeply into the sinister web of the occult, where unspeakable acts of evil occur, when she said, "I don't know how I got involved. It was like knowing everything was one thing, and then having it be something else. If I had known it was like this, I wouldn't have gotten in it."[34]

WHAT YOU CAN DO

Curiosity, power, materialism, parental influence or lack of, indoctrination, sexual lure, and strong personalities are all part of the above tragedy. It is a story that could be retold many times over, and not just in foreign countries but in the U.S. as well.

John Kilroy, father of Mark, wrote,

> Before Mark's death I never thought much about the power of the Devil, but since then I have seen his great powers of deception. I believe that the basic cause of the alarming expansion of satanism in the last twenty years is illegal drug abuse. The fun and the riches promised through drug use is one of Satan's greatest deceptions.
>
> The satanic cult leaders actively recruit young people with the pledge of unconditional acceptance, drugs, sex, and protection against authority. Once they are drawn into the cult, these kids are kept quiet with death threats, secretive blood rituals, and by implicating them in criminal activities. One young boy said that his own brother threatened to kill him if he left the cult.[35]

Jesus made it very clear when He said, "no man can serve two masters" (Matt. 6:24). There can be no blending of voodoo practices with Christianity, no following of other gods—only *the* God and His Son, Jesus Christ. The tragedy Matamoros represents is that too many blindly follow Satan as master and never know the results until it is too late!

➤ Do not delude yourself. Christianity does not mix with other practices. It stands alone without equal. It is not possible to combine it with voodoo, witchcraft, or other occult religion. To believe it can be done, is to delude oneself. The reader should accept this and help others to see this.

➤ Realize that minorities are pouring into the United States every day, altering the composition of our basic society. Because they come to America does not mean they become "Americanized" the moment they touch our shores. They bring their religious faith with them, which may include their belief in voodoo. These people, like all others, must be loved and greeted with the good news of the gospel. Your witness to them is imperative.

➤ Be concerned with what is being taught in our public schools. Whether you have a child in school or not, the teaching of voodoo beliefs and practices has no place in our school systems, either primary (elementary) or secondary (junior high through high school).

➤ Be alert as to the content of television programs and movies which glorify voodoo as a whole. Concerned parents and citizens can be mobilized to take a stand against these attempts to glamorize and desensitize the impressionable victims.

➤ Develop and support a forum to share the Christian alternative whether it is at a movie theater or on television. This can be done through a newspaper article (though it may be relegated to the religion page), a series of articles in the statewide denominational paper, your church's weekly mailout, a sermon(s) from the pastor, and/or a special study led by the youth/minister or another individual. By all means remember, you need to be informed.

LAUREN

Halloween night finally came. Lauren was both excited and nervous. She didn't know quite why she had these feelings.

"You're going out a little late, aren't you?" Lauren's mother asked after she noticed Lauren looking out the window for the third time in the last five minutes.

"It's okay, Mom," Lauren replied. "We're going to work on a float for homecoming." She hated lying, but she knew they wouldn't approve of her going out to the old Darkins place. There were stories of strange gatherings out there. Of course, they were just rumors. Lauren didn't believe them, but her parents would.

A car horn blew and Lauren was off.

"You two are dressed for the night. Solid black from head to toe," Lauren greeted them as she got in the car.

"This is a big night," Caroline responded seriously.

"All Hallow's Eve," added Pam.

The darkness seemed to increase as they left the lights of the city behind and sped silently deep into the countryside. There was little conversation between the girls. The gentle swaying of the car maneuvering over country roads rocked Lauren to sleep.

When Lauren awoke, she wondered how long she had been asleep. She did know that Caroline and Pam were not in the car, nor were the keys in the ignition. All she could see was the orange glow of a fire in the distance.

Like a moth to a flame, Lauren made her way toward the fire in front of the old vacant house. She would never forget the sights she was about to behold. Caroline and Pam were around the fire, as well as other men, women, teenagers, and even some children. In the middle of the crowd, Lauren gasped at the sight of the blood-stained altar, a circle with strange drawings, covered with the remains of the recent animal sacrifice. She suddenly remembered reading about similar altars in some of the books she had recently read.

The worst sight of all was the behavior of the people. It was incredible, and Lauren soon realized that she was the only one dressed at the gathering. Several groups were involved in orgy-like activities, while drugs and alcohol were also in abundance.

This is not for me, Lauren thought and quickly turned to go back to the car.

"Don't go," she heard Pam and Caroline hiss behind her. Their hands were on Lauren's arms, keeping her from going any further.

"No!" Lauren cried as she broke away and ran for the road.

"Stop her!" Caroline screamed, and in response, four young men threw on their jeans and set out in pursuit of Lauren.

She had a short lead on them, and she ran as if the devil himself was behind her. "God, if you are truly here, please help me," she sobbed as she ran up the road.

T E N

But when the Pharisees heard this, they said,
"It is only by Beelzebub, the prince of demons,
that this fellow drives out demons."
— MATTHEW 12:24

What's Got into You?
Demon Possession

Earlier we examined various theories as to the origins of demons, demonic characteristics, and territorial demonic spirits. As troublesome as these issues are to many, the most confusing of demon-related matters seems to be that of possession.

DEMONS ON THE LOOSE

Newspaper accounts of demonic activity seem to be in abundance these days. You need only to look at the strange circumstances surrounding the death of young actor Brandon Lee to realize the truth of this statement. The media was quick to cover all angles of Lee's death and *People* magazine made it the cover story. The following is based on these media reports.

Brandon Lee

In April 1993, actor Brandon Lee, son of the late famous martial arts movie star, Bruce Lee, was tragically killed on the set of a movie he was making. Ironically, *The Crow* had an occult theme in which the main character comes back to life after having been murdered by a drug dealer. Followers of Brandon wasted no time in establishing a demonic explanation to the untimely death of young Lee.

First, they said, the scene in which Lee was killed bore an eerie resemblance to the last of the six films his father made. In *Game of Death*, Brandon's father played an actor who was shot after mobsters substituted a live round for a fake bullet on a movie set. By some of the elder Lee's fans, this was seen as a foreshadowing of Brandon's death and the legend of the "Lee Family Curse" was revived.

The legend began shortly before Bruce died in 1973. Bruce Lee, whose Chinese name, Lee Shao-lung, means Little Dragon, had bought a house in a Hong Kong suburb called Kowloon tong (Pond of the Nine Dragons), incurring, as the legend has it, the jealous wrath of the neighborhood's resident demons. The curse lasts, it is said, for three generations.[1]

Indeed, outsiders felt the entire set was cursed. Just two months prior to the shooting, a carpenter from the set was severely burned after the crane in which he was riding struck high-power lines, hospitalizing him in critical condition. A disgruntled sculptor who worked on the set did extensive damage to the studio's plaster shop by driving his car into it, while another crew member slipped and drove his screwdriver through his hand. Lee's shooting added confirmation to many of an "other worldly influence in a movie that probes the dimensions beyond the grave."[2]

The Roman Catholic Church and Exorcism

Roman Catholic theologians found themselves explaining the church's teachings about Satan and exorcism after Cardinal O'Connor remarked in a New Year mass that two exorcisms had been performed the previous year by the church. Cardinal O'Connor admitted, however, that demon possession which calls for exorcism seemed very rare and that psychological, medical, and other causes of what appears to be possession must be ruled out first.[3]

Tragic Consequences

Unfortunately, time and time again tragic consequences are the result of misunderstandings attributed to demon possession. Marcos Morales, fifty-six, of Santa Ana, California, was sentenced to twenty-five years to life in prison for drowning his five-year-old daughter in a bath tub during an attempted exorcism. This attempted exorcism was undertaken because Morales thought his daughter was possessed by demons after pushing a sister down a flight of stairs.[4]

Tragic events such as that above do not happen in the United States alone nor do they affect only children. In Melbourne, Australia, a woman died of internal injuries after her husband and other members of a fundamental Christian sect held a four-day rite to rid her body of demons. The woman's husband told the Australian Associated Press that his wife was possessed by "two strong male evil spirits. When they finally released their hold on her, she was hissing and frothing and they came out with a groan."[5]

Stories like these are troublesome and though they happen with greater frequency than we might like to admit, they do take place many times with the general public unaware of the circumstances. The film, *The Exorcist*, however, called the attention of the public to demonic possession more than any other film of its kind.

The Exorcist

In 1974, the movie ranked fifth in the list of "All-Time Box Office Champion Films" according to *Variety* magazine, while the book by William Peter Blatty sold more than nine million copies. To say that the film and the filmgoers' reactions to the film bedeviled theater owners, employers, clergy, mental health officers, and others is an understatement.

"My janitors are going bananas wiping up the vomit," complained Frank Kenton, manager of the United Actors Cinema 150 in Oakbrook, California. Kenton also had to replace doors and curtains damaged by unruly crowds and even re-landscape the McDonalds' plaza across the street where movie-goers parked their cars. "I've never seen anything like it in the 24 years I've been working in movie theaters," said H. Robert Honahan, division manager at the ABC/Plitt theaters in Berkeley. "We've had two to five people faint here everyday since this picture opened. More men than women pass out, and it usually happens in the evening performance, after the crucifix scene."[6]

The film affected others in a different way. Leighton Ford, evangelist with the Billy Graham Evangelistic Association, reported that one man who had been waiting in line to purchase tickets punched an attendant in the nose when told there would not be another showing that evening. Ford also reported that a Chicago psychiatrist had to place two of his patients under restraint and four others were complaining of mental anguish after seeing the film. Some of his colleagues who had seen *The Exorcist* agree that there is no way to sit through it without receiving some lasting negative effects.[7]

In Ft. Worth, Texas, a cinema close to Southwestern Seminary placed a blue sign with white letters above the entrance which read, "The management does not recommend *The Exorcist* to anyone who is unfamiliar with its content." And what was the content exactly?

Truth or Fiction?

Author William Blatty based his book by the same title as the movie on a real-life event, the possession of fourteen-year-old Douglas Deen of Mount Rainier, Maryland, outside Washington. It began simply enough at the Deen home in January 1949. The family began hearing scratching noises in the attic and in the walls and thought that the sounds had an animal origin. They searched the attic and found nothing. The scratching became louder. Dishes flew from shelves. Pictures fell from walls. And in Douglas' room, the bed shuddered and shook. The family was terrified. When Douglas stayed overnight at a neighbor's house, the mysterious noises and bed-shaking moved with the boy. The neighbors were terrified.

Then the Rev. Mr. Winston, pastor of a church in Mount Rainier, decided to test the boy. On February 17, the minister took Douglas home with him. At 10:20 P.M., he spread two blankets on the floor beside the bed. Douglas lay on the blankets. The minister lay on the bed, watching Douglas. Suddenly the blankets began moving. With Douglas aboard, the blankets slid across the floor, bumped the boy into a wall, moved backward, spun in a circle, then slipped under the bed. All the time, Douglas was wide-eyed and frightened.

What convinced the minister was that "during the entire ordeal, Douglas' body was rigid, his hands were fully in sight and there was no wrinkling of the blankets," he admitted at a closed meeting of the Society for Parapsychology.[8]

THE PSYCHOLOGICAL SIDE OF DEMON POSSESSION

To convince a person that he is indeed possessed is of no small consequence. Consider, for example, how a person feels to be told that he is possessed by a demon or demons. This diagnosis can have three unhealthy aspects.

First, it tends to remove the responsibility of recognizing and confessing one's own sinfulness. The devil made me do it becomes literally true here. Second, to view ourselves as a battleground upon which forces of good and evil alternately rampage without volitional control robs us of a sense of potency. Third, by suppressing and repressing our own urges, viewing them as demonic by-products rather than as parts of ourselves, we are building an unhealthy personality structure. Large portions of ourselves remain dissociated rather than integrated.[9]

To further complicate the matter, multiple personality disorders and undifferentiated schizophrenia have overlapping symptomology with demon possession. For many, diagnosis on the basis of symptom analysis is preferable. Those in favor of this method logically argue that one or two symptoms are held in common with the two forms mentioned above, but none share the entire system complex.

The symptoms complex may be divided into physical, psychological and spiritual symptoms.[10]

Physical Symptoms of Demonic Possession

➤ Preternatural (more than natural) strength

➤ Change in facial demeanor (usually one of intense hatred and evil)
➤ Change in voice tone and pitch (usually the voice deepens and becomes harsher or takes on a mocking tone)
➤ Epileptic-like convulsions with attendant symptoms
➤ Anesthesia to pain

Psychological Symptoms of Demonic Possession

➤ Clairvoyance
➤ Telepathy
➤ The ability to predict the future
➤ The ability to speak in languages not known by the possessed person
➤ The clouding of consciousness while in the trance state
➤ Amnesia about things which happened while in the trance state.

Three Spiritual Changes from Demon Possession

➤ A significant change in moral character
➤ Becoming verbally or physically aggressive or falling into a trance if someone prays
➤ An inability to say Jesus' name reverently or to affirm that he is God's Son in the flesh (1 John 4:1–3)

In the case of Douglas Deen, every precaution was taken to ensure that there was not some other explanation for what appeared to be demonic possession. He was taken to St. Louis, Missouri, where he was thoroughly examined by doctors and psychiatrists of St. Louis University Hospital. Nothing was found to account for the noises and movements around Douglas. A Jesuit priest, said to be a quiet man in his fifties, began to make the necessary preparations for the exorcism.

The ridding of Douglas' devil consumed two and a half months. During all that time, the priest kept the "black fast," eating only bread and water. He lost fifty pounds. More than thirty times the Jesuit performed the ancient ritual which begins, "I command you, whoever you are, unclean spirit, and all of your associates obsessing this friend of God."

Douglas reacted violently to all the rituals with the exception of the last try. He went into angered frenzies. His body trembled violently. His voice became high and shrill. He cursed and spoke obscenities. He even spoke in classic Latin, a language unknown to him. The bed shook and rose from the floor. Furniture moved, fell, and rose. The room became alternately hot and cold.

Finally, the priest spoke the ritualistic words and Douglas was quiet. The ordeal was over. The devil had been exorcised.[11]

THE BIBLE AND DEMONIC POSSESSION

The term "demonic possession" does not appear in the Bible. Apparently, it originated with the Jewish historian Flavius Josephus in the first century and then passed into ecclesiastical language.[12] Scholars seem divided as to whether the Old Testament refers to demon possession or not. Unger writes,

> The presence of demonic phenomena in the Old Testament, if not actual cases of possession, is strongly suggested by such instances as the orgiastic rites of the priests of Baal (1 Kings 18:28) and Nebuchadnezzar's sudden manifestation of practices of lower animals (Dan. 4:33). David's feigned dementia (1 Sam. 21:13–14) argues for the frequency of such phenomena at that date, and Saul's persecution mania, which Josephus attributes to actual demon possession, is clearly a case of demon influence (1 Sam. 16, 18–21).[13]

The opposite view states that there was no belief in demons by the Israelites except in allusion to popular language and a few references to superstition among Hebrews. Even the encounter of Jesus with the demonic is not above battles over interpretation.

The Synoptic gospels contain numerous references to Jesus casting out demons. Mark alone accounts for ten instances (1:23–27, 32–34, 39; 3:11–12; 5:1–20; 7:25–30; 9:27–29, 38; 16:9, 17). These scriptures and others may be "exorcised" of any connection with possession by either of two theories: the accommodation theory and the psychopathological theory.

Scholars who hold the accommodation theory concede that Jesus appears to have believed in Satan and demons but only as an accommodation to the concepts of the age. They see it as in no way representing the content of Jesus' teachings. Jesus' purpose was ethical, and He used the concepts of His time as symbols to serve ethical ends.

Scholars who accept the psychopathological theory suggest that Jesus was a child of His day and was mistaken in His belief about demons. What the ancients then called demon possession is now called mental illness.[14]

George Ladd, in *Jesus and His Kingdom*, offers one interpretation that does justice to the gospel data as well as the integrity of Christ's person. This view accepts the existence of demons and demonic possession as an object reality. While acknowledging the ancient world's belief in demonic possession, a difference is held between the teachings of Jesus and Jewish literature. Jesus used sobriety and restraint in His references to demons and the magical element is absent altogether.[15]

CAN THE CHRISTIAN BE POSSESSED?

When we come to this issue, we find once again a diversity of opinions. Before looking at both sides and examining God's Word, a few clarifications would be in order. First, demons do not own anything as a "possession," as implied by some. Demons should be viewed as invaders. Second, demonic invasion takes on many forms from mild to more severe or enslaving, as in the demoniac of Gadara in Mark 5:1–20. Third, many authorities do not prefer the term "demon possession," but rather the term "demonization" or "demonized," taken "from the Greek *daimonizoma*, meaning being demonized, i.e., under the control of one or more demons."[16]

Three Views of Demonization and the Christian

Merrill F. Unger states in his book, *What Demons Can Do to Saints*, that Christians tend to hold one of the three following views of demonization.

> First, many Christians naively assume that the potential of Satanic power in the life of the regenerated is practically nil. They live in a sort of fool's paradise, imagining that becoming a Christian magically shields them from attack or demonic invasion.

Second, others maintain a more realistic view. They are fully convinced that Satanic powers may not only tempt and attack but that, if they are not reprised, they may affect the saint's life and do serious harm in his experience. These powers may influence him, delude him, despoil him. Always, however, Satanic powers attack the saint from without, never exercising total control over him. To such people, the possibility of a born-again believer being invaded by one or more demons is preposterous, and in their view, unbiblical.

A third class of believers holds to the most realistic view. Grievously sinning saints may go beyond the old nature. In cases of serious, persistent sin such as gross immorality or participation in occultism or occult religionism, demons may exercise control over the believer for a time until his sin is confessed and forsaken and deliverance from the evil powers is gained.[17]

The Biblical Evidence in Support

C. Fred Dickason offers the following passages which he believes support the idea that believers may be inhabited by demons: Genesis 31:19, 34–35; Numbers 22—24; Matthew 8:16; Acts 5:1–3; 8:9–24; 1 Corinthians 5:1–13; 10:14–22; 2 Corinthians 11:3–4; 12:7–8. As further evidence, he suggests several examples of believers who were inhabited, such as King Saul, the woman bent double, Judas Iscariot, and the Corinthian tongues-speaker.[18]

The Biblical Evidence Against

Dickason divides these passages into four categories: the defeat of Satan (John 12:31; 16:11; Rev. 20:1–3; Heb. 2:14–15; Col. 2:14–15), deliverance from Satan's domain (Col. 1:13; Acts 26:78), Christ's defense of saints (John 10:22–29; 17:15; Matt. 6:13; 2 Thess. 3:3; 1 John 4:4; 5:18), and denial of participation with demons (Ps. 5:4; 1 Cor. 10:21; 2 Cor. 6:14–16). According to Dickason, none of these passages can, with any fair treatment, be construed to eliminate the possibility of a genuine believer's being inhabited by wicked spirits.[19]

I personally do not believe that a demon can inhabit the body of a Christian. Romans 8:35–39 and 1 Corinthians 6:19–20 are as clear as they need to be in regard to demonic invasion. A believer may be oppressed, but not possessed.

The believer is further assured by the following scriptures:

➤ John 14:30; Romans 8:17; 1 Corinthians 2:16; Colossians 3:4. In the first Scripture, we see that Jesus had nothing to do with Satan, while the remaining three refer to the believer's intimate relationship with Christ. As we are possessed by Christ and live for Him, we cannot be inhabited by a demon or demons.
➤ 1 Corinthians 12:13; Ephesians 4:4; and 1 Corinthians 6:17 tell us of one spirit for the believer, not two or more.
➤ Romans 8:15 speaks of the "spirit of Sonship" in which we are adopted by grace as we give our hearts to Jesus Christ. Demonic inhabitation, on the other hand, is a spirit of fear.

THE CHRISTIAN'S RESPONSE

In his thorough volume, *Christian Counseling: A Comprehensive Guide*, Gary Collins writes that "exorcism should be used rarely and only with the full support of spiritually mature and biblically astute church leaders."[20]

Kent Philpott responds to the question from personal experience:

> How do you minister to someone who's demonized? They're sick, you have to understand that. They take on bizarre kinds of behavior, neurotic or psychotic expression. Even after they're delivered of the demon, they still may be emotionally ill.
>
> But there is a difference, a genuine difference. This is where the spiritual gift of discernment comes in. Many times you see it in counseling, you hear it in the way a person talks.
>
> We talk about Jesus, and if I feel there is a possibility of demon possession, I ask if they'd like to pray to be rid of this evil spirit.
>
> On these occasions, I like to have another person with me, because at this point, the evil spirit realizes what is happening and it will attack you; it will either try to destroy you or the person it possesses.
>
> I usually lay on hands. It seems appropriate, although it isn't necessary. Just have faith that your prayers can make this person free, that the work of the cross is sufficient for this person's

freedom. I pray simply without emotion. I ask God to rebuke this evil spirit and send it right back to hell.

Also, you want this binding of the spirit in hell, because those evil spirits can cause trouble unless there's some kind of binding. I know that sounds weird, but I've had too much trouble when it didn't happen.

Then I encourage the person to resist the devil and turn from any sin he has in his life. If he continues to sin, it's not going to work, for the spirit will come right back. If the person is not a Christian, he is really going to have to pray to receive Jesus Christ, or he is going to be continually exposed to demonic influence.[21]

A distinction may be made between performing an exorcism which is an inhabitation, possession, or complete domination of an individual, and deliverance, a minor degree of demonic influence. In Roman Catholic circles, the exorcism is performed only by priests with the authorization of the local bishop. Deliverance can be practiced by anyone with certain characteristics.

Eight Essential Elements for the Deliverer

Roger K. Bufford, in his fine book, *Counseling and the Demonic*, suggests eight qualifications for the individual who feels God leading him to the deliverance of the afflicted:

➤ Personal salvation of the individuals involved
➤ Consistent life of personal holiness
➤ Significant degree of personal spiritual maturity
➤ Confession of all known sin
➤ Renewed personal commitment to God, affirming His sovereignty and submitting to His will
➤ Good biblical knowledge of the character of Satan and demons
➤ Prayer for spiritual wisdom, including discernment of spirits
➤ Support team of others with similar spiritual maturity who are prepared to help in the process of casting out evil spirits[22]

Other truths should also be considered at this point:

➤ The demon will resist the exorcism.
➤ If possible, the individual should have given his consent to the exorcism.

➤ Immediate spiritual follow-up is essential by leading the individual to faith in Christ and/or personal discipleship.

Six Ways to Minister to the Individual

Finally, Bufford mentions six practical ways to minister to an individual experiencing demonic influence or control. They are entitled, "Six Spiritual Interventions in the Life of the Victim" and are the following:

➤ A person experiencing demonic influence may also need non-spiritual counseling in addition to spiritual intervention.

➤ The Christian must prepare himself for spiritual warfare involving his own spiritual condition.

➤ The effectiveness of spiritual intervention is greatly enhanced by combining the efforts of several people who work well together.

➤ The key to effective spiritual intervention is to recognize the complexity of the problem. Simple solutions can leave the individual worse than before the intervention (Luke 11:24–26).

➤ The Christian should focus on four important dimensions of a person:

1. Thoughts—The mind is one of Satan's first places to attack. A part of Satan's character is that he lies. Lead the individual to recognize Satan's subtle and persuasive lies and help him understand the truth found in the Bible. Reading, memorizing, and meditating on the Bible is essential.

2. Behavior—Bad habits are easier to replace than merely discard. Lead the individual to replace bad habits with positive habits.

3. Emotions—Anger, fear, anxiety, and doubt are disabling emotions. Lead the individual to see God's love for them and the forgiveness available to any person asking God for forgiveness. Sharing that the individual was created in the image of God may be helpful. Lead the individual to begin practicing those things which remind him of God's love and forgiveness.

4. Relationships—Many people become involved in the occult because of broken or sinful relationships. For example, incest or other sexual abuse is frequently part of the individual's hidden life. The Christian should seek opportunities to minister to spouses or

parents as he ministers with the individual. Lead the individual to more positive relationships, such as that with God (Matt. 22:37).
➤ Other parts of spiritual intervention include:

1. Support groups for prayer, group Bible study, mutual encouragement, service, and personal discipline

2. Candid and brief individual and corporate prayer

3. Individual and corporate worship

4. Practice of godly living

5. Spiritual giving (financial and personal)

6. Service in God's name

7. Church discipleship[23]

The best protection against demonization is total submission to God. As James reminds us, "Submit yourselves, then, to God. Resist the devil, and he will flee from you" (4:7).

WHAT YOU CAN DO

➤ An individual may be strongly influenced by what he or she opens his mind to, whether movies, television, or books. Guard your mind against such negative influences as demonic themes.
➤ Be alert to children's unhealthy interest in demonic related items, whether they take the form of music, posters hung on bedroom walls, drawings on school notebooks, notebook paper, etc., television movies, and books.
➤ Be well informed on the subject, to be able to dialogue with the individual of your concern and clearly state your viewpoint.
➤ Seek professional help. Mental illness and demonic possession are not always easily definable to the layperson. Any questions of this nature should be addressed by a competent professional, which can include your pastor or priest, followed by further consultation with a mental health professional.
➤ Pray. In addition to studying prayerfully the Scripture passages in this chapter and others in appendix C, you may also consult the suggested readings in appendix B. As you prayerfully consider what God would have you to do, you can trust Him, that He will reveal it to you.

LAUREN

What's going to happen to me? Lauren thought as she ran. She looked over her shoulder to see her four pursuers rapidly closing the gap between them. She might have a minute at best. *Why did I ever get involved in this? This is so disgusting, so perverted. I never dreamed it was really like this.*

Lauren's tears were flowing down her cheeks as she continued to run. *If they catch me, they may rape me or worse*, she agonized. She could hear footsteps just a few feet away.

"Oh, God, please save me!" she cried out loud.

As if on cue, the road was bathed with the headlights of an oncoming car, with the horn blaring series of beeps.

"Quick, hide!" she heard one of her assailants say. They disappeared behind some bushes.

The car screeched to a halt and the passenger door swung open.

"Get in quick!" a familiar voice shouted. It was Heather! The tires squealed as the car sped off, taking Lauren further from the tragic scene behind.

Lauren dissolved into sobs that seemed to last forever. Eventually the car re-entered the city and pulled into a vacant service station. Heather gently put her arm around Lauren and held her while she wept.

"I feel so ashamed, so stupid. How could I have been so blind?" Lauren said between sobs. "How could you have known where I was?" Lauren questioned when she realized what had just happened.

"I knew," Heather said. "It happened to me, too. I became a victim just like you were intended to be."

"Who saved you from them?" Lauren asked as she began to regain her composure.

"Jesus Christ," Heather responded happily, knowing that the moment of Lauren's real deliverance was at hand.

That night was a turning point in Lauren's life in more ways than one. It was in the quiet of that car that Heather led Lauren to a saving faith in Jesus. Lauren would never be the same again. She had seen the darkness around her. Now she would be a light in that darkness!

E L E V E N

I am the light of the world.
Whoever follows me will never walk in darkness,
but will have the light of life.
— JOHN 8:12

Turning the Darkness into Sunshine

There is no question but that we have to deal with Satan in our everyday lives. It would be wonderful if we never had to deal with temptation. Our efforts to be Christlike would go unhindered. You and I both know, however, this is not the case. Satan is alive and well. We have but only to read our newspapers or watch the nightly news to see evidence of his works all around us. Satan loves darkness, and you can rest assured that much of what he does we cannot always see. That should truly concern us.

Undoubtedly you have become concerned as you have read the previous chapters, just as I have been in writing them. So many more illustrations could have been added to give weight to my points.

After reading these chapters, you are either more convinced about the reality and danger of the occult than you were before; open-minded where you were once close-minded; or still close-minded to the reality of the occult.

Before closing, I would like to take a final look at ten of Satan's strategies for influencing individuals into the occult. Coaches and athletes know that the best competitive effort is, in part, based on knowing your opponent and his strategies. Hours and hours are spent scouting the opposition, watching the opponent on film, talking with others who have competed against the opponent, etc. In order to best defend ourselves against Satan and his armies, we must apply the same basic principles and study Satan's strategies.

STRATEGY NO. 1: CONFUSION

I would not argue that there are exaggerations concerning the occult. However, I also believe that the occult does pose a real threat to the believer today. The worst mistake we could make would be to write the occult off as fantasy.

Isn't it interesting that the media has been full of discrediting stories in evangelical work countering the occult? These reports can help confuse the believer as to the reality of the occult and to its power over many people by emphasizing the "failures" of those who openly argue against the occult.

In *Christianity Today*, Mike Warnke, the focus of a journalistic investigation of a 1992 *Cornerstone* magazine article, admitted that he exaggerated his role as a Satanist. Best known as author of the book, *The Satan Seller*, Warnke insists that he was involved as a Satanist, but does admit to inaccuracies and problems with details. "It was never meant to be a blow by blow academic description of every facet and fact of my life," Warnke explained.[1] As a result, Word Records severed their eighteen-year relationship with Warnke, who has in turn, submitted himself to a disciplining body.

In this same article, Bob Larson, a Christian radio talk show host and author of twenty-two books, was questioned about his alleged exploitation of Satanism victims, employee abuse, and obsession to raise money to remain on the more than 180 radio stations across North America. These criticisms were published in an exposè featured in the January 1993 issue of *World*, a weekly newsmagazine written from a Christian perspective.[2] Additional criticisms were made regarding his first novel, *Dead Air*, and his conspiratorial view of Satanism. Larson says his critics report he is "some type of gullible sensationalist who believes everything (he is) told on every story as if it were the absolute truth." Larson counters, "From a Biblical standpoint, there unquestionably is a conspiracy. Ephesians 6 tells us all about that and explains it in detail. Do I think these are conspiratorial groups? Absolutely."[3]

For some, these "exposés" are all the proof they need to write off ministries against the occult as a sham. This would be as logical as writing off the ministries of evangelists like Billy Graham, because of the exposés on evangelists Tipton, Swaggart, Baker, and Hinn. Nothing would please Satan more than a cynical, skeptical attitude toward him and the works of his army.

STRATEGY NO. 2: SHORTCUTS

Genesis chapter 3 offers one of the first lessons taught in the Bible: that Satan is the master in promising shortcuts. Eve was promised that she would "be like God, knowing good and evil" (Gen. 3:5) and that the fruit was "desirable for gaining wisdom" (v. 6), so she ate it and gave it to Adam. But Satan lied, as he always does. The wisdom she gained was not as God's—it set her against Adam and vice versa. Thus, they were both separated from God. What a price to pay for a little bit of "wisdom."

Satan draws the teenager, the young, the middle-aged, and even the older adult into the occult by promising such shortcuts. It may be a shortcut to power, fame, or riches.

I recently talked with a young minister who played in a band which backed some of the hottest groups in rock music. He said, "Bill, I've heard people say they promised Satan they would do anything for him if he would help them gain recognition. They really could not explain the 'talent' they seemed to have other than to attribute it to Satan's keeping his part of the bargain." What a price to pay—an eternity of separation from God in exchange for a few years of fame on earth!

STRATEGY NO. 3: DISILLUSIONMENT

This is not an easy world in which to live, and it grows even more difficult with each passing day. So many things happen which cause us to be disillusioned.

A chilling story was told to me in Brazil by an American who was on a missions trip in Belo Horizonte. According to this individual, a minister was en route to his destination via airplane and was served a meal while in flight. It was quite enjoyable, but he noticed a young man seated across the aisle from him had not touched his tray. Not wanting to be intrusive, but still concerned, he inquired as to why the young man had not eaten anything.

"Are you feeling bad?" he questioned.

"No," replied the young man, "I'm fasting."

"Oh," exclaimed the minister, "are you Jewish?"

"No, I am a Satanist. I am on my way to a gathering and we have made a pledge to fast and ask for the marriages of ministers to be destroyed," he explained.

It is one thing whether you believe that story or not, although this incident has been confirmed to me by several different sources. It is another thing altogether to deny the fact that divorce among ministers is an increasingly significant problem today.

Divorce among ministers is only one of many disillusionments suffered by people today. When people in whom we have placed our trust fall, it is easy for us to become disillusioned. We must, however, be careful to take our hurts to the throne, not the tempter.

STRATEGY NO. 4: ANGER WITH GOD

You remember how Satan questioned Eve and asked, "Did God really say, 'You must not eat from any tree in the garden?'" (Gen. 3:1) Satan assured her that she would not die in the following verse. Did she know God well enough that she thought He would not punish her?

People think of God as love and do not believe that He would ever allow anything bad to happen to His children. Satan likes for us to think that way. When something unfortunate happens, we often get angry with God. This suits Satan just fine.

When I was a seminary student in my first master's program, my brother called me to share the news that my mother had been diagnosed as having a brain tumor. We would not know whether it was malignant until exploratory surgery was performed and a biopsy report was given. I was concerned, but not overly worried. At sixty-four, my mother had never been ill a day in her life that I could remember.

I was surprised when the biopsy came back positive; I could not believe my mother had cancer. My wife, Susan, was pregnant with our first child, and we were looking forward to sharing this baby with my mother. Still, I would not let myself get upset. My mother was a woman of faith. She even witnessed to her surgeon only to discover that he was a committed Christian. *It's going to be okay*, I assured myself.

I was dealt still another blow when the surgeon regretfully told us that he took all of the cancerous growth he could, but he simply could not get it all without causing permanent brain damage. "We'll use chemotherapy and do all we can," he told us.

My faith was strong, or so I thought. God and I made a deal in my mind. "Lord," I said, "Your Word says if we have faith as small as a mustard seed, nothing will be impossible [Matt. 17:20–21]. Lord, I believe You can heal her, as she knows You can. You'll heal her because I believe as she believes. Everyone will know You healed her. She'll praise You and give You the glory and so will I." I was quite content and at peace with this "biblically-based logic." I grew less content as my mother seemed to go downhill.

Shortly after Christmas 1973, she went to be with the Lord. I was so hurt and angry with God. "You let me down," I raged within my heart. "You promised me if my faith was strong enough, You would come through for me," I bitterly said to Him.

I don't know how long I stayed angry with God, but fortunately Satan did not gain that victory. Certainly anger with God can and does lead to an individual's downfall. Unresolved anger which leads to involvement in the occult is a giant step in the wrong direction. I believe God understands our anger and hurt, but He wants us to trust Him completely. Faith is not dictating terms to God; it is trusting Him in whatever He decides to do.

STRATEGY NO. 5: THE CURSE OF THE PAST

Tiffany and Michelle (not their real names) are two very different women in terms of age. One is barely out of her teens while the other is thirty-something. They are beautiful people as God's creation, but they share a haunting common bond; both are victims of Satanic Ritual Abuse (SRA).

My heart breaks as I hear them describe the unspeakable atrocities they suffered at the hands of those they trusted. The average reader might well question the reality of what these two women have seen, heard, and felt as well as what they have done. Tiffany and Michelle's participation spanned well over fifteen years each.

As I have counseled with them, I have watched them climb ever so slowly from what one described as "the pits of hell." I have heard their anguished cries wondering if they will ever truly find healing from the past. When you have counted on Satan for so long, one told me, it is hard to let go and trust God.

God is God over the past, present, and the future as the writer of Hebrews reminds us: "Jesus Christ is the same yesterday and today and forever" (Heb. 13:8). He and He alone can bring healing into the life of the believer. He and He alone can grant the forgiveness for whatever you have done and give you the grace to live each day for Him!

How Satan loves to bring up your past to bother and discourage you. It needn't be that way, however. I like the way one person put it: "The next time Satan reminds you of your past, remind him of his future!"

STRATEGY NO. 6: FEAR OF THE FUTURE

If Satan cannot snare us with our past, he may well try to instill within you a fear of the future.

I believe at some point in occult involvement an individual passes over the line of marginal involvement to commitment. Once that person is hooked, his descent into bondage becomes a nightmare trip straight down. That person may well believe there is no hope, and he may see other attempts to help him fail.

One school administrator shared with me an unfortunate incident of a teacher who tried to fight the influence of occult groups operating in his community. He wound up losing his job and moving from the community. This is not to say that there is no hope. Those who care enough to help will be required to take some risks. As God burdens your heart to help someone and you follow His leadership, keep in perspective that the outcome is not solely dependent upon you, but Him. As the classic hymn states: "Our hope is built on nothing less than Jesus' blood and right-eousness."[4]

Over and over again God's word tells us that He is the source of our strength. Psalm 46:1–2 reminds us, "God is our refuge and strength, an ever-present help in trouble. Therefore we will not fear." Moses and the Israelites sang, "The Lord is my strength and my song; he has become my salvation. He is my God, and I will praise him" (Ex. 15:2). To that one who wants to escape Satan's web, no matter how bleak or uncertain the future may seem, God is able to deliver him.

STRATEGY NO. 7: ENTICEMENT

I have met those who were so blinded by Satan that they could not see how far down they had gone. They outwardly seemed content that Satan was delivering what he had promised, though he never truly does. No amount of reasoning would lead them to understand the ultimate price tag for what they were getting. As I have thought of these tortured souls and prayed for them, I have reflected on the thought if they could only "fast forward" their lives and see the end, some would likely bail out of the occult right now.

God's words are crystal clear in regard to the outcome of following the wrong path. As Jesus reminds us in Matthew 7:13, "broad is the road that leads to destruction, and many enter through it."

STRATEGY NO. 8: BLINDNESS

I have been a student of human behavior for twenty-seven years, and I still marvel at the complexities of the human personality. My own experience growing up in a loving Christian home, the typical Cleaver family of the fifties, makes it impossible for me personally to relate to what I have seen and heard from those deeply involved in the occult. However, my understanding of Scripture and my comprehension of God leads me to believe that God does not desire anyone to perish, but everyone to come to repentance (2 Pet. 3:9). It also leads me to believe that God's patience with us is not endless. Our mortality can bring about the beginning of an eternity apart from God for the unrepentant heart (Gen. 6:3). Second Peter 3:10–13 assures us that the day of judgment is coming. John 3:19 tell us that many prefer darkness to light because of their penchant for doing evil. In Luke 12:54–56, Jesus tells us that many will fail to recognize the signs of the end times because of their blindness.

The difference falls on your shoulders and mine. Jesus challenges us in Matthew 5:13–16 to be the salt and light in this world. May God use us to deliver people from Satan's stronghold.

STRATEGY NO. 9: SELF-RELIANCE

It's no secret that emphasis on self is a "buzz word," a key concept in the New Age movement today. Satan, of course, wrote the textbook on self-indulgence and selfishness.

When I was a boy growing up in the church, I remember my Sunday School teacher writing the word SIN on the blackboard with the middle letter greatly exaggerated. That, of course, says it all: the enhancement of self.

With the exception of children inducted into the occult or those who have been deceptively manipulated, most people enter the occult for what it will do for them. Whatever advantage they think they may gain is quickly replaced by the realization that they are going to be used as well. Satan always gets something out of those who permit him to use them.

There is also a sense of self-reliance in trying to battle Satan in our way and on our own terms. If I have learned anything over the years, it is to respect the wiles of Satan. It's like my feelings for snakes. I respect them and give them all the room they need to maneuver. I respect them, but I do not like them.

Satan does have power. He is ever so crafty and I know he wants to compromise me in any way he can. I also know he would like to destroy me as he does every creation of God. I respect him from the point of view that my wisdom and strength alone is no match for him. He will win every time *unless* I fight him in the strength of the Lord. We must fight him with the spiritual armor of Ephesians 6:13–18. We must remember Paul's words to the Philippians when he wrote, "I can do *everthing* through him who gives me strength" (Phil. 4:13).

Satan is defeated when we die to self and live in Christ. Paul tells us to "do nothing out of selfish ambition or vain conceit" (Phil. 2:3). We are not to be self-centered, but rather to have the mind of Christ (1 Cor. 2:16).

STRATEGY NO. 10: THE WINNER IS THE LOSER

Many Satanists believe that in the end they will emerge victorious, not Christians.[5] Of course their belief will not hold true and many will be rudely awakened on that glorious day when Jesus returns and every knee shall bow and every tongue confess that Jesus Christ is Lord (Phil. 2:10–11).

I am reminded of a story told to me by a Brazilian psychiatrist in Sao Paulo. He was treating a young homosexual man who had acquired the AIDS virus and was dying. He abruptly quit coming for treatment during the time of Brazil's Carnival following Lent. This is a time of unparalleled debauchery, self-indulgence, and sexual excess. After the carnival, the young man returned to continue therapy. When asked why he had quit therapy earlier, he bitterly replied, "I know I am going to die, so I went to Rio (de Janeiro) to party. I wanted to infect as many as I could and take them with me."

Satan will infect as many as he can. There will be no ultimate victory for Satan. God's Word assures us of this. But Satan will be victorious in the lives of many. He will succeed in compromising some Christian testimonies, and he will destroy some ministries. However, we must stand strong in Jesus Christ and not only resist Satan personally, but fight him with every ounce of strength in Christ for the souls of those already in Satan's grasp.

May we recall the words of the great hymn: "Rescue the perishing, duty demands it. Strength for my labor the Lord will provide back to the narrow way patiently win them; tell the poor wanderer a Savior has died."[6]

May we never forget the Great Commission that is our awesome and challenging responsibility: "Therefore go and make disciples of all nations, baptizing them in the name of the Father and of the Son and of the Holy Spirit, and teaching them to obey everything I have commanded you. And surely I will be with you always, to the very end of the age" (Matt. 28:19–20).

I am always interested in hearing from those who have questions or experiences involving the occult which they would like to share. If you are such a person, please write me at OBU, P.O. Box 3637, Arkadelphia, AR 71998-0001.

Appendix A

ORGANIZATIONS

You may want to contact one of these organizations, arranged by state, for additional information. If you should want to correspond with me, write to the address listed in the Arkansas section below.

ARKANSAS

Dr. William C. Viser
Ouachita Baptist University
410 Ouachita Street, Box 3637
Arkadelphia, Arkansas 71998-0001
501/245-5524 or 246-5547

CALIFORNIA

ACT-Affirming Children's Truth
Jackie McGauley
P. O. Box 417
Redondo Beach, CA 90277
213-376-5652
(A child advocacy group for sexually and/or ritually abused children)

Answers in Action
P. O. Box 2067
Costa Mesa, CA 92626

Believe the Children
Leslie Floberg
P. O. Box 1358
Manhattan Beach, CA 90266
(Nat'l headquarters—association for parents and children of ritual abuse)

Beyond Survival Foundation
M. K. Gustinella, MS., MFCC, President
1278 Glenneyre No. 3
Laguna Beach, CA 92651

Beyond Survival Magazine
Craig Lockwood, Editor
P. O. Box 20063
Fountain Valley, CA 92728
714/563-6330
(Articles for all areas of abuse, individual and group counseling)

Breaking Out
P. O. Box 6782
Salinas, CA 93912-6782
(Information, crisis counseling, referrals)

Calvalcade Productions
Dale McCulley
7360 Potter Valley Road
Ukiah, CA 95482
702/743-1168
(Company offering educational tools on satanic cults)

CARA (Churches Against Ritual Abuse)
P. O. Box 584
Pasadena, CA 91102

CARIS
Box 2067
Costa Mesa, CA 92626
(Christian apologetics and information on cults and the occult)

Child Help U.S.A.
P. O. Box 630
Hollywood, CA 90028
800/422-4453
(For survivors and therapists)

Christian Research Institute
Dr. Walter Martin
P. O. Box 500
San Juan Capistrano, CA 92693
(Information on cults and the occult)

CRCIA (California Ritual Crime Investigators Association)
808 Alamo Drive, Suite 290
Vacaville, CA 95688
209/575-5550

Dolter, Steve
School Psychologist
9401 South Painter Ave.
Whittier, CA 90605
213/698-3121 Est. 361
(Counselor offering seminars on heavy metal and the occult)

FOCOS (Families of Crimes of Silence)
P. O. Box 2338
Canoga Park, CA 91306
805/298-8768

Healing Hearts Project
357 MacArthur Blvd
Oakland, CA 94610
510/465-3890
(Sponsored by Bay Area Women Against Rape)

Jewish Family Services of Los Angeles Cult Clinic
6505 Wilshire Blvd.
Los Angeles, CA 90048
213/852-1234

Jude 3 Missions
P. O. Box 1901
Orange, CA 92668

Monarch Resources
P. O. Box 1293
Torrance, CA 90505-0293
310/373-1958
(Information, publications, counseling for ritual abuse survivors)

Real Active Survivors
P. O. Box 1894
Canyon Country, CA 91386-0894
805/252-6437
(Offers multiple personality disorder workshops, anger workshops, retreats, a listening-line service, and consulting)

Spiritual Counterfeits Project
P. O. Box 2418
Berkely, CA 94702
Referral Hotline: 415/540-0300
(Provides information on all cults, especially Eastern mysticism, and the occult. Publishes the *SCP Newsletter*.)

Survivor Newsletter
3181 Mission St., No. 139
San Francisco, CA 94110
415/334-5979
(Supported by the California Consortium Against Child Abuse. Newsletter devoted specifically to ritual abuse and recovery)

Task Force on Ritual Abuse, L. A. Co. Commission for Women)
383 Hall of Administration
500 W. Temple St.
Los Angeles, CA 90012
213/944-1455

UBC Rape Prevention & Education Program
Building T-9, Room 201
University of California
Berkely, CA 94729
(Office providing educational materials on occult crime)

Witness, Inc.
Duane Magnani, Director
Box 597
Clayton, CA 94517
415/672-5979
(Witness to cult members and informs Christians about the dangers of cults. Provides books and training aids)

Writeway Literary Associates
David Balsiger
P. O. Box 10428
Costa Mesa, CA 92627
714/850-0349

COLORADO

Bob Larson Ministries
P. O. Box 360
Denver, CO 80236
303/985-HOPE
(Crisis counseling, referrals)

Justus Unlimited
P. O. Box 1121
Parker, CO 80134
303/643-8698

CONNECTICUT

FACES
71 Haynes Street
Manchester, CT 06040
203/646-1222

DISTRICT of COLUMBIA

National Center on Child Abuse and Neglect
P. O. Box 1182
Washington, DC 20013
301/251-5157
(Clearinghouse for child abuse information)

National Center for Missing & Exploited Children
1835 K Street, N.W., Suite 700
Washington, DC 20006
202/634-6795
(Clearinghouse for missing and abused children)

National Child Abuse Coalition
1125 15th Street, N. W., #300
Washington, DC 20006
202/293-7550
(Resource group on child abuse problems)

FLORIDA

Adam Walsh Resource Center
1876 N. University, Suite 306
Fort Lauderdale, FL 33322
(A clearinghouse for kidnapped children information)

American Family Foundation
P. O. Box 2265
Bonita Springs, FL 33959
212/249-7693
(Information packet, books, bibliography)

Justice for Sexually Abused Children (J-SAC)
Andrea Landis
9703 S. Dixie Highway
Miami, FL 33156
305-284-0485
(Activist group offering help in ritual abuse cases)

Reel to Real Ministries
P. O. Box 4145
Gainesville, FL 32613
(Specific research on the occult and Satanism in rock and rap music)

GEORGIA

Home Mission Board, Southern Baptist Convention
Interfaith Witness Dept.
1350 Spring St., N. W.
Atlanta, GA 30367
404/898-7000
(Provides information on cults, the occult, and world religions)

ILLINOIS

Cornerstone Religious Research
4704 N. Maiden
Chicago, IL 60640
(New Age tracts and *Cornerstone* magazine)

Cult Awareness Network
2421 W. Pratt Blvd., Suite 1173
Chicago, IL 60645
312/267-7777

National Commission for Prevention of Child Abuse
332 S. Michigan Avenue, Suite 950
Chicago, IL 60604
(Agency providing information and training materials)

VOICES (Victims of Incest Can Emerge Survivors)
P. O. Box 14309
Chicago, IL 60614
312/327-1500
(VOICES support groups all over the United States)

KANSAS

Jerry Johnston Association
P. O. Box 12193
Overland Park, KS 66212-0193
(Youth specialist organization)

MASSACHUSETTS

American Family Foundation
Kay H. Barney, Director
Box 336
Weston, MA 02193
617/893-0930
(Collects information on cultic groups and shares this with other professionals, the general public, and those needing help with cultic involvement. Publishes *The Cult Observer* and *Cultic Studies Journal*)

District Attorney Office/Victim Witness Service
Janet Fine
40 Thorndike
Cambridge, MA 02141
617/494-4232
(An advocate in child abuse, ritual abuse cases)

MICHIGAN

Michigan Protection and Advocacy Services
109 West Michigan Avenue, Suite 900
Lansing, MI 48933
517/487-1755
(Child advocacy agency)

MINNESOTA

Christian Ministries International (CMI)
7601 Superior Terr
Eden Prairie, MN 55344
612-937-8424
(Seminars, video and audio cassete tapes on cults and the occult.

MINNARA (Minnesota Awareness of Ritual Abuse)
Hennepin County Sexual Violence Center
1222 W. 31st Street
Minneapolis, MN 55408

MISSOURI

Concordia Publishing House
3558 S. Jefferson Ave.
St. Louis, MO 63118
314/664-7000
(Publishes booklets and tracts on major cults)

Lutheran Church—Missouri Synod
Philip Lochlaas, Director
Commission on Organizations
1333 S. Kirkwood Rd.
St. Louis, MO 63122
314/965-9000
(Supplies information and/or counsel regarding general cults)

NEW JERSEY

Institute for Contemporary Christianity
Box A
Oakland, NJ 07436
201/337-0005
(Cult information)

NEW YORK

Cult Hot-line and Clinic
1651 Third Ave.
New York, NY 10028
212-860-8533
(Assists people who are in or have left a cult, family and friends of someone involved in a cult, and groups who want to know more about cults)

Cult Hotline/Crisis Clinic
Jewish Board of Family and Children's Services
120 W. 57th St.
New York, NY 10019
212/632-4640
(Counseling)

Incest Survivors Resource Network, Int.
15 Rutherford Place
New York, NY 10003
513-935-3031
(Agency offering information on incest/ritual abuse)

Interfaith Coalition of Concern About Cults
711 Third Ave., 12th Floor
New York, NY 10017
212-983-4977
Director: Philip Abramowitz
(Provides information on cults to all members of the community.
Sponsors conferences on the cults)

Interfaith Council on Cults
Fr. James LeBar
2 Harvey Street
Hyde Park, NY 12538
(Consultant on the occult)

International Cult Education Program
P.O. Box 1232
Gracie Station
New York, NY 10028
212/439-1550
(A resource list including general and law enforcement information, coun-
selors and treatment, support groups, and research agencies)

OHIO

Dr. Dale W. Griffis, Ph.D.
Chief of Police
P.O. Box 309
Tiffin, OH 44883

TEXAS

EXODUS
Yvonne Peterson
San Antonio, TX
512/733-4208

Michael Paul and Associates
Sr. Paul Carlin
P.O. Box 151
Crockett, TX 75835
409/544-5400

Sunny von Bulow Victim Advocacy Center
307 W. 7th Street, #1001
Fort Worth, TX 76102
917/877-3355
(Agency advocating victims' rights)

The Educational Research Analysis
P.O. Box 7518
Longview, TX 75607
214/753-5993

Victims' Hotline (Texas)
713/779-7979

W.A.T.C.H.
Susan Joiner
P.O. Box 12638
El Paso, TX 79913
(Group monitoring occult activity)

VERMONT

CHILD LURES
P.O. Box 4345
Shelburne, VT 05482
802/985-8458

National Coalition for Chidren's Justice
Mr. Ken Wooden
P.O. Box 4345
Shelburne, VT 05482
802/985-8458
(Consultant and educator on all forms of child exploitation)

VIRGINIA

Occult roleplaying games, involvement, and crime.
804/883-5616

Parent's Music Resource Center
1500 Arlington Blvd. Suite 300
Arlington, VA 22209
703/527-9466
(Occult lyrics in music)

WISCONSIN

C.A.R.I.S.
Jack Roper
P.O. Box 1659
Milwaukee, WI 53201
414/771-7397 or 771-2940
(Occult crime and satanic education organization)

Appendix B

SUGGESTED READING

The following books are suggested readings for those who want to read deeper into the subject area:

The Occult

Guiley, Rosemary Ellen. *Harper's Encyclopedia of Mystical and Paranormal Experience*. New York: Harper Collins Publishers, 1991. A comprehensive volume including major figures in the field, in-depth explanations of different mystical and divinatory techniques, mystical traditions, places and phenomena.

McDowell, Josh, and Don Stewart. *The Occult*. San Bernardino, Calif.: Here's Life Publishers, Inc., 1992. Stewart and McDowell examine the occult from a spiritual point of view, including New Age occultism.

Wilson, Colin. *The Occult: A History*. New York: Random House, 1971. A secular overview of the occult written in three parts, Wilson begins with the correlation between creativity and psychic sensitivity and spans the gap to include in depth histories of the various personalities ending with metaphysical questions that arise out of occultism, etc.

Satanism

Lyons, Arthur. *Satan Wants You.* New York: The Mysterious Press, 1988. A secular look at the dark world of the occult. Lyons has studied Satanism for over thirty years.

Raschke, Carl A. *Painted Black.* New York: Harper and Row, Publishers, 1990. A well-documented four-part examination of the occult, including occult crime, heavy metal music, and an extensive look at the victimization of children.

Ryder, Daniel. *Breaking the Circle of Satanic Ritual Abuse.* Minneapolis, Minn.: Compcare Publishers, 1992. An excellent, easy-to-read volume on S.R.A. Rider's dedication says it all: "This book is dedicated first of all to all those who have been victims of ritual abuse; to the ones who have died and to the ones courageously struggling to recover. It is also dedicated to the therapists, police, social service workers, cult researchers, and friends and families of the victims, who are just as courageously working to expose the abuse, fight back and support the victims in their recovery."

Sellers, Sean. *Web of Darkness.* Tulsa, Okla.: Victory House, Inc., 1992. An easy-to-read volume for both teenagers and parents, born again Sellers tells his own story of his involvement in Satanism by discussing Satanism, occult games, rock music, suicide, and a number of other pertinent issues.

Witchcraft

Buckland, Raymond. *Complete Book of Witchcraft.* St.Paul, Minn.: Llewelyn Publishers, 1990. A protege of the late Gerald Garner, Buckland is regarded as one of the leading authorities on witchcraft, voodoo, and the supernatural. In this volume Buckland covers every aspect of the practice of occult in a workbook fashion.

Burnett, David. *Dawning of the Pagan Moon.* Nashville: Thomas Nelson Publishers, 1991. Burnett has done an excellent job of expressing the broad appeal of paganism today, including witchcraft. His charts are fine aids to help the reader understand how witchcraft and the other religions fit into the neopagan movement so popular today and the challenge this affords the church.

Guiley, Rosemary Ellen. *The Encyclopedia of Witches and Witchcraft.* New York: Facts of File, Inc., 1989. This secular approach traces the history and development of modern witchcraft and its personalities as well as a definition of terms and practices common to witchcraft.

Spiritism

Christopher, Milbourne. *Mediums, Mystics and the Occult.* New York: Crowell, 1975. Christopher does a fine job of exposing the trickery behind spiritism and other aspects of the occult but fails to see the harm in these deceptions.

Pike, James A. *The Other Side*. New York: Dell Publishing Company, 1969. The late Episcopalian bishop's controversial occult experiences in communication with his son Jim, who took his own life at twenty years of age.

Unger, Merrill. *The Mystery of Bishop Pike*. Wheaton, Ill.: Tyndale House Publishers, 1971. As a biblical scholar, Unger explains, from a biblical point of view, the events surrounding Bishop Pike's efforts to communicate with his son.

Multiple Personality Disorders

Friesen, James G. *Concerning the Mystery of MPD*. San Bernardino, Calif.: Here's Life Publishers, 1991. A licensed minister and psychologist, Friesen explores the controversy of MPD, combining both the psychological and spiritual in its treatment.

Mayer, Roberts. *Satan's Children*. New York: B.P. Putnam's Sons, 1991. A secular examination of case studies and the links between Satanic cults and personality disorders.

Occult Crime

Kahaner, Larry. *Cults That Kill*. New York: Warner Books, Inc., 1988. A knowledgeable look at the dark side of the occult through the eyes of those in law enforcement across the country.

Terry, Maury. *The Ultimate Evil*. New York: Bantam Books, 1987. Terry traces the correlation between a satanic cult, the process, and twenty years of ritual murder including the David Berkowitz ("Son of Satan") and the Charles Manson murders.

Counseling and the Occult

Bufford, Roger K. *Counseling and the Demonic*. Dallas: Word Books, 1988. Buford, a committed Christian and professional psychologist, examines the demonic from a scriptural and counseling point of view, including the relationship with mental illness, disorders, possession and spiritual interventions as well as counseling approaches in treatment.

Koch, Kurt. *Christian Counseling and Occultism*. Grand Rapids, Mich.: Kreger Publications, 1972. Renowned authority Koch covers the occult, combining the theological, psychological, and medical fields in a thoroughly biblical manner.

Demonology

Koch, Kurt. *Demonology, Past or Present*. Grand Rapids, Mich.: Kregel Publications, 1973. Each of Koch's six chapters comprise a unit standing on its own. Nonetheless he does a good job of dealing with several issues as Christian counseling and occultism, demonology, occult subjection and mental illness, miracle healing, and deliverance from demonic possession.

Newport, John P. *Demons, Demons, Demons*. Nashville: Broadman Press, 1972. A scholarly and yet readable work on the occult undergirded with a strong theological base.

Unger, Merrill F. *Demons in the World Today*. Wheaton, Ill.: Tyndale House Publishers, 1971. Unger's biblically-sound study of occultism in light of Scripture.

Unger, Merrill F. *What Demons Can Do to Saints*. Chicago: Moody Press, 1991. Unger examines the controversial issue of the question, Can a Christian be demonically possessed? This was Unger's last book prior to his death in 1980.

Spiritual Warfare

Anderson, Neil T. *The Bondage Breaker*. Eugene, Oreg.: Harvest House Publishers, 1990. Anderson, a seminary teacher and pastor, examines the bondage in spiritual warfare, the hows and whys of it all, and how the individual can find freedom from bondage.

Bubeck, Mark I. *The Satanic Revival*. San Bernardino, Calif.: Here's Life Publishers, 1991. Bubeck addresses the occult explosion across the nation today and the spiritual battle that involves every Christian as well as our weapons in fighting it.

Bubeck, Mark I. *The Adversary*. Chicago: Moody Press, 1975. In this well-known work Bubeck proceeds from the point of view that the best way to defeat the enemy is to know the enemy. Solidly scriptural, Bubeck reassures the Christian of the victory over the adversary which we have in Jesus Christ. The reader will appreciate the prayers Dr. Bubeck has composed.

Wagner, C. Peter. *Engaging the Enemy*. Ventura, Calif.: Regal Books, 1991. Wagner writes from a belief in territorial spirits, demons from Satan's ranks assigned to specific geographical areas. Wagner enlists the help of seventeen different authors to address the issue of how to prepare and how to fight the spiritual battle.

Appendix C

SCRIPTURE INDEX

OLD TESTAMENT

Genesis
1:1–2/*91*
1:26/*85*
2/*160*
3/*86,205*
3:1/*206*
3:1–5/*82,205*
3:1–7/*93*
6:1–4/*91*
6:3/*210*
31:19/*196*
31:34–35/*196*
44:5/*155*

Exodus
4:8/*152*
7:10–11/*92*
7:22/*92*
8:7/*92*
15:2/*209*
15:20/*152*
22:18/*108,109,*
  117
22:19–20/*109*
28:30/*107*
32/*166*

Leviticus
16:8/*155*
19:31/*108*
20:6,27/*108*

Numbers
22/*196*
23/*196*
24/*196*
24:17/*166*
26:55/*155*

Deuteronomy
4:9/*46*
13:1–5/*152*
18:9–10/*92*
18:10/*109,119*
18:9–15/*118*
18:21–22/*152*
32/*94*
34:5–6/*86*

Judges
2:18/*152*
4:4/*152*
5:20/*166*

1 Samuel
15:23/*109,118*
16:18–21/*194*
18:3–20/*109*
21:13–14/*194*
25:1/*107*
28/*107,108,118*
29:4/*82*

2 Samuel

12:23/*113*
14:20/*92*
24:1/*86*

1 Kings

18:28/*194*

2 Kings

9:22/*118*
21:6/*109,118*
22:14/*152*
23:24/*108*

1 Chronicles

10:13/*108,118*
10:13–14/*108*
21:1/*86*

2 Chronicles

24:22/*152*
33:6/*109, 118*

Nehemiah

6:14/*152*

Job

1:6/*85, 91*
1:7–12/*82*
1:12/*89*
2:1/*91*
2:6/*89*
38:7/*91*
38:33/*166*

Psalms

5:4/*196*
19:1/*166*
46:1–2/*209*
91:13/*87*
103:20/*92*
109:6/*87*

Proverbs

3:6/*166*

Isaiah

7:11/*152*
7:14/*152*
8:3/*152*
8:19/*98, 109*

8:19–20/*152*
14:12/*82*
14:13–14/*50, 91*
19:3/*109*
47:9/*108*
47:13–14/*165*

Jeremiah

5:23–28/*37*
10:2/*165*
10:7/*165*
27:9/*109*
29:8/*155*

Ezekiel

21:21/*155,160*
28:12–15/*83, 84*
28:14/*91*

Daniel

2:1–49/*166*
2:2/*108*
4:1–37/*166*
4:33/*194*

5:7–15/*166*
10/*94*

Hosea

4:12/*155*

Micah

3:6/*155*
5:12/*118*

Nahum

3:4/*118*

Zechariah

3:12/*87*
10:2/*155*
13:2/*92*

Malachi

3:5/*109*

NEW TESTAMENT

Matthew

4/*87*
4:3/*83,93*
5:13–16/*210*
6:13/*196*
7:3/*47*
7:13/*209*
7:15/*152*
7:16/*42*
8:16/*196*
8:29/*92*
9:32–33/*92*
10:1/*92*
12:22/*92*
12:24/*91,188*
12:29/*92*
12:45/*92*
13:38f/*87*

13:38–39/*93*
13:38–43/*87*
16:23/*88*
17:20–21/*207*
22:37/*200*
24:41/*91*
25:41/*5,90*
27:52–53/*108*
28:19–20/*212*

Mark

1:13/*87*
1:23–27/*194*
1:24/*92*
1:27/*92*
1:24–27/*90*
1:32–34/*194*
1:39/*194*

3:11/*92*
3:11–12/*194*
4:15/*88*
4:25/*90*
5:2–3/*90*
5:6–7/*92*
5:1–20/*194,195*
5:10/*91*
7:25/*90*
7:25–30/*194*
9:27–29/*194*
9:38/*194*
13:22/*152*
16:9/*194*
16:17/*194*

Luke

2:36/*152*

4/*87*
4:6/*89*
4:34/*91*
4:36/*92*
11:24–26/*199*
12:54–56/*210*
13:11–17/*92*
13:16/*88*
22:3/*88*
22:31–32/*88*

John

3:19/*210*
4:1–6/*91*
8:44/*83,88*
9:4/*preface*

John, cont'd

10:22–29/*196*
12:31/*83,*
  90, 170, 196
13:2/*88*
13:27/*93*
14:30/*83,*
  88, 196
16:11/*90, 196*
17:15/*198*

Acts

5:3/*89, 93*
5:1–3/*196*
5:16/*90*
7:41–43/*166*
8:7/*90, 92*
8:9–11/*109*
8:9–24/*196*
13:1/*152*
13:6–11/*109*
13:10/*89*
16:9–21/*171*
19:12–16/*90*
19:19–20/*46*
21:8/*152*
26:18/*90*
26:78/*196*

Romans

1:18–32/*109*
1:30–32/*46*
8:15/*197*
8:17/*196*
8:35–39/*196*
12:2/*166*
16:20/*81, 90*

1 Corinthians

2:16/*196,211*
5:1–13/*196*
5:5/*89*
6:3/*85*
6:17/*197*
6:19–20/*196*
7:5/*89*

10:13/*89*
10:14–22/*196*
10:20/*3*
10:21/*196*
12:13/*197*
14:33/*37*
15:55/*113*

2 Corinthians

4:4/*83, 93*
6:14–15/*171*
6:14–16/*196*
6:15/*82*
11:3–4/*196*
11:13–15/*171*
11:14/*82, 85*
12:7/*89*
12:7–8/*196*

Galatians

5:20/*109, 171*
5:19–21/*108,*
  117, 118

Ephesians

2:1–2/*83*
2:2/*151, 170*
4:4/*197*
4:26/*27, 92*
5:11/*42*
6:12–17/*77, 94*
6:13–18/*211*

Philippians

2:3/*211*
2:10–11/*211*
2:11/*94*
4:13/*211*

Colossians

1:13/*196*
2:14–15/*196*
2:15/*171*
3:4/*196*

1 Thessalonians

2:18/*89*
3:5/*28, 93*

2 Thessalonians

2:8–10/*92*
2:9–10/*171*
2:9–11/*109*
3:3/*196*

1 Timothy

4:1–2/*91, 92,*
  113
4:1–3/*92*
6:20/*46*

2 Timothy

3:8/*171*

Hebrews

2:14/*83, 90*
2:14–15/*196*
13:8/*208*

James

1:14–15/*62*
4:7/*200*

1 Peter

5:8/*83*

2 Peter

2:4/*85, 91*
2:11/*92*
3:9/*46, 210*
3:10–13/*210*

1 John

2:1–3/*92*
2:13/*83*
2:17/*92*
3:8/*90*
3:10/*89*
4:1–2/*91*
4:1–6/*92*

4:4/*196*
5:18/*196*

Jude

1:6/*85, 91*
1:7/*90*
1:9/*86*

Revelation

2:20/*152*
4:1–21/*92*
9:4/*92*
9:11/*82*
9:21/*109*
12:3–4/*83*
12:9/*83*
12:7–11/*85, 91*
12:10/*83*
12:15/*83*
13:15/*92*
16:13/*83, 90,*
  92
16:13–14/*92*
20:2/*83*
20:1–3/*85, 92,*
  196
20:10/*90*
21:2, 7, 13/*89*
21:8/*109*
22:15/*109*

Endnotes

CHAPTER I

1. *Webster's New World Dictionary*, 1972, s. v. "occult."
2. *The World Book Encyclopedia*, 1986, s. v. "occultism."
3. Brenda Lee Sims, "Where There's Fire, There Could Be the Occult," *Texas Firemen* (December 1976), 14.
4. C. S. Lewis, *The Screwtape Letters* (New York: Macmillan Co., 1948), 9.
5. Ken Sidey, "Bedeviled in D. C.?" *Christianity Today* (December 17, 1990), 40.
6. David Alexander, "Giving the Devil More Than His Due," *The Humanist* (May/June, 1990), 41.
7. Ibid.
8. Ken Sidey, "Publisher Withdraws Satanism Story," *Christianity Today* (February 19, 1990), 34.
9. David Alexander, "The Devil Didn't Make Her Do It," *The Humanist* (May/June, 1990), 35.
10. Sidey, 35.
11. Ibid.
12. Ibid.
13. Pete Simmons, executive producer, taken from transcript for "Devil Worship: Exposing Satan's Underground," October 25, 1988.

14. Robin D. Perrin and Les Parrott III, "Memories of Satanic Ritual Abuse," *Christianity Today* (June 21, 1993), 21.

15. David Gates, "Networking to Beat the Devil; But Are the 'Satan Sleuths' Really on to Something?" *Newsweek* (December 5, 1988), 29.

16. Chip Alford, "Students Warned," *Arkansas Baptist Newsmagazine* (October 19, 1989), 20.

17. Karen Rafinski, "Psychic Fair Draws Seekers, Doubters," *Arkansas Gazette* (March 17, 1991).

18. Steven Komarow, "Soldiers Narrowly Miss Four of Noriega's Witches," *Arkansas Gazette* (December 23, 1989).

19. Clinton E. Arnold, "Giving the Devil His Due," *Christianity Today (August 20, 1990), 18.*

20. Jeff Brookings and Alan McEvoy, "Satanism and Schools," *School Intervention Report* (April/May 1990), 18.

21. Paul Bendelow, "Taking Diabolical Liberties: Occultism Attracting West German Youth," *Times Educational Supplement* (April 1, 1990), 1.

22. Ibid.

23. Peter Muello, "Brazil Allows Cult for Drug/Tea," *Arkansas Democrat* (April 21, 1991), 6H.

24. Marcia Rudin, "Cults and Satanism: Threats to Teens," *National Association of Social Science Professors* (May 1990), 46.

25. *The Arkansas Gazette* (April 8, 1990).

26. John Whitmere, "Satanic Youths Unnerve El Paso," *The Houston Post* (February 23, 1986).

27. N. Kilham, "Satanism," *Seventeen* (August 1990), 284.

28. Ibid., 285.

29. "U. S. Teens' Future Troubled, Report Says," *Arkansas Gazette,* (June 8, 1990).

30. Ibid.

31. David D. Burns, "An End to Loneliness," *Bottom Line Personal 6* (June 30, 1985), 9–10.

32. Henri J. M. Nouwen, *Reaching Out* (Garden City, N.Y.: Doubleday, 1975), 15.

33. Suzanne Gordon, *Lonely in America* (New York: Simon and Schuster, 1976), 15.

34. David Haywood, "Baptist Youth Facing Frustrating Problems," *Facts and Trends* (April 1985), 7.

35. "Meditators Reach a New High in the '90s," *USA Weekend* (July 26–28, 1991).

36. Paul Harvey, "From Ghetto to High Rises: Is Peer Pressure to Blame for Drugs?" *The Arkansas Democrat* (May 17, 1991).

37. Billy Graham, "My Answer," *Fort Worth Star Telegram* (April 13, 1972).

38. "Police Chiefs Warned Against Occult Crime," *Charisma and Christian Life* (January 1991), 26.

39. Peter Leithart and George Grant, *A Christian Response to Dungeons and Dragons* (Ft. Worth, Tex: Dominion Press, 1988), 16.

40. Taken from the book *Painted Black* by Carl A. Raschke. Copyright 1990 HarperCollins. Reprinted by permission of HarperCollins, 10 E. 53rd St., New York, NY 10022.

41. "NCTV News," *National Coalition for Television Violence* (January-February 1985).

42. Ted Schwartz, "Diary of a Phoenix Boy's Death," *Phoenix Magazine* (December 1985), 97.

43. Sean Sellers, *Web of Darkness* (Tulsa: Victory House, 1990), 23.

44. David Ward, "Teenagers Vulnerable to Occult Influence," *Winston-Salem Journal (November 5, 1988)*.

45. Ibid.

46. John Brzybys, "Divorce, Career Interests Changing the Way We Live," *Siftings Herald* (July 25, 1991), 12.

47. Arthur J. Norton, "Families and Children in the Year 2000," *Children Today* (July/August, 1987), 6-9.

48. Paula Schwed, "Li'l Dividend Can Dim Glow of Finances," *Arkansas Gazette* (April 19, 1991).

49. Dean Register, "Facing the Challenge of the Changing Family," *Search* (Summer 1990), 17.

50. Michelle Green, "A Boy's Love of Satan Ends in Murder, A Death Sentence and Grisly Memories," *People Weekly* (December 1986), 154.

51. Cited in Brookings and McEvoy, 3.

CHAPTER 2

1. Stewart Powell, et. al., "What Entertainers Are Doing to Your Kids," *U.S. News and World Report* (October 28, 1985), 46.

2. Cheryl Clark, "But Are Teens Worse Today?," *Arkansas Democrat-Gazette* (March 29, 1992), 10.

3. Stuart Goodman, "That Old Devil Music," *National Review* (February 24, 1989), 28.

4. Paul King, "Heavy Metal: A New Religion," *Journal of the Tennessee Medical Association* (December 1985), 754.

5. John Podhoretz, "Metallic Rock That's Designed to Shock," *U.S News and World Report* (September 7, 1987), 51.

6. Dan and Steve Peters and Cher Merrill, *Why Knock Rock?* (Minneapolis: Bethany House Publishers, 1984), 29–30.

7. Podhoretz, 51.

8. Ibid.

9. Ibid.

10. Ibid.

11. Ibid.

12. *Hit Parader* (February 1975), 24.

13. Richard Ostling, "No Sympathy for the Devil," (March 19, 1990), 55.

14. *Hit Parader* (Fall 1983), 37.

15. Peters and Merrill, 183.

16. Lynn Minton, "Is Heavy Metal Dangerous?" *Parade Magazine* (September 20, 1992), 12.

17. Tamara Jones, "Experts Debate Influence of Violent Music on Youths," *Los Angeles Times* (October 19, 1988), 23.

18. Charles Dickson, "Christian Parents Cope with Teen Suicide," *Living with Teenagers* (October–December, 1990), 38.

19. Ibid.

20. John Q. Baucom, "The Teenage Suicide Crisis," *Light* (June-July, 1987), 4.

21. Gary Collins, *Christian Counseling* (Dallas: Word, 1988), 167.

22. Judy Keen, "Suicides Blamed on 'Subliminal' Lyrics," *Arkansas Gazette* (July 16, 1990), 44.

23. Esther Davidowitz, "Die, Mother, Father, Brother," *Redbook* (April 1989), 132.

24. Ibid.

25. Ibid.

26. J.R. Beck, "Subliminal Perception," in *Baker's Encyclopedia Psychology*, ed. by David G. Benner (Grand Rapids, Mich.: Baker Book House, 1985), 1127.

27. Arthur Lyons, *Satan Wants You* (New York: The Mysterious Press, 1988), 169.

28. R.C. Morse and David Strother, "The Hidden Message That Breaks Habits," *Science Digest* (September 1982), 28.

29. Peters and Merrill, 171.

30. Jeff Brookings and Alan McEvoy, "Satanism and Schools," *School Intervention Report* (April/May 1990), 6.

31. Eric Holmberg, "Transcription 'Hell's Bells: The Dangers of Rock and Roll,'" (Cleveland: American Portrait Films, 1989). For a more in-depth examination of how backmasking is done, see chapter 8, Schwarz and Epley's *Satanism* (Zondervan).

32. The following information is based on Peters and Merrill, 115–126.

33. "Backlash," *Newsweek* (April 7, 1969), 31.

34. Dan Peters and Steve Peters, *The Truth About Rock* (St. Paul, Minn.: Truth About Rock, 1985), 26.

35. Mark Marymont, "Hastings Enters Battle Against Explicit Lyrics," *Arkansas Gazette* (June 25, 1989), 5G.

36. "Not all Heavy Music Corruptive, Conservative Group Concedes," *Arkansas Gazette* (December 8, 1988), 1E.

37. "Heavy Metal: Selling Satan or Songs," *The Press Enterprise* (April 12, 1987), C1.

38. Cal Thomas, "Officials Must Say 'No' to Violence at Concerts," *Arkansas Gazette* (September 25, 1988), 9B.

39. Peters and Peters, 149.

40. Ken Tucker, "Love and Lust in Minneapolis," *Rolling Stone (February 19, 1981), 54.*

41. Richard Price, "Totally Outrageous," *USA Weekend* (June 8-10, 1990), 4.

42. Richard Rothenstein, "Porn Rock," *Seventeen* (March 1986), 70.

43. New York Times News Service, "Obscenity Drive Heats Up; Rap Gets a Record," *Arkansas Gazette* (June 7, 1990), 1.

44. Zimmerman, 6D.

45. "Rap Group 'Clean as They Wanna Be,'" *Arkansas Gazette* (June 16, 1990), 2A.

46. "Doctors Support Record Labeling," *Arkansas Gazette* (June 19, 1990), 4A.

47. Rosemary Ellen Guiley, "Aleister Crowley," in *Harper's Encyclopedia of Mystical and Paranormal Experience* (New York: Harper Collins, 1991), 129.

48. Stephen Davis, *The Hammer of the Gods* (New York: William Morrow and Company, 1985), 246.

49. John Symonds, "Aleister Crowley," in *Man, Myth and Magic: An Illustrated Encyclopedia of the Supernatural,* vol. 4, ed. Richard Cavendish (New York: Marshall Cavendish Corporation, 1970), 559.

50. Andy Secher, "Led Zeppelin: The Second Coming," *Hit Parader* (July, 1982), 7.

51. Davis, 291.

52. Robin Richman, "An Infinity of Jimis," *Life Magazine* (October 2, 1969), 74.

53. Eric Holmberg, "Hell's Bells," 26.

54. Ibid.

55. Ibid., 125.

56. Lyons, 167.

57. *Rolling Stone* (August 19, 1971).

58. "Rock Music! What Is Spiritual Adultery?" *Onward Christian Courier* (November, 1983), 14.

59. Bernard Gotfryd, "Mick Jagger and the Future of Rock," *Newsweek* (January 4, 1971), 44.

60. Holmberg, 29.

61. Ibid., 29.
62. Jerry Hopkins and Danny Sugarman, *No One Here Gets out Alive* (New York: Warner Bros., 1980), 327.
63. "Paul McCartney: The Rolling Stone Interview," *Rolling Stone* (September 11, 1986), 48.
64. Tipper Gore, *Raising PG Kids in an X-Rated Society* (New York: Bantam Books, 1987), 130.

CHAPTER 3

1. "Reflections," *Christianity Today* (June 16, 1989), 45.
2. Gary Abrams, "Study Finds Young Generation of Americans Light on Morals," *Arkansas Democrat-Gazette* (November 13, 1992), 18A.
3. Ibid.
4. Curtis Knight, *Jimi* (New York: Praeger Publications, 1974), 7.
5. Fletcher A. Brothers, *The Rock Report* (Lancaster, Pa: Starburst Publishers, 1987), 11.
6. Richard Price, "Totally Outrageous," *USA Weekend* (June 8-10, 1990), 7.
7. Ibid.
8. Denise Worrell, "NOW: Madonna on Madonna," *Time* (May 27, 1985), 83.
9. Roy M. Anker, "Yikes! Nightmares from Hollywood," *Christianity Today* (June 16, 1989), 20.
10. Ibid., 20.
11. Ibid., 23.
12. Ibid., 21.
13. Vernon Scott, "Valenti Earns Respect in Film Rating System," *Arkansas Gazette* (November 17, 1988), 2E.
14. Ibid.
15. Susan Wloszczyna, "R Rating Doesn't Always Keep Kids From Films," *USA Today* (June 12, 1990), 1.
16. "Henry and June," in *Movies on TV and Videocassette, 1992–1993* (New York: Bantam Books, 1991), 465.
17. "NC Rating Gives Edge to 'Henry,'" *Arkansas Gazette* (October 10, 1990), 3E.
18. Larry Rohter, "X Marks the Porn, But High-Browed Adult Films Get New Label," *Arkansas Gazette* (September 29, 1990), 2E.
19. John Horn, "'NC-17' Replaces X Rating," *Arkansas Gazette* (September 28, 1990), 3A.
20. Wioszczyna, 1.
21. Ibid.

22. "Ratings Board Grows Lax, Film Watchdog Group Says," *Arkansas Democrat-Gazette* (March 31, 1992), 3E.
23. Ibid.
24. Ibid.
25. Murphy, 7G.
26. Letter from James Dobson, October 1991.
27. "Police Chiefs Warned Against Occult Crime," *Charisma and Christian Life* (January 1991), 26.
28. James D. Tagliarini, "Occult Crime: The Dark World of Satanism," *The Florida Police Chief* (October 1990), 39.
29. Walter Scott's Personality Parade, *Parade* (November 29, 1992), 2.
30. John Horn, "'Dracula' Bites Off a Record Opening," *Arkansas Democrat-Gazette* (November 19, 1992), 8F.
31. John Horn, "'Good Men' Early Cruises Into First Place," *Arkansas Democrat-Gazette* (December 17, 1992), 8F.
32. Horn, "'Dracula.'"
33. "See the Movie, Buy the Automobile Air Freshener," *New York Times* (December 6, 1992), 121t.
34. Excerpted from James V. Hart's "Screenwriter's Note" which appears in *Bram Stoker's Dracula: The Film and the Legend*, copyright © 1992 Newmarket Press. Reprinted by permission of Newmarket Press, 18 E. 48th St., New York, NY 10017.
35. Ibid.
36. Trish Deitch Rohrer, "Coppola's Bloody Valentine," *Entertainment Weekly* (November 20, 1992), 24.
37. Excerpted from Francis Ford Coppola's "Introduction" which appears in *Bram Stoker's Dracula: The Film and the Legend*, copyright © 1992 Newmarket Press. Reprinted by permission of Newmarket Press, 18 E. 48th St., New York, NY 10017.
38. Mike Clark, "A Lush, Lustful Dracula," *USA Today* (November 13, 1992), D1.
39. *New York Times* (December 13, 1992), 184.
40. Rohrer, 23.
41. Hart, 8.
42. Hugh A. Mulligan, "Dracula Remained Popular Since the Beginning," *Daily Siftings-Herald* (Arkadelphia, Ark., January 4, 1993), 6.
43. Radu R. Florescu and Raymond T. McNally, *Dracula, Prince of Many Faces* (Boston: Little Brown and Company, 1989), 234.
44. Ibid., 224.
45. Richard Noll, *Vampires, Werewolves and Demons: Twentieth Century Reports in the Psychiatric Literature* (New York: Brunner/ Mazel, 1992), 10.
46. Copolla, 5.

47. Rohrer, 23.
48. Frank Rich, "The New Blood Culture," *New York Times* (December 6, 1992), section 9, 11.
49. Charles R. Rogers, "What's TV Doing to Our Children?" *Home Life* (December 1990), 37.
50. "Working Women, College Students Don't Miss Soaps," *Arkansas Gazette* (July 17, 1989), 1E.
51. Lloyd Shearer, "Too Much Television=Too Much Fat," *Parade Magazine* (May 27, 1990), 13.
52. Phil Phillips, *Saturday Morning Mind Control* (Nashville: Oliver Nelson, 1991), vii.
53. Howard Kurtz, "Clinton 'Mortified' by What Gets on TV," *Arkansas Democrat-Gazette* (November 13, 1992), 16A.
54. Mark Kelly, "Clinton, Others Knock Entertainment Industry," *Baptist Reflector* (December 9, 1992), 2.
55. Allan C. Brownfield, "How Television Is Shaping America," *American Family Association Journal* (March 1992), 5.
56. Ibid.
57. Lyons, 115.
58. Letter to AFA Supporter from Donald E. Wildmon, President of the American Family Association, n.d.
59. Ibid.
60. "Homosexuals Hail 'L.A. Law' Kiss," *Arkansas Gazette* (February 10, 1991), 18A.
61. Brownfield, 6.
62. Cynthia Crossen, "Is TV Too Sexy?" *McCall's* (October 1991), 100.
63. "That's Why They Call It the Boob Tube," *Youthworker Update* (December 1992), 2.
64. Michael J. Martin, "Television and Families," *Kansas State University Cooperative Extension Service*, n.d., 3.
65. Paul Johnson, "Networks Use Sneak Attacks with Sex," *Arkansas Gazette* (May 12, 1990), 4E.
66. Phillips, 87.
67. Crosser, 102.
68. Ibid.
69. Cathleen McGuigan with Janet Huck, "What Makes Arnold Run?" *Newsweek* (December 7, 1987), 84.
70. "Should You Censor What Children See?" *First* (January 21, 1991), 92.
71. Ibid.
72. Saralie Faivelson, "Verdict on TV Violence," *Women's Day* (October 1, 1987), 24.

73. "TV Linked to Behavior of Children," *Arkansas Gazette* (April 17, 1990), 7.

74. Mark Kelly, "Challenging Hollywood Values," *Arkansas Baptist Newsmagazine* (December 17, 1992), 11.

75. Quoted by Phil Phillips and Joan Hake Robie, *Horror and Violence: The Deadly Duo in the Media* (Lancaster, Pa.: Starburst Publishers, 1988), 14.

76. Duncan and Priscilla Jaenicke, "Married to Television," *Focus on the Family* (November 1989), 15.

77. Quoted by Joe Stumpe, "TV Turns Off Educators, Counselors," *Arkansas Gazette* (May 5, 1991), 1B.

78. T. Berry Brazelton, "Strive to Balance TV's Influence on Children," *Arkansas Democrat-Gazette* (January 19, 1992), 100.

79. "New Movie Ratings Count Each 'Offensive'" *USA Weekend* (September 20–22, 1991), 22.

80. Rhonda Owen, "'Shudder' Combines Two Genres," *Arkansas Democrat* (June 23, 1991), 7H.

81. Steve Garbarino, "Interview with the Vampire's Chronicles," *The Times-Picayune* (October 30, 1988), D1.

82. Charles Evans, "Confessions of a Teenage Satanist" (American Tract Society, n.d.).

83. James C. Dobson and Gary L. Bauer, *Children at Risk* (Dallas: Word Publishing, 1990), 19.

84. Neil T. Anderson and Steve Russo, *The Seduction of Our Children* (Eugene, Oreg.: Harvest House Publishers, 1990), 68.

85. Jack Canfield and Paula Klimek, "Education in the New Age," *New Age Magazine* (February 1978), 28.

86. Brian and Bertie Adrian, "Is Disney Safe?" *Focus on the Family: Citizen* (October 15, 1990), 13.

87. Berit Kjos, *Your Child and the New Age* (Wheaton, Ill.: Victor Books, 1990), 27.

88. Pete Winn, "What's New in School? Lesbians and Wizards," *Focus on the Family: Citizen* (June 18, 1990), 10.

89. Ibid.

90. "'Impressions' Case Goes to Judgment in California," *Journal of the American Family Association* (March 1991), 13.

91. Quoted in Johanna Michaelsen, *Like Lambs to the Slaughter* (Eugene, Oreg.: Harvest House Publishers, 1989), 46.

92. Ibid., 47.

93. "New Trading Cards Feature Notorious Murderers," *New York Times* (December 6, 1992), 2D.

94. Ibid.

95. Ibid.

96. Ibid.
97. "Canadians Try to Keep 'Killer' Out," *Arkansas Democrat-Gazette* (December 18, 1992), 2A.
98. Dobson and Bauer, 17.
99. "Citizen Writes Letter, Porn Videos Disappear," *American Family Association Journal* (March 1992), 13–14.
100. "Goodness" in *The Treasure Chest*, ed. Charles L. Wallis (New York: Harper and Row, Publishers, 1965), 111.

CHAPTER 4

1. "Lucifer," *Holman Bible Dictionary*, ed. Trent C. Butler (Nashville: Holman Bible Publishers, 1991), 899.
2. John T. Bunn, "Ezekiel," *The Broadman Baptist Commentary*, vol. 6, ed. Clifton J. Allen (Nashville: Broadman Press, 1971), 318.
3. Ralph H. Alexander, "Ezekiel," *The Expositor's Bible Commentary*, vol. 6, ed. Frank E. Gaebelein (Grand Rapids, Mich.: The Zondervan Corporation, 1986), 882.
4. Ibid.
5. Hal Lindsey, *Satan Is Alive and Well on Planet Earth* (Grand Rapids: Zondervan Publishing House, 1972), 48-50.
6. W. A. Criswell, *The Criswell Study Bible* (Nashville: Thomas Nelson Publishers, 1979), 948.
7. Billy Graham, "Why Does God Permit Satan to Exist?," *Arkansas Democrat-Gazette* (February 4, 1992), 4E.
8. L. L. Morris, "Satan," *The Illustrated Bible Dictionary, Part 3* (Wheaton, Ill.: Inter-Varsity Press, 1980), 1396.
9. Mike Martin, "Angels," *Holman Bible Dictionary*, ed. Trent C. Butler (Nashville: Holman Bible Publishers, 1991), 51.
10. Morris, 1396.
11. *Zondervan Pictorial Encyclopedia of the Bible* (Grand Rapids: The Zondervan Corporation, 1974), 284.
12. S. E. McClelland, "Demon, Demon Possession," In *Evangelical Dictionary of Theology*, ed. Walter A. Elwell (Grand Rapids: Baker Book House, 1984), 307.
13. Merrill F. Unger, *Biblical Demonology* (Wheaton: Scripture Press, 1952), 16–17.
14. Lewis Sperry Chafer, *Satan* (Chicago: Moody Press, 1942), 63.
15. John J. Owen, "The Demonology of the New Testament," *Bibliotheca Sacra and Biblical Repository*, 16 (January 1859), 119–139.
16. G. Campbell Morgan, *The Gospel According to Mark* (New York: Fleming H. Revell Company, 1927), 114.
17. A. A. Hodge, *Outlines of Theology* (New York: A.C. Armstrong and Son, 1891), 255.

18. Charles Hodge, *Systematic Theology I* (Grand Rapids: 1940), 643.

19. A. H. Strong, *Systematic Theology* (Philadelphia: The Judson Press, 1907), 455.

20. A.C. Gaebelein, *The Gospel of Matthew* (New York: Our Hope Publication Office, 1910), 247.

21. Unger, *Biblical Demonology*, 16.

22. From *Demons in the World Today* by Merrill F. Unger, copyright © 1971 by Tyndale House Publishers, Inc. All rights reserved.

23. Louis Matthews Sweet, "Demon, Demoniac Demonology," *The International Standard Bible Encyclopedia*, ed. James Orr (Chicago: The Howard-Severance Company, 1915), 828.

24. Michael G. Maudlin, "The Life and Times of the Prince of Darkness," *Christianity Today* (August 20, 1990), 21.

25. C. Peter Wagner, "Territorial Spirits," *Engaging the Enemy*, ed. C. Peter Wagner (Ventura, Calif.: Regal books, 1991), 43.

26. C. Peter Wagner, "Territorial Spirits" *Wrestling with Dark Angels*, eds. C. Peter Wagner and F. Douglas Pennoyer (Ventura, Calif.: Regal Books, 1990), 78–79.

27. Maudlin, 22.

Chapter 5

1. Roger Elwood, *Strange Things Are Happening* (Elgin, Ill.: David C. Cook Publishing).

2. William Watson, *A Concise Dictionary of Cults and Religions* (Chicago, Ill.: Moody Press, 1991), 217.

3. Frank S. Mead, *Handbook of Denominations in the United States*, 8th ed. (Nashville: Abingdon, 1988), 235–36.

4. Ibid.

5. *Arkansas Democrat-Gazette* (April 21, 1993), 1A.

6. "Seance Held in Court," *Arkansas Gazette* (August 13, 1988), 4A.

7. Cyd Tabyanan, "150 Attend Seance to Hear Story of Hotel Visitors' Former Lives," *Arkansas Democrat Gazette* (1992), 1.

8. Peter Swet, "Just Give This Man Some Hard Work," *Parade Magazine* (February 23, 1992), 12.

9. Sue Leonard, *Quest for the Unknown: Life Beyond Death* (Pleasantville, N.Y.: The Reader's Digest Association, Inc., 1992), 75.

10. Ibid., 83.

11. Cited in ibid.

12. "Spiritualism," *Man, Myth, and Magic*, edited by Richard Cavendish (New York: Marshall Cavendish Corporation, 1970), 2656.

13. James W. Sire, *Scripture Twisting* (Downer's Grove, Ill.: Inter Varsity Press, 1980), 109.
14. Marvin Olasky, "The Return of Spiritism," *Christianity Today* (December 14, 1992), 20.
15. Ibid.
16. "Religious Requirements and Practices of Certain Select Groups," *A Handbook Supplement for Chaplains* (U.S. Department of Defense, n.d.), 3-4.
17. Merrill F. Unger, *Biblical Demonology* (Wheaton, Ill.: Scripture Press, 1952), 148.
18. Kurt Koch, *Christian Counseling and the Occultism* (Grand Rapids, Mich.: Kregel Publishers, 1972), 268.
19. Rosemary Ellen Guiley, *The Encyclopedia of Witches and Witchcraft* (New York: Facts on File, 1989), 320.
20. Unger, *Biblical Demonology*, 150.
21. Kurt Koch, *Occult ABC* (Grand Rapids, Mich.: Kreger Publications, 1970), 33.
22. Herbert Lockyer, *All the Trades and Occupations in the Bible* (Grand Rapids, Mich.: Zondervan Publishing House, 1969), 215.
23. W. A. Criswell, *The Criswell Study Bible* (Nashville, Tenn.: Thomas Nelson Publishers, 1979), 103.
24. Douglas Hill and Pat Williams, *The Supernatural* (New York: Hawthorne, 1965), 128.
25. James E. Alcock, "Spirits Cannot Speak Through Human Mediums," *Paranormal Phenomena*, ed. Terry O'Neil (San Diego: Greenhaven Press, Inc. 1990), 217.
26. George Plagenz, "Spiritualists Search for Belief in Afterlife," *Siftings Herald* (April 30, 1993), 4.
27. Walter Martin, *The Kingdom of the Cults* (Minneapolis: Bethany House, 1985), 231–32.
28. John P. Newport, *Demons, Demons, Demons* (Nashville: Broadman Press, 1972), 132.
29. Ibid.
30. Merrill Unger, *The Mystery of Bishop Pike* (Wheaton, Ill.: Tyndale House Publishers, 1971), 7.
31. James A. Pike and Diane Kennedy, *The Other Side* (New York: Dell Publishing Company, 1968), 321.
32. Unger, *The Mystery of Bishop Pike*, 108-9.

CHAPTER 6

1. Rosemary Ellen Guiley, *The Encyclopedia of Witches and Witchcraft* (New York: Facts on File, 1989), 320.

2. Herbert Lockyer, *All the Trades and Occupations in the Bible* (Grand Rapids, Mich.: Zondervan Publishing House, 1969), 215.
3. Merrill F. Unger, *Biblical Demonology* (Wheaton, Ill.: Scripture Press Publications, Inc., 1952), 153.
4. Ibid.
5. Ibid., 154.
6. "Witchcraft Evangelism," *Youthworker Update* (April 1992), 2.
7. *Arkansas Democrat-Gazette* (May 28, 1992), 1.
8. "Witches Complain of Harassment," *Group Magazine* (October, 1992), 57.
9. Ibid.
10. "Shopping Center Owner Evicts Witches," *Arkansas Democrat-Gazette* (June 14, 1992), 4.
11. "Witches' Rites at Stake on Military Base," *Arkansas Democrat-Gazette* (November 24, 1992), 2A.
12. "Parliament of Faiths Showcases Diversity," *Arkansas Democrat-Gazette* (August 29, 1993), 3A.
13. "Self-Styled Office Witches Ply Wares," *Arkansas Democrat-Gazette* (October 25, 1992), 5A.
14. "Question of the Week: Robey—Bewitching On and Off Camera," *Arkansas Gazette U.S.A. Weekend* (January 15, 1989), 2.
15. "Witchcraft Ruled a Religion," *Arkansas Gazette* (August 9, 1989), 7A.
16. M. Thomas Starkes, "Hog Fat on Anxiety" in *Home Missions*, ed. Walker L. Knight (January 1972), 7.
17. "Witchcraft" in *The Occult* (IWA Manual) Home Mission Board, SBC (September 26, 1990), 30.
18. Raymond Buckland, *Buckland's Complete Book of Witchcraft* (St. Paul, Minn.: Llewellyn Publications, 1986), 5.
19. Ibid.
20. Taken from the book *Dictionary of Cults, Sects, Religions, and the Occult*, by George A. Mather and Larry A. Nichols. Copyright © 1993 by Mather, Nichols, and Alvin J. Schmidt. Used by permission of Zondervan Publishing House.
21. Ibid., 315–16.

CHAPTER 7

1. Robin D. Perring and Les Parrott III, "Memories of Satanic Ritual Abuse," *Christianity Today* (June 21, 1993), 23.
2. Ibid.
3. Anton LaVey, *The Satanic Bible* (New York: Avon Books, 1969), 96.

4. Johanna Michaelsen, *Like Lambs to the Slaughter* (Eugene, Oreg.: Harvest House Publishers, 1989), 185–86.

5. Bob Larson, *Satanism: The Seduction of America's Youth* (Nashville: Thomas Nelson Publishers, 1989), 42.

6. Josh McDowell, and Don Stewart, *Understanding the Occult* (San Bernardino, Calif.: Here's Life Publishers, Inc., 1982), 176.

7. Larson, 41.

8. John Symonds, "Aleister Crowley," *Man, Myth, and Magic,* vol. 4, edited by Richard Cavendish (New York: Marshall Cavendish Corporation, 1970), 559.

9. Ibid.

10. Ibid., 561.

11. John Godwin, *Occult America* (New York: Doubleday and Company, Inc., 1972), 242–43.

12. Eric Holmberg, Transcript of "Hells Bells: The Dangers of Rock and Roll" (Cleveland: American Portrait Films, 1989).

13. Maury Terry, *The Ultimate Evil* (New York: Garden City, 1987), 303.

14. John Charles Cooper, *The Black Mask* (Old Tappan, N. J.: Fleming H. Revell Company, 1990), 50.

15. William Watson, *A Concise Dictionary of Cults and Religions* (Chicago: Moody Press, 1991), 71.

16. Walt Harrington, "The Devil in Anton LaVey," *Washington Post Magazine* (February 23, 1986), 4.

17. Arthur Lyons, *Satan Wants You* (New York: The Mysterious Press, 1988), 107.

18. Cited by Buron H. Wolfe, "Introduction" in Anton LaVey, *The Satanic Bible* (New York: Avon Books, 1969), n.p.

19. Lyons, 107.

20. Taken from the book *Painted Black* by Carl A. Raschke. Copyright 1990 HarperCollins. Reprinted by permission of HarperCollins, 10 E. 53rd St., New York, NY 10022.

21. Lyons, 108.

22. William C. Viser, "Satanism," *Arkansas Baptist Newsmagazine* (July 19, 1973), 5.

23. Raschke, 119.

24. Ibid., 39.

25. Arthur Lyons, *The Second Coming: Satanism in America* (New York: Dodd, Mead, and Company, 1970), 171.

26. Ibid., 181.

27. "Church of Satan," *Religious Requirements and Practices of Certain Selected Groups: A Handbook for Chaplains* (Washington, D.C.: Department of the Army, 1978), section 7, 17-22.

28. LaVey, 26.

29. *Handbook for Chaplains*, 5-6.

30. Larry Kahaner, *Cults That Kill* (New York: Warner Books, 1988), 42.

31. Ibid.

32. James G. Friesen, *Uncovering the Mystery of MPD* (San Bernardino, Calif.: Here's Life Publishers, 1991), 96.

33. Ibid.

34. Kahaner, 160.

CHAPTER 8

1. Merrill F. Unger, *Biblical Demonology* (Wheaton, Ill.: Scripture Press Publications, Inc., 1952), 123.

2. Herbert Lockyer, *All the Trades and Occupations of the Bible* (Grand Rapids: Zondervan Publishing House, 1969), 258.

3. Joan Quigley, What Does Joan Say? (New York: Carol Publishing Group, 1990), 73.

4. *The Chronicle of Higher Education* (November 6, 1991), 45A.

5. Abigail Van Buren, "Dear Abby: Forget Ouija Board 'Bunk.'" *Fort Worth Star Telegram* (February 16, 1977), 6C.

6. Patrick Fairbairn, *Fairbairn's Bible Encyclopedia* (Grand Rapids: Zondervan Publishing House, 1957), 81.

7 John Stevens Kerr, *The Mystery and Magic of the Occult* (Philadelphia: Fortress Press, 1971), 31.

8. Carl Sagan, *Cosmos* (New York: Random House, 1980), 51.

9. Alan Bunce, "Searching for Secrets in the Stars," *Christian Science Monitor* (July 5, 1988), 1-2.

10. Sonya Ross, "Atlanta Board Licenses, Monitors Astrologers to Protect Its Citizenry," *Arkansas Democrat-Gazette* (June 16, 1992), 5B.

11. Ibid.

12. "North American Scene: What New Age?," *Christianity Today* (October 1992), 54.

13. Ibid.

14. David Burnett, *Dawning of the Pagan Moon* (Nashville: Thomas Nelson Publishers, 1991), 202.

15. "New Age Groups Target Baptist Youth," *Mission USA* (November-December, 1992), 6.

16. From *Demons in the World Today* by Merrill F. Unger, copyright © 1971 by Tyndale House Publishers, Inc. All rights reserved.

17. John Newport, *Demons, Demons, Demons* (Nashville: Broadman Press, 1972), 95.

18. M. Thomas Starkes, "Hog Fat on Anxiety," *Home Missions* (January 1972), 7.
19. J. J. Thompson, "Forecaster," *Arkansas Gazette* (April 23, 1990), 1E.
20. Ibid.,
21. Ruth Montgomery, *A Gift of Prophesy* (New York: William Morrow and Company, 1965), 21.
22. Ibid., 16.
23. Ibid., 14–16.
24. Morris Cerullo, *The Backside of Satan* (Carol Stream, Ill.: Creation House, 1973), 137.
25. Montgomery, 22.
26. Starks, 7.
27. Roger B. Culver and Phillip A. Ianna, *Astrology: True or False?* (Buffalo, N.Y.: Prometheus Books, 1988), 29.
28. Paul Kurtz, *The Transcendental Temptation: A Critique of Religion and the Paranormal* (Buffalo, N.Y.: Prometheus Books, 1986), 46.

CHAPTER 9

1. Clinton E. Arnold, "Satan and Company," *Christianity Today* (August 20, 1990), 17.
2. Arthur D. Moore, "Missions and the Demonic," *Christianity Today* (August 20, 1990), 18.
3. Ibid.
4. Ibid.
5. Ibid.
6. *Missionary Occult Survey*, Furlough Conference and Southern Baptist Missionaries (March 9–11, 1993).
7. "Texas Lifts Hex on Voodoo Beer," *Memphis Commercial Appeal*, (July 4, 1991), 2.
8. "Removed Mayor Returns Pledging No New Voodoo," *Arkansas Democrat-Gazette* (August 16, 1992), 4A.
9. "ACLU Sues Over Voodoo Book Ban," *Arkansas Democrat-Gazette* (October 16, 1992), 4A.
10. "Florida Ban on Animal Sacrifices Tests Religious Freedom in U.S.," *Arkansas Democrat-Gazette* (March 24, 1992), 2A.
11. "Justices Hear Animal Sacrifice Case," *Arkansas Democrat-Gazette* (November 5, 1992), 5A.
12. "Afro-Caribbean Groups" in *The Occult* (IWA Manual), ed. Gary Leazer, Home Mission Board, Southern Baptist Convention, (September 1990), 55.
13. *Across the Border,* copyright © 1989 by Gary Provost, p. 13, reprinted by permission of Pocket Books, division of Simon & Schuster, Inc.

14. Ibid., 122–24.
15. "13th Victim Found on Ranch; Key Suspects Believed in U.S.," *Arkansas Gazette* (April 14, 1989), 8A.
16. Ibid.
17. *Sacrifice*, Jim Kilroy and Bob Steward, copyright 1992, Word, Inc., Dallas, Tex. Used with permission.
18. Ibid.
19. Ibid.
20. Ibid., 137.
21. Leonard Maltin, *Leonard Maltin's Movies and Movie Guide* (New York: Signet Books, 1991), 81.
22. Provost, 81.
23. "Satanic Cult Suspected in Slaying of College Student, 12 Bodies Found," *Daily Siftings Herald* (April 12, 1989), 8.
24. Richard Woodbury, "Cult of the Red Haired Devil," *Time* (April 24, 1989), 30.
25. Kilroy and Steward, 137.
26. Ibid, 138.
27. Ibid.
28. Ibid., 177–78.
29. Provost, 242.
30. Ibid, 176.
31. Ibid., 233.
32. Ibid., 255.
33. Ibid., 246.
34. Ibid., 229.
35. Kilroy and Steward, 186.

CHAPTER 10

1. Michael A. Lipton, "Lethal Weapon," *People* (April 19, 1992), 84.
2. Ibid.
3. Peter Steinfels, "Rise in Satan Cult Activity Alarms Cardinal," *The New York Times* (March 6, 1990), B1.
4. *Arkansas Democrat-Gazette* (January 31, 1993), 1A.
5. "Woman Dies After Four-Day Exorcism Rite," *Arkansas Democrat-Gazette* (February 4, 1993), 6A.
6. Kenneth L. Woodland, "The Exorcism Frenzy," *Newsweek* (February 11, 1974), 61.
7. Leighton Ford, "God's Exorcist," *Decision* (May 1974), 1.
8. Jerry Flemmons, "Movie Is Only Fiction; Douglas Deen Is Real," *Fort Worth Star Telegram* (February 22, 1974), 6F.

9. H. A. Virkler, "Demon Influence and Psychopathology," *Baker Encyclopedia of Psychology*, ed. David G. Benner (Grand Rapids, Mich.: Baker Book House, 1985), 296–97.

10. Ibid., 297.

11. Flemmons, 6F.

12. From *Demons in the World Today* by Merrill F. Unger, copyright © 1971 by Tyndale House Publishers, Inc. All rights reserved.

13. Merrill F. Unger, *Biblical Demonology* (Wheaton, Ill.: Scripture Press, 1952), 80.

14. John P. Newport, *Demons, Demons, Demons* (Nashville: Broadman Press, 1972), 68–69.

15. George Eldon Ladd, *Jesus and His Kingdom* (New York: Harper and Row, 1964), 145–47.

16. Taken from p. 97 of *What Demons Can Do to Saints* by Merrill F. Unger. Copyright 1991, Moody Bible Institute of Chicago, Moody Press. Used by permission.

17. Ibid.

18. From *Demon Possession and the Christian* by C. Fred Dickason, copyright © 1987, 101–27. Used by permission of Good News Publishers, Crossway Books, Wheaton, IL 60187.

19. Ibid., 81–100.

20. Gary Collins, *Christian Counseling: A Comprehensive Guide* (Dallas: Word Publishing, 1988), 72.

21. "Lying Spirits and Teaching of Demons," *Home Missions* (January 1972), 45.

22. *Counseling and the Demonic*, Royce K. Buford, copyright 1988, Word, Inc., Dallas, Tex. Used with permission.

23. Ibid.

Chapter 11

1. Perucci Ferraivola, "Warnke Admits 'Failure,'" *Christianity Today* (May 17, 1992), 88–89.

2. Timothy C. Morgan, "Bob on the Block," *Christianity Today* (May 17, 1993), 74.

3. Ibid.

4. Edward Mote, "The Solid Rock," *The Baptist Hymnal* (Nashville: Convention Press, 1991), 406.

5. Arthur Lyons, *The Second Coming* (New York: Dodd, Mead, and Company, 1970), 202.

6. Fanny J. Crosby, "Rescue the Perishing," *The Baptist Hymnal* (Nashville: Convention Press, 1991), 559.